"This book is an invitation to a sober conversation, away from the sound and fury of social media. You've heard the whispers of this conversation, when people hint at their fear of cancellation, or wonder at how good intentions pave the way for hellish loops of toxic behaviour. Rhyd Wildermuth has lived enough of this first-hand, it gives his writing an edge of hard-won wisdom. In fighting monsters, he tells us, we risk to become monstrous; yet this bestiary he offers is also an invitation to come to terms with the monstrosities within us, the parts of ourselves that don't fit onto any map of identities. And it culminates in a call to a politics that is grounded in friendship, surely the starting point for building a common life in the troubled times around and ahead of us."

Dougald Hine, author of *At Work in the Ruins: Finding Our Place in the Time of Science, Climate Change, Pandemics & All the Other Emergencies*

"Rhyd writes about some of the toughest, most contentious issues of our society — and he does so with empathy and wisdom. A great, highly informative book."

Yasha Levine, author of *Surveillance Valley: The Secret Military History of the Internet*

T0023218

HERE BE MONSTERS

HERE BE MONSTERS

HOW TO FIGHT CAPITALISM
INSTEAD OF EACH OTHER

Rhyd Wildermuth

Published by Repeater Books

An imprint of Watkins Media Ltd

Unit 11 Shepperton House

89-93 Shepperton Road

London

N1 3DF

United Kingdom

www.repeaterbooks.com

A Repeater Books paperback original 2023

1

Distributed in the United States by Random House, Inc., New York.

Copyright © Rhyd Wildermuth 2023

Rhyd Wildermuth asserts the moral right to be identified as the author of this work.

ISBN: 9781914420467

Ebook ISBN: 9781915672087

Printed and bound in the United Kingdom by TJ Books Limited

MIX
Paper from
responsible sources
FSC® C013056

CONTENTS

INTRODUCTION: REALISTS OF A LARGER REALITY

I once went on a date with a bat.

He was really nice, quite attractive, and very well spoken. We had a few beers together, and then I invited him home as the bar closed. He agreed, and we walked back to my place together, talking. But it wasn't until we were sitting on my bed, about to kiss, that he told me he was a bat.

You'll perhaps forgive me for not noticing before. I mean, *he looked human*. He even spoke like a human, rather than employing the high-pitched inaudible chirps and clicks bats use for echolocation. Maybe you'll also forgive me for laughing when he told me that he was a bat.

"You mean you want to role-play?" I asked, naively. "Okay, maybe that could be fun."

"That's insulting. It's not role-playing: I am really a bat," he said, making clear his disappointment.

I suddenly felt bad, so I apologized, and then asked him to explain. He told me he had only recently discovered that he was a bat, so he could understand why it was hard for me. He had known something was different about him for a long time; then, one day, someone online had told him, "I see you are really a bat," and this had changed his life.

He explained to me that it wasn't like being a furry, the subculture of people who dress up like animals to have sex. He didn't need to "dress up" like a bat, because he *actually* was one. And most importantly of all, if we were to have sex, I needed to have sex with him as he truly was.

"What... what does that mean, exactly?"

"You will be having sex with a bat, not a human."

1

This finally all got a little too weird for me. "I... I don't know how to have sex with a bat," I said. I had that weird dizzy feeling in my head, the way you feel when you realize you've been talking to a conspiracy theorist or a religious fanatic. I don't know exactly what that feeling is, but it's like an internal alarm, or a mental shutdown, something telling you to get out of there.

"I can show you how to have sex with a bat," he said.

This was finally too much. I told him, "No, I'm sorry. I can't do this."

I received angry texts from the guy over the next few days, messages about how he'd thought I wasn't a bigoted speciest but now saw I was, and how could I possibly even justify such prejudice. I eventually blocked his number, and mostly blocked the incident out of my memory until, years later, I was part of a social media discussion about the surge in the use of "neo-pronouns,"[1] such as "dragon/dragons/dragonself."

What followed was a more-than-250-comment argument about the matter, with a really surprising amount of people taking weather- or mythic-based pronouns seriously. "Cloudselves" and "faeselves" faced significant oppression, I was told. Another person reported that fascists were targeting neo-pronoun users online by exposing them to their triggers (apparently listing your deepest triggers in a Twitter bio is a "thing") in order to cause them psychological harm. Yet another supporter of neo-pronouns angrily accused me of taking the side of the fascists themselves, claiming that the arguments used against people identifying as animals or weather phenomena are the same used against non-binary and trans-identified people.

---

1 See Marcus, 2021.

Needless to say, I didn't engage further in that discussion. It felt as if there would be no way to talk about these matters without becoming trapped in endless accusations and arguments.

What's Really Real?

Especially online, but also quite often in person, discussions of this sort can leave us with the sense that reality itself is a politically contested territory. Extreme and sometimes incomprehensible examples of self-identification often make great fodder for right-wing or tabloid-style commentary about the excesses — or what is often labeled "insanity" — of radicals or leftists. For instance, the very popular and controversial Twitter account called "Libs of TikTok"[2] rose to prominence by reposting videos of "pronoun reveals"[3] and of people discussing the subtle distinctions between newly created sexual orientations.[4] Popular and often acerbic right-wing critics such as Matt Walsh have used apparent internal contradictions within the matter of gender identity as the basis for popular documentaries and articles, mocking those they interview

---

2 1.7 million followers as of 1 January 2023.

3 Videos in which a person announces their new or neo-pronouns to an audience.

4 Or newly identified, since, according to an article discussing sexual orientations in *Cosmopolitan*, "because this number is evolving (there are already over 100 terms to describe sexuality), there may also be more to add in the future. It's important to know, though, that these are not *new* sexual orientations, simply ones that don't have names yet. Clear, specific definitions help us get closer to inclusive representation." In other words, the ever-expanding list of sexual orientations is merely a more accurate classification of what has always existed. See Igoe, 2022.

and presenting them as representatives of the "woke" or of leftists.

From the left, on the other hand, we usually encounter denials that such excesses even occur — or that they are even excesses at all. Any criticism is often turned back upon the critic and their motives made suspect. Suggesting that someone cannot actually be a cloud, or that there are problems — including abuses — in populist iterations of identity politics, can lead a person quite quickly to be smeared as hateful, bigoted, or even a fascist.

We seem trapped in a position where there appears to be two — *and only two* — competing narratives about what is happening. Each narrative is in turn part of a larger framework opposed to the other, two containers into which all thought and all political action must be assigned. Each presents itself as the diametric opposite of the other, and sees everything outside its boundaries as automatically the territory of its dangerous enemy. Shadows of each other, they are locked in a struggle for "the real" that pulls all the rest of us into their shouting matches.

This all leads leftists and those sympathetic with leftist goals — an end to capitalist and industrialist exploitation of the Earth and of people — to a very difficult and confusing place. Previous projects and theories of liberation seem to have become unrooted from their original grounding. Worse, at least within the English-speaking world, right-wing demagogues have been able to dominate these discussions, to set the terms for the debate, and even to position themselves as speaking for the Real, for really existing things. This has meant that the left seems to many to be out of touch with everyday reality, or to be lost in fantasies and utopian dreams.

Accusing leftists and leftist goals of being utopian or lost in fantasy is hardly a new thing, nor is it really an insult. In fact, fantasy and dreams are where any significant positive change begins. Every revolution must first start with a dream, since we must be able to imagine the kind of world in which we wish to live in order to fight for it.

After all, what we are told at any given time is possible is never very inspiring. We are told that if we work for someone else at low wages, we may perhaps one day save up enough money to rent a slightly larger apartment in the dreary and expensive cities where most of us live. We are told that if we vote hard enough for politicians who repeatedly sell us out, we may one day get higher wages, less government corruption, less exploitation, fewer jails, fewer wars, or less climate change. We are told that this is all that is possible, and that to dare dream of something more is "unrealistic" or "utopian."

The left, if it has been anything, has been the province of dreamers, of fantasies, and especially of the "impossible." More than this, the left has been the province of tricksters and rogues, those who pull back the curtain on the fantasies of this world, who reveal the magic tricks that keep capital and the powerful in place. It's been the leftists who've shown this political and economic system, this "reality," to have been born from other fantasies and other dreams. And if this world was dreamt up in conspiracy, then can we not dream up and conspire a better one?

Realists of a Larger Reality

We live in capitalism, its power seems inescapable — but then, so did the divine right of kings. Any human power can be resisted and changed by human beings. Resistance and change often begin in art. Very often in our art, the art of words.[5]

---

5 See Le Guin, 2014.

The prolific fantasy author Ursula K. Le Guin spoke those words as part of her acceptance speech for the National Book Foundation Medal for Distinguished Contribution to American Letters. This part of her speech has lived on in the radical imagination — including in political slogans and leftist T-shirts — and it's quite inspiring. However, it's taken out of context. Le Guin's specific point was her opposition to the growing corporate dominance over the publishing industry, as well as the tendency of writers to shape their works for sales strategies rather than to create as artists create.

Despite being very rarely quoted, an earlier part of her short speech is much more powerful and deeply relevant to this question of leftism and reality:

> Hard times are coming, when we'll be wanting the voices of writers who can see alternatives to how we live now, can see through our fear-stricken society and its obsessive technologies to other ways of being, and even imagine real grounds for hope. We'll need writers who can remember freedom — poets, visionaries — realists of a larger reality.

"Realists of a larger reality" is quite a phrase. It seems to evoke the legacy of the popular Situationist slogan during the late Sixties in France: "Be realistic: demand the impossible." For the Situationists, who were Marxist artists and theorists, capitalism had led to the degradation of all life experience, alienating us from ourselves, each other, and the possibility of authentic social relations. Similar to the French philosopher Jean Baudrillard, they believed that we were no longer able to determine what was really "real," and so we thus instead mistook spectacle and representation for reality.

We can see the truth in these ideas quite easily when we think of advertising and social media. In advertising, we view images or videos with upbeat or sweeping music in which happy and beautiful people seem to be happy and beautiful precisely because of the product being sold. Of course, we might tell ourselves that we see through the manipulation, yet advertising wouldn't exist if it didn't work.

On social media, especially on image- or video-heavy platforms such as Instagram and TikTok, we are presented — and present others with — similar visions of a real that doesn't really exist. When someone posts a selfie, for instance, they've often selected that image from dozens of other photos which they decided weren't good enough to show. "Spontaneous" scenes of laughter with friends, stunning vistas, and even restaurant meals are never actually spontaneous. Getting the camera just right, making sure your friends are all looking the same direction, ensuring you've gotten the right angle on the landscape or the plate in front of you: these actions and many more are part of the creation of the "candid" glimpses of our lives we try to show the world.

We all know this because we all do this, yet even still, we often experience the images and videos of others as if they are actually not staged. We might then feel a bit depressed: that intimate photo of a man with ripped muscles — how does he just wake up with perfect hair in the morning like that? The tanned woman laughing with her friends at the club on a Friday night — why does her life look so exciting compared to our own?

We know it's not actually "real," yet we find ourselves nevertheless treating it all as if it were. Worse than this, we find ourselves unknowingly trying to emulate these false representations, posing our friends around a table at a club, arranging our hair and getting back into bed just to show that we, too, are happy and beautiful. And who are we trying to prove this all to? Others, or maybe also ourselves?

To be a "realist of a larger reality" is thus not only to dream of something different from what is, nor is it to be lost in the spectacle of the world of representations. Instead, it's to see the scene presented to you *as well as what created the scene*. It's to see not just the Instagram picture but also the camera with which it was taken, the person holding the camera, the staging and posing beforehand, and all the discarded shots afterwards. It's also to see the social media network itself, the influence of "influencers" and the algorithms that determine which images you see and which ones you never do. It's to see the effects of these representations on the way we see ourselves and each other, the profit motive behind the corporations which own, shape, and control the way we represent the world and which limit our ability to see what else is possible.

Being "a realist of a larger reality" requires we refuse to be lost in the world of images and representation. The way not to be lost is quite simple: we need only be faithful to the rules, or internal coherence, of larger reality. At the beginning of her acceptance speech, Le Guin references a particular political point about her receipt of the award:

> And I rejoice in accepting it for, and sharing it with, all the writers who've been excluded from literature for so long — my fellow authors of fantasy and science fiction, writers of the imagination, who for fifty years have watched the beautiful rewards go to the so-called realists.

Le Guin was long a critic of what she saw as an artificial division between "realist" fiction and "fantasy" or "speculative" fiction. Fiction is by its very definition imaginary, "not real," in the sense that it didn't actually happen. Despite this, some fiction is seen as more realistic than other fiction because it tells stories with elements that look more like everyday occurrences than fantastic or magical actions. For Le Guin, however, both kinds of fiction serve the same purpose, telling us something about life, about humans, and about the way they act with each other.

A crucial element in any good fiction is internal coherency. Whether or not there are flying dragons and magical schools for children, there are reasons for — and most importantly consequences of — their existence. Flying dragons fly because there is such a thing as flying, which means there is such a thing as not flying. Magical schools for children exist because there is such a thing as a school and such a thing as children. The imagined world has limits and structures and consequences because our own world, "reality," also has those things.

What Monsters Show Us

Not everything that looks like liberation actually is, nor is every political idea which claims to help people actually helpful. Sometimes, we can dream up things which become nightmares. Sometimes, the left is actually out of touch with reality, with "larger reality." Sometimes, the theories and frameworks crafted to fight oppression only lead to more oppression. Sometimes, the "impossible" is actually really impossible.

That's the purpose and reason for this book. In this time of politically contested reality, the left must become realists of a larger reality. This does not mean abandoning our capacities and obligation to dream of a different world; on the contrary, it means becoming more faithful realists for that world. What is possible is much larger than what we allow ourselves to imagine, because our imaginations themselves are shaped, controlled, and commodified by the capitalist order. To break free of that control, we must first admit that false visions and representations have captured too much of our political and cultural dreaming, leading only to more strife, which feeds and strengthens the order we wish to see end.

To do this, I'll present several fantastical figures, creatures drawn from myth and history, to show how we've failed to be realists of a larger reality. These figures function as archetypes in the Jungian sense, mythic containers of larger meanings and historical forces which are themselves neutral. They are "monsters" in the original Latin sense. Our word monster derives from the Latin word *monstrum*, itself coming from the verb *montere*. As with another English word sharing its root, *demonstrate*, monsters "remind, bring to (one's) recollection, tell (of); admonish, advise, warn, instruct, teach."

In older times, the appearance of a monster was seen as a sign, an omen, or a warning. They meant that something was wrong in the world, or with the relationship between humans and the world and the divine. In other words, monsters were a symptom of a greater problem, and they were also messengers pointing to the solution.

"The old is dying and the new cannot be born; in this interregnum a great variety of monsters appear."

These oft-quoted words were penned by Antonio Gramsci, a young Marxist theorist imprisoned in Italy until his death at forty-six. A bit like the earlier Le Guin quote, there's some context missing, but this time that context is what some believe is a translation error. The Italian phrase Gramsci used was *"fenomeni morbosi"* which means literally "morbid phenomena," and it is elsewhere translated as "morbid symptoms." However, as we just saw, monsters were once likewise considered symptoms, signs that point to some greater underlying problem.

The Nigerian philosopher, writer, activist, and professor of psychology Bayo Akomolafe points us to something else we should know about monsters. In his beautiful essay "When You Meet The Monster, Anoint Its Feet," he reminds us that monsters and "the monstrous" arrive as part of moments of transformation:

> Monsters are admittedly horrific entities. But monsters did not sprout autonomous of context or history; they have always been in dynamic interaction with the "city" that exiles them to the wilderness. This is why monstrosity can serve as a cultural means to examine ourselves. To meet ourselves as if for the first time....
>
> I read monsters as cultural technology — as mythic figures that have always been intimately entwined with human becomings. From a time past remembering, we've needed monsters to define ourselves, to teach our children what not to do, to sound warnings about the future, to define the territorial boundaries of our habitats (and therefore carve out the wilderness), and to dream about the impossible. Indeed, monsters play a crucial social role: they challenge our addictions to particular forms and disturb the familiar.[6]

That is, we need monsters not merely as stories but also as messengers from that larger reality. They bear with them not just warnings but also instructions and maps. They show us what we have become, and what we can also be.

Thus, the monsters we'll look at are not creatures to eradicate, nor are they symbols of what we do not like. They are not things to fear, but rather beings from which to learn. Some are ancient monsters, drawn from antiquity and folklore yet persisting throughout our modern imagination. Others are very new monsters, born from technological shifts to which humans have not yet had

---

6 See Akomolafe, 2018.

time to adapt. Each of these monsters are *monstrums*, signs or symptoms that point us to a larger morbidity, a greater calamity or illness which we struggle to otherwise explain. Most of all, they point back to us, challenging, guiding, and inspiring us to birth the world waiting to be born.

CHAPTER ONE: MORBID SYMPTOMS

Early in the year 2017, one of the most progressive colleges in the United States saw a series of "anti-racist"[7] protests demanding the firing of a science professor, Bret Weinstein. These protests were sparked by his stated opposition to a call for white students and professors to stay off campus for the day.

A year before these protests, I stayed several days on the campus of this college, called Evergreen State College. This was not the first time I'd been there. I lived in nearby Seattle, Washington, and the city of Olympia, where the college is located, is one of three cities in the United States renowned for a particularly high concentration of anarchists. Many of my friends who lived there were anarchists, and at that time I considered myself one as well. Also, several of my friends and two partners of mine during the sixteen years I lived in the Pacific Northwest were at one time or another students at Evergreen.

This particular time I was visiting a friend and staying in his communal dormitory apartment. It was an otherwise uneventful stay, except for two rather weird incidents involving interactions between him and two of his roommates, incidents which I think might explain the protests that occurred the next year better than any of the official narratives.

---

7 I've put "anti-racist" in quotation marks here to distinguish it from other forms of opposition against racism. The difference will be extensively discussed in Chapter Four.

Things were really strained in that apartment, to put it mildly. Though I did not know it then, the four students who lived there represented a kind of microcosm of the much larger identity strife that has come to define leftist politics in the United States and elsewhere. My friend, a gay man, is white and had grown up very poor in a trailer with a single mother and two younger brothers from different fathers. His lesbian roommate was also white and from slightly better economic circumstances. The other two identified as BIPOC (Black Indigenous People of Color), were from solidly middle-class families, and though they might have appeared heterosexual (they were a couple), they both identified as queer non-binary people.

The first night I slept there, I was woken in the middle of the night by the slamming of a very heavy door at 3am. The couple had arrived back, very drunk, to the apartment, and they were being very, very loud. My friend, who had class early the next morning, went to ask them to please be quiet so he could go back to sleep. The ensuing argument became even louder than the original door slamming, finally ending when one of the couple shouted at him: "Check your white privilege."

The second incident happened on the last day of my stay. My friend had planned to prepare a meal for us before I left, but when he searched the refrigerator for the ingredients he had bought, he found them missing. When he asked, the two aforementioned roommates admitted to having eaten his food. He then rather cautiously explained to them how this made him feel frustrated, and one of them replied, "White people owe us much more than that as reparations. Consider it your down payment."

Two decades ago, the incidents I've recounted would have been more fit for a comedy script than a book of theory. I know that I never suspected that the radical leftist traditions which first captured my imagination in the early

2000s would ever have manifested in this way. I certainly never thought Evergreen State College — where so many of my friends were first introduced to leftist theory — would ever take the turn it did.

That turn became quite famous in the US media, drawing attention particularly from conservative journalists. Evergreen became a symbol for them of the "intolerant left," as well as of a new radical politics of "woke" identity. It also served as a warning to many of us on the left as well, a sign that a fundamental re-alignment had occurred that could not easily be understood. What occurred at Evergreen the year after my visit was hardly the beginning of this deep shift, but rather it was the first time that shift could no longer be denied.

What happened at Evergreen in the spring of 2017? Let me try to recount it to you in as balanced a way as possible, which can only be done by giving you historical context first.

The first thing to understand is that Evergreen State College isn't a traditional sort of university: it was founded specifically as a kind of radical experiment in alternative higher education. In the 1960s, many such colleges arose as part of a movement to introduce anti-hierarchical principles into society, with a focus on empowering students to design their own educational experience and curriculum.

One of the radical features of Evergreen is that professors do not assign grades at the end of a course but rather issue written evaluations of the student's experience and engagement with the subject. Those courses themselves could likewise be described as something other than traditional. Consider, for example, some of the courses on offer as part of the 2021–2022 Evergreen academic catalog, cited along with excerpts of their descriptions:

American Popular Music: A People's History (16 credits):

We will historicize, consider, and complicate questions of authenticity, regionality, the division of high and low culture, and appropriation. We will have a particular emphasis upon the ways popular music has served as a way to include and exclude along lines of race, gender, and sexuality, with focused explorations of music created by Black Americans, women and queer or gender-non-conforming Americans, and how that music has been popularized and consumed by Americans from less marginalized groups....

Processing Our Wool: Relating with Indigenous and Modern Fibers

All peoples have an original calling to fulfill, a gift that is meant to be shared within the circle. In this course you will be introduced to various fibers, whose gifts we will begin to understand and synthesize by examining our connections to others — including fungi, plants, animals, and humans....

The Authentic Self: Becoming an Instrument of Change

You are the most powerful and versatile tool you have. Do you know who are you and what you stand for? Is that who you want to be? How can you use your presence as an instrument of change? How do you know what you evoke/provoke in others? How do you move in the world with awareness of your authentic self? The ability to communicate and influence is crucial to our effectiveness as we move through many systems. This program is designed for students who want to develop skills of self-knowledge and "use of self" as an instrument of social change. [8]

---

8 See Evergreen State College, 2022.

Because of such courses and its alternative academic structure, Evergreen College developed quite a reputation both with its supporters and its critics as a factory of radicalism and alternative understandings of the world. As such, many who knew of the place were not surprised that the campus erupted in anti-racist protests for several days. What was surprising, however, was how those protests came about and how "anti-racism" came to be defined.

Day of Absence

For decades, a tradition — at first informal and then later officially recognized — had been practiced every year in April called "Day of Absence." Inspired by a drama written by a black playwright and led by black students, the tradition was meant to highlight the contributions of black people to society through their sudden absence, a kind of black people's strike. Each year, black students (and by extension all non-white students) who wished to participate would skip classes and instead hold solidarity meetings off-campus to discuss their personal struggles.

That year, however, citing the larger political movement of Black Lives Matter and a need for more anti-racist action, student organizers decided that the tradition should be flipped on its head. Rather than black students, faculty, and staff choosing to leave the campus for the Day of Absence, it was decided that it would be whites who should be "invited" to leave. According to the student newspaper announcing the decision:

> This year, however, it was decided that on Day of Absence, white students, staff and faculty will be invited to leave the campus for the day's activities. This decision was reached through discussion with POC Greeners who voiced concern

over feeling as if they are unwelcome on campus, following the 2016 election.[9]

It was this shift — or rather the publicized reaction of one Evergreen professor to this shift — which led to the protests that occurred that year. Bret Weinstein, who at that time taught evolutionary biology, protested in a faculty email later leaked to the student body that

> there is a huge difference between a group or coalition deciding to voluntarily absent themselves from a shared space in order to highlight their vital and under-appreciated roles... and a group or coalition encouraging another group to go away. The first is a forceful call to consciousness, which is, of course, crippling to the logic of oppression. The second is a show of force, and an act of oppression in itself.[10]

The incidents on campus which followed the leaking of Weinstein's email — along with national attention from right-wing and mainstream media — led to several days of protests a few weeks later. Video footage of the events soon flooded social and traditional media. Students took over buildings and prevented white faculty members and staff from leaving through physical coercion and social pressure, telling them leaving would be taken as proof that they were racist and white supremacists. At the height of the protests, campus police told Bret Weinstein and his wife, Heather Heying (also then a professor at Evergreen), that it was unsafe for them to be on the campus: students had been stopping cars entering and leaving, apparently looking for Weinstein.

---

9 See Manchester
10 See Volokh

As with many similar events in recent years, the explanation for why these protests became so severe — and of what precisely the protesters were angry about — is quite contested. Some social media posts from student organizers accused Weinstein of being a white supremacist or even a Nazi; others stated that the protests were in response to the arrest of two black students who had physically fought each other on campus in the previous days. Video footage from several of the events tells conflicting stories about the protests: in some, white faculty and staff speak of their support for the protestors, while other footage shows white faculty and staff frustrated that they were being prevented from using the bathroom. Student reactions are likewise divergent: organizers attested to the solidarity of the students, contradicting video footage of an Asian student harassed and heckled by activists for saying that her professor, Weinstein, was not in any way a white supremacist.

Complicating the narrative even further was the outside reaction, especially from right-wing media, to the incidents occurring on campus. Though even mainstream news media known for putting a progressive spin on events (such as the *Washington Post* and the *New York Times*) admitted that some of the student protestors appeared chaotic and even abusive, commentators such as Tucker Carlson and the alt-right news site *Breitbart News* directed relentless attention towards the extremes of some of the protesters as proof of the rising power of the "intolerant left." And even from the side of the student protestors, some pointed to the unsolicited involvement of the local Olympia anarchists in the campus events — especially the stopping of cars entering and leaving campus in search for Weinstein — as an explanation for some of the more extreme actions.

A New World Struggling to Be Born

Because of my own experience with Evergreen College and the radicalism of the Pacific Northwest, what happened there seemed almost inevitable, a manifestation of much larger cultural and political shifts.

I myself was a radical, an anarchist mostly, and I lived most of my adult life in the Pacific Northwest. I also worked for a little while as a labor organizer, and had both organized and participated in many anarchist, anti-racist, anti-war, socialist, and gay rights events. In the sixteen years that I lived in Seattle, I had made quite a few friends and "comrades" within the various radical movements there. I had participated in Occupy, where I volunteered my time to teach workshops on non-violent crisis-management techniques, made large pots of lentil soup and chai to feed the crowds, and spent many evenings listening to speeches during general assemblies. I also co-organized Pride events, including the largest anti-war contingent in the Seattle Pride Parade that had ever existed.

I held many large parties — often with more than one hundred people — in the communal house I rented. These parties brought together anarchists, socialist party organizers and members (Socialist Alternative, Freedom Socialist Party, and the now defunct International Socialist Organization), trans-rights activists, environmentalists (especially the more radical sort: tree-sitters and tree-spikers who self-identified as eco-saboteurs and attributed their actions to the Earth Liberation Front), as well as some stodgy and dour-faced communist friends who mostly sat in the corner. Along with all these people came the more artistic sorts and the "gay-orgy seekers" (as one of my roommates described them — and yes, often these parties ended as such guests were hoping) whose politics were somewhat aligned with the others, people who in the 1950s one might have called "fellow travelers."

I didn't fully understand at the time, but regardless I had a sense I was a kind of node for the many diverse and intersecting radical currents of the city. Of course, there were many other people functioning that way, and our communal house was not really remarkable compared to the many others I knew and visited. Their parties were often larger — though a lot less gay — and brought together other combinations of radical currents. Some of these were in squats or warehouses, while others occurred in large community spaces lent out by the non-profit organizations for which the hosts worked.

All through my twenties and well into my thirties, the radicalism which I saw, experienced, and in which I participated while living in Seattle and the Pacific Northwest felt deeply tangible and immediate. Often, it felt like I was living in the early days of a revolution, something that many friends there also felt. We discussed books constantly, arguing about theory and historical events the way others might football statistics or celebrities. Accounts of the struggles against capitalism and the state around the world — whether they occurred in Venezuela, Oaxaca, or Syria — were to us the equivalent of local news: anyone recently returned from those places was immediately invited to dinner, or to a bar or a bookstore, so they could tell us everything they'd seen.

I recount my experiences in radical leftist communities not as a brag or as a repudiation of leftism and radical politics, despite the many critiques these pages convey. Instead, I recount them as an attempt to unravel the historical and ideological forces which I and others couldn't quite understand at the time. These forces have now brought us to a point where many leftists — including myself — are often terrified of what now passes for "leftism." What conservative commentators have called "the intolerant left" or "the woke left" (as well as many less kind terms) once seemed to many of us as mere hyperbole at best. Their accusations seemed at most a kind of manufactured outrage over misunderstood events meant to smear with broad strokes a powerful movement for liberation. Unfortunately, I and others like me — those of us who have long histories within radical communities — have come to understand that something significant has indeed shifted. The leftism we once knew and fought for has been replaced with something else entirely.

This ideological shift has been defined by many names. When I first noticed the beginnings of this shift, these newer iterations were usually called "social justice identity politics." Others, especially those heavily steeped in anarchist theory, identified what was happening as an expansion of "anti-oppression work," a term which had come into significant vogue in the decade before. For a little while, it was also called "intersectionality," a term derived from the work of Kimberlé Crenshaw.

Terms and labels change fast, especially with the breakneck speed of communication we now see on the internet. As I write this, there are currently two major ways of describing this new political ideology — though of course there is still intense debate as to whether it is actually a political ideology or even new. One of those terms, "successor ideology," derives from the work of UK conservative theorist John Gray and has been popularized by the writer Wesley Yang. In this conception, what is occurring is a kind of replacement or succession of earlier political agreements by a newer one more suited to a neoliberal order. But where John Gray first introduced this idea in an essay for *New Statesman*, he also uses other terms: "wokery" and the "woke movement":

Wokery is the successor ideology of neo-conservatism, a singularly American world-view. That may be why it has become a powerful force only in countries (such as Britain) heavily exposed to American culture wars. In much of the world — Asian and Islamic societies and large parts of Europe, for example — the woke movement is marginal, and its American prototype viewed with bemused indifference or contempt.[11]

"Woke," in fact, has come to be the current dominant name for this ideological shift. However, it's also become a meaningless word employed to describe all manner of ideas, beliefs, and behaviors that are often contradictory and not always related to each other. "Woke" isn't a name most of the people it is used to describe actually call themselves any longer (though there were a few years when activists indeed described their own politics as "woke"). Those who strongly reject the use of the term often deny there is any such a thing, or point to the term's origin in AAVE (African American Vernacular English) as evidence that there are anti-black or white supremacist inclinations in those who use the term negatively.

Regardless, the word's origins provide an informative starting place for understanding these shifts. "Woke's" original usage was to describe a state of liberated enlightenment, a sudden awareness of how the world "really" works. The phrase "stay woke" was an admonition to others to keep their eyes open to the true state of the world, especially regarding societal oppression and the systems which reproduced that oppression. This core sense explains why the term was initially taken up by radicals to describe their own politics, until it made its way into the mainstream and took on negative connotations.

---

11 See Gray, 2020.

An argument can be made that since those described as "woke" do not use the term for themselves, it's a false label. This is a fair argument, except that we might also mention that people labeled as racist, fascist, or white supremacist likewise do not use those terms for themselves. There is a larger argument to be made here, however: rarely are the terms of identification for groups, movements, and even religions ever initiated by those within these groups.

Religion, especially, is one of the identity categories most instructive with regard to this problem, and — as you will see throughout this book — it is deeply relevant to understanding these shifts. For instance, the term "Christian," which for very few Christians would ever be considered a derogative term, started out as an insult. That is, "Christian" was not what the early believers in the Christ actually called themselves but was rather a label applied to them by people outside of their movement.

Related to the way "Christian" developed as a slur are the words "pagan" and "heathen." "Pagan" predates "Christian" as a term, and was originally a pejorative used to describe rural people who were considered backwards by the Romans. Once Christianity became the dominant and official religion of Rome, the term was then used to describe the "backwards" sorts who continued to worship the old gods and keep to older customs. "Heathen" had a similar development and was likewise related to geographical position. A heathen was originally a "dweller on the heath," but through the writings of Christian bishops, priests, and missionaries, "heathen" then came to describe not just the people who lived on those heaths but also the customs, cultures, and beliefs of such people. Regardless of what the people who identified themselves as Christian, pagan, or heathen actually called themselves in the beginning, the terms are now seen as meaningful descriptors of actual belief systems.

The question of whether or not we should call these ideological shifts "woke" or some other name points to a much deeper problem, and is itself one of those "morbid symptoms." We've become caught up in — or perhaps even trapped within — a rapidly shifting world in which new labels and their meanings change before their older meanings even have a chance to be settled. New words for things seem to arise almost overnight, while older words are suddenly repurposed for new uses. Perhaps in five years no one will even remember that anyone thought there was such a thing as "woke."

What's more important than what these shifts are called is that we recognize they are actually shifts and find some way to talk about them. What we name them is probably irrelevant, but behind the drive to name is the awareness that there is something new, a phenomenon, a system, a *monstrum* we need to heed.

CHAPTER TWO: LET THEM EAT PRONOUNS

Especially in the last ten years, a lot of political strife has arisen over the matter of gender identity. Trans and non-binary identities have become particularly contentious, and they've been the subject of protests and large pushes for new laws to either expand legal definitions and protections or to reinforce protections for more traditional definitions of "man" and "woman."

On the left, this strife is often narrated as a war between progress on the one hand and reactionary or even fascist beliefs on the other. The right often also describes what is happening as a war: a war against traditional beliefs, against the safety of women and children, and even against biology itself. What neither of these primary narratives take into account, however, is that our current ideas about gender, sexuality, and gender identity are extremely new and were originally not even rooted in politics at all. Instead, they came about quite recently, and were effects of massive technological and economic changes in society.

To move beyond the contention and strife of these issues — especially in regards to the matter of identity — we need to understand how our conceptions of ourselves, our behaviors, and our relationships are rooted in larger frameworks or cosmologies. These frameworks or cosmologies are in constant flux, yet we often perceive them as static and unchanging.

The Shifting Frameworks of Sexuality

To get a small sense of the larger problem here, consider someone like myself, a man who exclusively desires other men. I'm very happily married to a man, and I have only ever had any sexual desire for men throughout my entire life. In our current order and current way of seeing such things, the sort of person I am is labeled "gay" or "same-sex attracted." Until just a few years ago, I'd have been called a "homosexual," but this term is now included among "terms to avoid" by GLAAD, a LGBTQ media advocacy organization.[12] Regardless, I and many others like me continue to use the term.

One hundred and thirty years ago, "homosexual" and "gay" were not terms in use for what I am. Instead, there were other terms, each situated in specific ways of thinking about human sexuality. One such term was "invert." Invert comes from a now abandoned scientific framework in which men who have sex with men were seen to have "inverted" genitals. In other words, I — as a man who desires men — would be considered to actually be a woman whose vagina was "inverted" into a penis. A woman who desires women (what we'd now call "lesbian") likewise suffered from this condition: her penis was "inverted" into a vagina. The underlying belief within this scientific framework was that no "real" man would desire other men; because only women desired men, an invert man must be somehow really a woman.

Another term often used during that same period of history was "Uranian," and it stemmed from a mythic, rather than scientific, framework. In Greek myth there are

---

12 See GLAAD (2022)

two Aphrodites. The first and most well-known is Aphrodite Pandemos, and she was said to be born from Zeus and Dione. The other Aphrodite is a much older goddess found in Semitic cultures and later imported into Greek culture: Urania, or Aphrodite Urania. Aphrodite Urania was said to have been born not from a woman but a man, specifically from the severed genitals of Uranus. Therefore, she was a kind of "celestial" love rather than a physical love. When it was in use, Uranian denoted a man whose desire didn't require a woman to manifest it, just as Aphrodite Urania didn't need a mother to be born. The idea here was that the erotic desire of a person was a larger force, and for most men it could only be consummated or manifested with a woman. Uranians, on the other hand, could manifest love and desire with men.

"Pederast" was another common term, one which is still in use by the French as the slur "*pédé*." Pederasty was a Greek social form in which an older man became the guardian of an adolescent male of noble birth. The pederast's role was to be the adolescent's tutor, foster father, guardian, and sponsor into society. Greek male society had a peculiar sexual arrangement which persisted for a very long time also in Arabic, Persian, Slavic, and Turkish cultures. Sex between men was not seen as immoral at all, but it nevertheless had very specific rules. Men of higher social standing (age, class, rank, etc.) could only engage in penetrative sex with other men, never in receptive sex. Men of less social standing were thus more likely to have receptive sex, but of course they could have penetrative sex with men of even less standing or with women.

Like all the previously-mentioned labels, pederasty was a product of a certain way of thinking and part of a specific cultural understanding. It does appear to have continued outside of Turkish, Persian, and Arabic societies into European society among certain nobles and also within priesthoods and monasteries, but the specific later use of the word was as a pejorative. A pederast was someone who was corrupting upper-class youth. For instance, the initial charges against Oscar Wilde hinged on his relationship with Alfred, Lord Douglas, a noble adolescent of higher social standing than Wilde.

Probably the most — and ancient — term for people who desire others of the same sex as themselves is "sodomite." The label is derived from the Biblical story of Sodom and Gomorrah, in which God rains down fire and turns Lot's wife into a pillar of salt (sparing Lot and his daughters, who then rape their father in the middle of the night) as punishment for the townsfolk's actions. The punishment for those two towns was actually not because the cities were full of men having sex with men, but specifically for the way they treated two visiting male angels. When the celestial messengers arrived, the men of the town demanded to be able to have sex with them. In Semitic society, as in Greek, this would have involved a loss of social status for the angels, so the morally-superior Lot offers his two virgin daughters to the mob instead. (It's those two daughters who later rape their father, perhaps in retaliation.) Later, Lot is warned that God will destroy the town for the way they treated the angels, and so he flees.

The belief that the "crime of Sodom" was that men were having sexual relations with men is obviously reductive, yet nevertheless this was the dominant understanding in Christian Europe, and sodomy laws even still persist in some states in America. In many cases, sodomy referred to all anal and often also oral sex, even between a man and a woman, since these were all sexual activities "contrary to nature" (non-reproductive sex).

There is a final term which shows us a peculiar problem for understanding how our ideas about sex and gender change, "bugger." Bugger as a verb specifically refers to the act of penetrating another person through the anus. As a noun, a bugger refers to someone who has buggered someone. However, the term doesn't imply or denote that a person who has buggered someone inherently desires to bugger, only that he has done so. The difference here may seem quite subtle and perhaps even irrelevant, but it's actually quite important. Whereas all the other terms in use now refer to something inherent or intrinsic to a person, bugger refers only to something one has done. In other words, a man who has buggered another man wasn't presumed to desire men over women, only that he had at one point engaged in buggery.

What's particularly fascinating about this term is that it's most likely derived from a heretical Eastern Orthodox sect, the Bogomils. Active in the Balkans (especially in Bulgaria) during the eleventh and twelfth centuries, they were Gnostics who rejected all church hierarchy, and were rumored to engage in sexual orgies and to consume their own ejaculate during rituals. Whether this actually happened is unclear, but at least as far as the legacy of same-sex activity in Semitic, Slavic, Greek, and Turkish cultures, it's unlikely that Christian ideas about sex had fully destroyed the older forms in such a short period of time.

The crucial difference in this term from the others I've mentioned — including the ones currently in use — is that it wasn't tied in any way to something intrinsic to the bugger. Buggery was something you engaged in, not a sexual desire or orientation. Unlike the modern terms we have to describe what is happening, there was never a sense that buggering another man made you a different kind of man, only that you've done something others thought you shouldn't have. Contrast "bugger" with "homosexual" or "gay" and you can see the deeper implications. A homosexual is someone who desires people of the same sex, being gay is being a man who is attracted to other men. Any man, on the other hand, could be a bugger. The term encompasses both the situational or singular male-male sexual activities common in prisons, ships, military deployments, or drunken nights with mates, and also the guys like me who do this sort of thing more often. In other words, it's part of a framework or cosmology where what you do doesn't define who you are. There is no identity attached to the activity: they are completely separate spheres.

Why does this all matter? First of all, in order to talk about what is happening now, we must understand that our categories and labels are products of larger frameworks, and they can only be understood within those frameworks. Secondly, and related to that point, frameworks change, shift, become displaced by other frameworks, are often quite temporary and transitional, and also recur in different forms. The framework which created the term invert, for example, lasted only a few decades. It was later displaced by the psychological model that birthed the idea of the homosexual, a term some now see as incorrect or even pejorative. There's a third reason that long discussion of varying labels and framework for same-sex activity is relevant: it gives us a sense that underneath the ideological frameworks is something very human which has always been with us. How sex among men or sex among women is explained changes according to the cultural framework in which it is occurring, but the important part is that is occurs and seems to always occur

The very same thing can be said about gender variance, or what we currently call transgender identity, non-binary identity, or gender non-conformity. These are all new labels that are produced within a specific framework, and these labels are in transition and flux along with that framework.

The Birth of Gender

With the reality of these larger cosmologies in mind, we can now look at the particularly contentious matter of gender and gender identity. "Gender" as a term to reference sexual distinctions between humans only began in the early 1900's. Before then, "sex" was the dominant term, but as noted by etymologists,

> as sex (n.) took on erotic qualities in 20c., gender came to be the usual English word for "sex of a human being," in which use it was at first regarded as colloquial or humorous. Later often in feminist writing with reference to social attributes as much as biological qualities; this sense first attested 1963.[13]

In other words, "gender" became a euphemism for sexual difference as a way to avoid embarrassment lest the listener blush thinking of the act of sex instead. Later, through feminist theory, gender then took on an extra meaning it never had before: that of "social attributes."

There was an intermediary step here, that of the concept of a "gender role." This concept was first deployed not by a feminist writer but by a controversial sexologist, John Money, best known for trying to turn a young boy into a girl (without his consent or even knowledge) after a botched circumcision destroyed the boy's penis.[14] In a paper he wrote in 1955 entitled "An Examination of Some Basic Sexual Concepts: The Evidence of Human Hermaphroditism," John Money defined the term "gender role" the following way:

---

13 See Etymonline, 2022.

14 That boy's name was David Reimer, and he later committed suicide. See Colapinto, 2014.

By the term, gender role, we mean all those things that a person says or does to disclose himself or herself as having the status of boy or man, girl or woman, respectively. It includes, but is not restricted to sexuality in the sense of eroticism. Gender role is appraised in relation to the following: general mannerisms, deportment and demeanor, play preferences and recreational interests; spontaneous topics of talk in unprompted conversation and casual comment; content of dreams, daydreams, and fantasies; replies to oblique inquiries and projective tests; evidence of erotic practices and, finally, the person's own replies to direct inquiry.[15]

In other words, Money asserted that there was a psychological phenomenon of gender that was not necessarily related to physical sex but rather to social identity. In his other writings, as well as in his controversial and sometimes abusive medical practices, he asserted that these roles were malleable and could therefore be changed by social, environmental, and medical influences and interventions.

John Money's concept of gender roles was quickly embraced by scientific journals and universities, but it got its strongest support from feminists. It took less than two decades for Money's concept of gender to become one of the primary fields of political discourse in feminism. Second-wave feminists — that is, feminists writing in the 1960s, 1970s, and up into the 1980s — expanded this social concept of gender into a discourse of resistance against something imposed upon them. For instance, the feminist writer Gayle Rubin described gender as "the socially-imposed division of the sexes," meaning that gender was how women were boxed into acting certain ways and doing

---

15 See Money, J., Hampson, J.G. and Hampson, J.L. (1955)

certain work and prevented from acting other ways and doing other kinds of work.

As with any other political and historical shift, it can be difficult to grasp how profound these changes really were or even to trace precisely how they occurred. Gender's original meaning referred to type, sort, or kind, and it was related to the concept of offspring. That is, it was a category marker that had no inherent relationship to sexual difference but referred rather to lineage or group belonging. We can see this in other words that share its root: engender, generation, general, and generic. More tellingly, we can get a sense of what gender meant when we consider the word *genre*, its French equivalent, used commonly in English. We speak of books as having a genre (fiction, noir, memoire, and so forth), meaning that we classify those books into certain categories by shared traits.

That's how "gender" was used in English before it became a euphemism for sex and then later a psychological, social, and political concept. What is usually meant now by gender is something completely different from what was intended in its original sense. Especially in feminist and radical conversations, gender usually means the "felt sense" of who you are: woman, man, non-binary, transgendered, cis-gendered, agendered, and so on.

Without getting too much into the meaning and consequences of these new ideas yet, it's essential we remember that this is a very new thing. The idea that gender is a thing separate from sexual difference (between males and females) is less than seventy years old (if we count back from John Money's introduction of the idea; it is even younger if we start from second-wave feminist uses of the term).

Sex and Gender as Social Constructs

"Gender's" shift from being a synonym for "sex" to describing biological or physical characteristics and then into being a concept which also describes social traits took several decades to fully manifest. A second shift occurred famously (and in a famously obtuse way) in 1990, with the publication of Judith Butler's book *Gender Trouble*. Whereas in the previous few decades gender had come to be seen by feminists as the social reality of sexual difference, Judith Butler introduced a wholly new idea. Butler argued that gender and sex were both mere "discursive" subjects. That is, neither sex nor gender had any physical reality or existence outside of the way we think about them, talk about them, and "perform" them in our lives and interactions.

To put this more plainly: in the 1960s and 1970s, second-wave feminist writers used gender as a term for the social aspects of sexual difference. In their thinking, there was a category difference between maleness and man-ness, as well as between femaleness and woman-ness. For most of them, a person was biologically or physically male or female; however, what made that person a man or woman on the social level wasn't their genitalia but rather their masculine or feminine expressions and the ways those interacted with societal expectations of masculinity and femininity.

This way of thinking led to a de-synchronization of the two concepts, such that you could be a feminine male or a masculine woman, and it also led to a de-prioritization of the physical or biological category of sex in favor of a focus instead on the study of gender and gender relations. Here, as in many other ideological shifts we'll encounter, the initial intention was good, or at least derived from a clear purpose. And as with many other shifts, there was often at least some tenuous connection to material or class analysis.

For earlier (second-wave) feminist theorists, gender was a negative thing to be overcome. Gender was the social construction overlaid upon the existence of women, an accumulation of restrictive and limiting ideas of what a woman is and what she is capable of. Domesticity in the role of housewife and subservience to a husband were both limiting aspects of this social construction. Politeness, a subdued social presence, fragility, beauty, and elegance accompanied by silence: these were gender roles that women were taught they should be, perform, and fulfil in order to be "real" women.

Subsequent feminist critiques went further than merely interrogating gender. They began to sever gender from sex altogether. Judith Butler was not the first to do this, as feminist theorists Catherine MacKinnon and Donna Haraway had previously written towards this end. Judith Butler's book *Gender Trouble,* however, represented the first full political argument for the severance of sex and gender.

Not only did Judith Butler sever the two, she went even further. Rather than merely suggesting (social) gender and (physical) sex were unrelated to each other, Butler argued that neither of these concepts referred to any physical reality at all. Gender and sex — and the differences they described — were mere constructs, artificial categories humans created. We only performed or acted out gender and sex, and it was our "performativity"[16] which gave these concepts any semblance of life.

16 If these concepts seem unnecessarily abstract or confusing
    to you as a reader, you're not alone. Judith Butler was the
    winner of a 1998 "Bad Writing" award for the following
    passage: "The move from a structuralist account in which
    capital is understood to structure social relations in

Gender Trouble had a profound influence on feminist thinking, and its publication is often seen as the moment when second-wave feminism ended and third-wave feminism began. This is because the framework Butler proposed deeply undermined many of the core foundations of earlier feminist critique. For instance, feminist writers before Butler had focused on the exploitation and subjugation of women through sex work, pornography, and highly-restrictive gender norms. These writers had shown how the physical qualities of women as females made them susceptible to violence from men, less able to escape domestic abuse, more likely to be sexually exploited, and more likely to be forced into subservient situations. Much of this was due to the sexual differences associated with being female: menstruation, pregnancy, and lactation were all things women experienced that men did not.

By arguing that both gender and sexual difference were mere social constructs, Butler eroded this entire way of thinking. Underneath what humans thought of as sexual difference was actually no difference at all. Thus, there was nothing peculiar or really different about women as bodies that made them vulnerable to men.

---

relatively homologous ways to a view of hegemony in which power relations are subject to repetition, convergence, and rearticulation brought the question of temporality into the thinking of structure, and marked a shift from a form of Althusserian theory that takes structural totalities as theoretical objects to one in which the insights into the contingent possibility of structure inaugurate a renewed conception of hegemony as bound up with the contingent sites and strategies of the rearticulation of power."

Gender Troubles

The consequences of this shift in thinking have been rather profound, and they have manifested particularly in the political strife and conflict regarding two particular issues: prostitution and pornography. Earlier feminists argued that both of these were inherently damaging to women and were essentially exploitative. They pointed out that it was primarily poor, homeless, drug-addicted, and otherwise vulnerable women who were most often prostitutes, and thus that they could not be honestly said to have willingly chosen to sell their bodies. For many feminists, prostitution was linked to the subjugation of women to men in abusive marriages as well: such women had to "put out" for their husbands in order to keep them happy and to benefit from their financial and physical protection. Oftentimes, this meant producing and raising children for their husband and devoting their bodies, their time, their labor, and all their social energy into taking care of others rather than attending to their own desires and goals. Some more extreme second-wave feminists even went as far as to suggest that being a housewife was itself a kind of prostitution or indentured servitude.

Related to this was the matter of pornography. Second-wave feminists criticized the increasing popularity of pornography both for its treatment of women's bodies as sexual commodities and for its perpetuation of very narrow standards of female beauty. Magazines such as *Playboy* (founded in 1953) and *Hustler* (1974) had made nude images of women in erotic contexts widely available to men, and feminists argued that the mass production of such images reduced women to mere sexual objects and trapped women in standards of unattainable beauty shaped by the "male gaze."

Often, warnings about pornography by second-wave feminists can seem prudish, conservative, or even ridiculous from our contemporary vantage point. After all, pornography is now widely available to anyone (including very young children) with access to the internet. What's on offer on sites like Pornhub makes the early centerfolds of *Playboy* look rather tame and commonplace, and women are also consumers of pornography (Pornhub claimed in 2019 that 32 percent of their website visitors were women), though not at the same rate as men.[17]

On the other hand, one could also see their criticisms as having an almost prophetic nature. Though writing before the birth of the internet, they warned that the prevalence of pornography would lead to an escalation, with ever more "hardcore" images being produced and consumed to sate the desires of people who had become desensitized to more common forms of erotic relations and desires. Also, the prevalence of violent and non-consensual pornographic videos and images and even child pornography on the internet — including on sites such as Pornhub — seems to give credence to their predictions.

Regardless of whether or not you agree with second-wave feminists' critiques, it's important to keep in mind that they were rooted in an analysis of physical subjugation of women as sexually distinct humans. Those sexual differences were specifically what pornography exploited: reducing women to breasts, lips, hair, and vaginas, all arrayed together at the service of male desire. That's the crucial part here: male desire. If sexual difference exists on a biological or physical basis, then male desire is different from female desire. In this view, what a man wants from sex is not the same as what a woman wants, and the political, social, economic,

17 See Salihbegovic, 2020.

and physical dominance of men over women means that the desires of women become secondary to those of men.

After the assertion that sex and gender had no real physical basis, there was no longer a straightforward way to argue for physical differences in desire. In the framework Butler introduced, both male and female desire were also socially created. Men were shaped into desiring certain things, while women were shaped into desiring other things. Those desires had nothing to do with actually existing physical differences but were just the result of social and psychological conditioning.

One result of this shift was that new feminists began to argue that sex work (prostitution and modeling or acting for pornography) was actually liberating for women, and that it was a way for women to embrace their own desires and agency. While often admitting that many women (usually poor and immigrant women) were forced into such situations rather than entering into them willfully, these feminists no longer saw sex work as being any more exploitative than any other kind of work.

This shift applied also to paid surrogacy, the act of carrying a child for another person. Surrogacy was seen by many earlier feminists as the quintessential form of sexual exploitation of women, since it reduced a woman to her reproductive capacity. Not only was a women compelled to gestate a baby inside her for nine months, surrogacy turned this very female act into a site of economic exchange. The surrogate mother's womb was being bought or rented for the period of surrogacy, and the child born from her uterus was the property of the buyer. Once sexual difference became merely a "discursive subject," feminist arguments against surrogacy no longer had any foundation.

Declarative Gender

The most contentious issue born from this shift — from sexual difference's transition from being seen as a physical reality to being a mere discursive subject — is that of trans-sexual and transgender identity. If sex and gender are, as Butler argued, only socially created categories sustained by our belief in their existence and our subsequent performance of that belief, then belief and performance can create other realities. Thus, if a person believes they are female or woman and then performs femaleness or femininity, any physical characteristics which might suggest otherwise (a penis and a body shaped from puberty by higher levels of testosterone than estrogen) are utterly irrelevant to that identity.

Perhaps as an unintended or unforeseen consequence of this, positing the performance of gender and sex as a mere social construction also raises other questions. For instance, what does it mean to "perform" masculinity if there is not really such a thing as males or men? What does sexual difference mean if sex itself is merely an artificial division in our head?

This has now led to the current phenomenon of declarative gender, or "self-identification" for gender. Now fully separated from any reference to physical traits, one need only declare oneself a man, a woman, non-binary, or trans for it to be so. Because none of these identities any longer reference anything really existing, what they consist of is fully up to the person self-identifying as such to decide.

Declarative gender is the core point of strife regarding gender identity for older feminists (including so-called TERFs), the traditional left, and much of the general public. The reason for this strife is that legal protections and cultural spaces for women were crafted on the basis of physical and biological differences between males and females. Women's sporting events, for example, were created upon the understanding that females are physically different from males and generally have certain disadvantages in many sports when compared to a typical or average[18] male athlete. Laws guaranteeing rights to abortion access and contraceptives, as another example, are premised upon the physical reality that females can become pregnant and require additional access to services to prevent or end those pregnancies, which males do not require (because males cannot become pregnant). Rape, though it absolutely also occurs to men and is also committed by women, is overwhelmingly a physical assault directed at females and overwhelmingly by males. And the logic of the existence of private spaces for women — for instance, changing rooms in gyms and schools — is predicated upon the physical reality that some males tend to seek out moments of female nudity for sexual arousal and that men can, on average, physically overpower and menace women in vulnerable spaces.

If, as Butler argued, gender and sex are merely constructs we perform, and if gender is merely a matter of declaration, then the recognition of difference upon which those legal and cultural rights and spaces were built crumbles.

Previous feminist frameworks sought to rectify inequality in the treatment, political access, and material conditions of women by crafting laws, increasing

---

18 This point of the word "average" is too often ignored by people on all sides of the political debates regarding this matter. An exceptional female athlete may absolutely beat an average male-bodied athlete (trans or otherwise), but an *average* male-bodied athlete will have advantages over an *average* female-bodied athlete.

educational access, and creating separate spaces that would both protect women and empower them based upon certain physical differences — for instance, differences in strength or based on the fact that they can become pregnant. Because a woman is more likely to be raped, for instance, or to be caught in difficult domestic abuse situations, segregated sex-specific services and spaces were created (women-only shelters, for example).

Without physical differences as a primary guide, it becomes quite difficult to explain precisely why women need access to certain services or spaces. That doesn't necessarily mean that new legal and cultural formulations cannot be created to address these concerns, but it's difficult to find evidence of such work being undertaken.

The Contentious Matter of the Wi Spa

Highly publicized incidents in which women report being sexually assaulted or harassed by people identifying as trans women in sex-segregated spaces have resulted in even deeper polarization on these questions. Incidents in prisons within the United States and in the United Kingdom in which women have been raped by people identifying as trans women have received a lot of media attention, as have sexual assaults on women and girls in bathrooms and changing rooms. On the other hand, assaults against people identifying as trans women for being in the "wrong place" (women's bathrooms, for example) also abound, and assaults in men's prisons against people identifying as trans women have been reported as well.

What is notable here is that the question of integrating trans-identifying people within sex-segregated spaces is far from straightforward, and highly publicized incidents of assault in either direction lead to political strife that often results in physical fights, with all sides accusing their opponents of supporting, instigating, and committing violence. Perhaps the best known incidence of this occurred in Los Angeles on 23 June 2021.

Darren Agee Merager, who identifies as a trans woman, was accused by five women, and later charged by the police, of lewdly exposing an erect penis to them in the women-only area of the Korean Wi Spa. The event was first brought to international attention through a viral video filmed by one of the women at the spa that day, who claimed Merager acted lewdly and sexually threatening to her. Soon, protests outside the spa erupted over several days, drawing in people upset about the incident and others there to defend trans rights, including those aligned with Antifa.[19] At this point, however, no one actually knew the name of the person accused, nor was anyone certain the incident had actually happened.

In fact, a popular theory in social and traditional media at that time was that there was actually no trans woman in the spa and that the woman whose accusations had become viral was part of a conspiratorial right-wing set-up. This theory derived from a similarly viral article in the *Los Angeles Blade* by an anonymous guest contributor using a pseudonym, "Robert Lansing," who cited anonymous sources in the Los Angeles Police Department and the Wi Spa. The headline declared, "Alleged Trans incident at upscale LA spa may have been staged":

> There is increasing doubt among law enforcement and staff at the Wi Spa whether there was ever was a transgender person there to begin with. Anonymous sources within the LAPD tell the Blade they have been unable to find any

---

19 Several posters and images were posted on social media in the days following the incident calling for protest actions against "fascists and transphobes."

corroborating evidence that there was a transgender person present on that day.

Similarly, a source at the Spa told the Blade there's no record of any of its usual transgender clients on its appointments guest list on the day in question. Treatment at the Spa is by appointment only, and most of its transgender clients are well known to the staff.

...it also remains a possibility that there was a person, unknown to the Wi Spa staff, who pretended to be transgender to create an inciting incident.[20]

Widely cited in other major American and international news sources (for instance, in reporting by the *Guardian* and the *Los Angeles Times*), the article later turned out to be completely untrue. Darren Agee Merager was charged several months later with five felony accounts of sexual misconduct. According to a follow-up by the *Guardian*:

LAPD said on Thursday that five individuals had come forward with indecent exposure allegations in July, and that the department "conducted interviews of victims and witnesses, reviewed the evidence, and ultimately corroborated the allegations of indecent exposure."

Police said Merager has been a registered sex offender since 2006 and has a history of previous indecent exposure charges. Merager was convicted of indecent exposure in LA in 2002 and 2003, and pleaded not guilty to seven counts of indecent exposure in an alleged December 2018 case, according to court records. That case is still open.

It was not immediately clear if Merager had an attorney, and Merager's gender identity was also unclear.[21]

---

20 See Lansing, 2021. Curiously, no other articles appear under this pseudonym.

21 See Beckett, L. and Levin, S., 2021.

The early rush to conclusions about the meaning of the incident, before any details were released, as well as the violent protests that ensued (including attacks on journalists by participants on both sides of the protest), clearly shows how contentious the matter of declarative gender has become.

It also shows how little effort has been put into reconciling the larger questions posed by this framework. Perhaps unsurprisingly, Butler herself weighed in on the matter in an interview with the *Guardian*, which later redacted the parts of the interview in which she cited the Wi Spa incident. The interviewer's original (later redacted) question was this:

> It seems that some within feminist movements are becoming sympathetic to these far-right campaigns. This year's furore around Wi Spa in Los Angeles saw an online outrage by transphobes followed by bloody protests organised by the Proud Boys. Can we expect this alliance to continue?

Butler replied, in her redacted answer:

> It is very appalling and sometimes quite frightening to see how trans-exclusionary feminists have allied with right-wing attacks on gender. The anti-gender ideology movement is not opposing a specific account of gender, but seeking to eradicate "gender" as a concept or discourse, a field of study, an approach to social power. Sometimes they claim that "sex" alone has scientific standing, but other times they appeal to divine mandates for masculine domination and difference. They don't seem to mind contradicting themselves.[22]

22 Unredacted parts of the essay are published on the interviewer's Patreon. See Gleeson, 2021.

In a later essay for the *Guardian,* Butler greatly expanded upon this argument that any kind of reaction to this newer conception of gender (socially-constructed, performative, declarative) is not just inherently right-wing, but also fascist:

> Anti-gender movements are not just reactionary but fascist trends, the kind that support increasingly authoritarian governments. The inconsistency of their arguments and their equal opportunity approach to rhetorical strategies of the left and right, produce a confusing discourse for some, a compelling one for others. But they are typical of fascist movements that twist rationality to suit hyper-nationalist aims.[23]

While there are certainly right-aligned movements that oppose this new conception of gender (and it is rather ironic that Butler suggests there is an effort by critics of this new conception to "produce a confusing discourse"), it's both spurious and a bit infantilizing to claim all such critiques are fascist trends. Again, this conception of gender is a very new one and was only recently popularized in the last ten years through social media and clickbait articles from sites like *Everyday Feminism*. Changes to the legal classification of people, from being based on sex to being based on gender, are hardly widespread, and only very recently have some governments begun to allow self-declaration of gender without medical or therapeutic documentation. For instance, as of writing only sixteen nations allow declarations of gender self-identification without other documentation, and some of those (for instance, Denmark) mandate a "reflection period" after filing the declaration in order to prevent potential abuse of the legal process.

---

23 See Butler, 2021.

Polling and surveys often show that people are more accepting of transgendered identity recognition when it's tied to medical diagnoses or mandated periods of social transition (living as one's declared gender for a time before legal recognition). In other words, there seems to be a general acceptance of transgender identity by large parts of the public, but not for declarative gender divorced from material conditions or physical reality. This would suggest that, rather than being merely a construct created through performance and belief, many people have a sense that sex and gender are tied at some level to physical traits.

If that is so, then Butler's assertion that opposition to this newer conception is "not just reactionary but fascist" is at best heavy handed. However, Butler is hardly the only theorist to assert this. Many activists who identify as transgender have also asserted there are connections between criticism of declarative gender and right-wing movements. Also, several feminist academics[24] have asserted there is an organized global right-wing and fascist populist movement against gender, and many Antifa websites and social media accounts make clear that to be critical of this new gender framework in any way is to be also a fascist.

Conflating any criticism or concern about this new conception of gender with extreme nationalist and racist movements certainly is politically effective: it casts the situation as a clear "progressive versus reactionary" dichotomy. On one side are all those who find this newer framework liberating, while on the other are all those who want to dismantle all gender equality and return society to patriarchal, medieval forms of social relations.

---

24 See Graff, A. and Korolczuk, 2022; Case, 2019; and Kováts Eszter, Poim, M. and Pető Andrea, 2015.

However, the question really needs to be asked: Is a woman who reports sexual harassment or assault by a person who identifies as a trans woman automatically therefore a fascist? What about a victim of rape in a crisis center — is she a fascist if she expresses a preference not to be housed in the same intimate space with someone she perceives to be male and therefore a potential abuser? Is it really fascist for an athlete to prefer competing against people of her biological sex rather than against people whose bodies were shaped by the higher amounts of testosterone found in males than in females?

You'll note in these questions that the primary concerns relate to women rather than men. This is because of something older feminist theorists pointed to long before gender became divorced from sex: men tend to dominate and physically abuse women much more often than women do men. The proposed reasons for why this occurs are varied (inherent differences between men and women, patriarchal legal regimes, differences in the socialization of boys and girls), but the material reality is nevertheless undisputed. Men lose very little in regards to rights and protections under this new conception of gender, because these older cultural and legal mechanisms were not created to protect men from women but rather to protect women from men and to allow women to have more access to resources and activities where men dominate.

Especially in regards to reproduction, women have a separate set of concerns which men lack. A man cannot be forced to conceive, carry, and give birth to a child, because he is physically incapable of doing any of things. He will not be fired from a job because he is pregnant and requires leave from work for the birth and early nurturing, because he cannot get pregnant or give birth.

The Haunting of the Real

Attempts to accommodate these older concerns into the newer ideological formation of gender have resulted in some very clumsy and revealing rhetoric. For instance, the stripping of reference to sexual or gender characteristics in order to be more inclusive of trans and non-binary identities has resulted in terms such as "uterus-havers," "chest-feeding," "menstruators," and "gestators." In these attempts, we get a glimpse of how the physical — otherwise deprioritized or even completely denied — reasserts itself back into these narratives.

Let's return again to the matter of Darren Agee Merager, the alleged perpetrator of the indecent exposure incidents at the Wi Spa in June of 2021. Merager claimed, in an interview for the *New York Post*, to have been in the correct place, and that she was being punished for being a woman using the spaces in a spa designated exclusively for women.[25] If so, then Merager was merely *performing gender* the way everyone else does, affirming the existence of women as such. Merager's allegedly erect penis notwithstanding, any other women in those spaces who rejected Merager's presence were, according to Butler, responding to a fascist trend or urge, or were at best clinging to an outdated and reactionary understanding of what constitutes a woman or man. But were the women who were in that women-only area along with Merager there because they were performing gender as well? That is, by choosing to enter the women-only area rather than the area designated for men, were they merely performing and reifying an outdated social construct? Or did they go into that space because

---

25 Merager gave an account early on to the deeply controversial journalist Andy Ngo. See Ngo, 2021.

going into the other space would put them among a lot of nude men?

Or in a larger sense, do you use a men's toilet or a women's toilet because you "feel" like you are a man or a woman? Are you merely responding to social pressure and constructs by doing so (the sign on the door, for example), or is it just a lot safer and more comfortable to have your pants down around your ankles among people who are physically more similar to you than to the other sex?

These kinds of questions reveal an unspoken and unresolved consequence of this newer gender conception. Gender as a mere social construct proposes that there is really no underlying sexual difference, only the different gender signs on the door. That is, women only see themselves as part of a category called "women" because society defines them as such. They are treated differently as infants, socialized differently by their parents, surrounded by living models (mothers, for example) of this constructed category, and constantly pushed into performing "woman" in all their interactions. Men are similarly socialized, and disciplined into performing "man" and thinking of themselves as part of that category.

In addition to all this, men are also enlisted through this socialization into performing dominance over women. According to this framework, a key part of male socialization into the category of "man" involves learning how to dominate, how to favor force and violence over care and nurturing, and how to replicate the oppression and exploitation of women in their social relations. For some feminist theorists, this exploitation begins even in young childhood, with boys being taught by their fathers that they should expect women to labor and care for them rather than to participate equally in such activities. Those women (mothers, often) also teach their sons that men can expect such things from women through their willingness to do these activities, their deference to their husbands, and their social performance of the construct of "woman."

These ideas are not unique to this new gender framework, however. Older feminist theorists also pointed to early socialization as a key to inequality between men and women, as well as to the way women also uphold this inequality through their many acts of subservience to men. These are general feminist insights, but they have been re-tooled in this newer framework to explain not just how inequality is reproduced but also how gender and sexual difference is constructed.

Earlier forms of feminism — along with still-current feminist frameworks such as Marxist feminism and eco-feminism — accepted that there are inherent differences between men and women, and argued that these differences are the site of exploitation of women. A woman's capacity to give birth and nurture infants especially made her different from men, and it was this capacity that patriarchal systems sought to exploit through rape, forced marriages, and punitive laws against the use of contraceptives and abortion.

So, there are really two competing frameworks within feminism. The earlier framework sees the differences between men and women as rooted in physical differences, while the newer framework locates the division in social constructs. Each framework then leads to different conclusions about what can and should be done about inequalities and abuses. According to the older framework, women require extra protections, laws, and access to things like maternity leave and abortion services because the things which make them physically different from men lead to disadvantages and positions of vulnerability. For the newer framework, the way sex and gender are constructed on the social level must be changed so that women are no longer seen as weaker, easily abused, or secondary to men.

As with so much else we'll look at in this book, this newer framework was constructed with good intentions and from important observations. The docile servility of the 1950s housewife, for example, was most definitely a socially created role that women were expected to play. So, too, were social expectations that women should prioritize having children and taking care of their family as their ultimate fulfilment. Because these are socially constructed roles — constructed especially through television, films, and, particularly, advertising — they can be changed through social means.

Also, in its attempt to liberate people from restrictive, socially constructed expectations about gender expression, this newer framework correctly understands that what it means to be a man or a woman is shaped by cultural and political forces, not just by sexual difference. Examples of these forces include the idea that a man or a woman must look a certain way, or must take on certain kinds of jobs and not others, or must only engage in heterosexual relations and desires. A woman who desires other women instead of men, and a man who keeps house and cares for children while his wife works — they are not any less a man or woman because of these things, and societies that try to force them into cultural norms regarding what they should be doing are absolutely oppressive.

Unacknowledged Problems

However, problems absolutely arise when underlying sexual differences are ignored, as the situation of the Wi Spa and Darren Agee Merager shows. Regarding that incident, there is yet another level of complication caused by the model of declarative gender. A few days after his arrest on 13 December 2022 — almost a full fifteen months after the incident — *Los Angeles Magazine* published an exclusive interview with Merager regarding the events and aftermath.

After explaining how her many sexual assault and harassment charges prior to the Wi Spa incident were just misunderstandings, Merager makes several claims which do not square with either of the dominant narratives that arose in defense of or opposition to Merager's presence in the spa. For one, Merager stated that he equally prefers he/him and she/her pronouns and is "very neutral, like non-binary." Further, in response to a question regarding sexuality, Merager explained:

> I have heterosexual sex because my penis fits in a vagina. I don't tell women I'm with that I'm transgender because that's not my sex. So I'm not faking anything. Gender is internal, sex is external.[26]

In other words, Merager's conception of gender and of sex is that they are separate things altogether. In the interview, Merager insists that people who get medical gender interventions such as hormone treatments or surgery (breast implants or removal, vaginoplasty or phalloplasty) are actually not transgender at all:

> Everybody's confusing your internal with your external. All these external people are doing what is being called transitioning. There's no transition. That's called deviation. I'm tired of that word, "transitioning." It's a fake word.[27]

And regarding Merager's own presentation and appearance, we learn from the interview that Merager changed legal sex merely by signing a piece of paper ("Basically, anybody

---

26 See Quinn, J.L., McGahan, J. and Dolak, K.A., 2022.
27 Ibid.

could walk in and get one"). Merager also acknowledges not having a female appearance:

> I'm legally female. But I have facial hair. I have a penis. I have no breasts. I don't have a feminine voice. I don't wear makeup or dress up like a female. So imagine you're a grocery store [clerk] and you're bagging my groceries and you say, "Excuse me, sir..." I mean, am I supposed to be offended? That'd be ridiculous. How would this person know? [28]

Because Merager doesn't present in obvious feminine ways, the women in the spa who reported harassment and sexual threats wouldn't have had any obvious way of knowing that Merager is "legally female." Also, because the process of getting legal recognition of a different sex in California doesn't require anything except a signed declaration, it's quite possible to abuse that process. Whether or not that was Merager's intention, it's very easy to see that such concerns have merit.

These are problems inherent to the declarative gender framework that have not been resolved. Complicating this further is the vehement denial by activists and theorists that such problems even exist. This is what has led us to the current place where right-aligned activists and theorists have been able to claim a position of speaking for "reality," while the left appears out of touch or even willfully blind to these problems.

---

28 Another interesting matter: according to the interview, even Antifa and other radical protesters mistook Merager for a right-wing protester when Merager showed up to the protest.

CHAPTER THREE: THE CYBORG

In the previous chapter we looked at the shifting understanding of sexual difference and gender, as well as at some of the consequences of that shift. Ideological shifts do not merely happen in a vacuum, however, and they are rarely if ever born only in academic, political, or scientific discourse. Larger events occurring in society often initiate these changes.

It's well known, for example, that the transformation of industrial societies during the Second World War changed the composition of the labor force. While millions of men were pulled into the war efforts as soldiers, millions of women filled the industrial and agricultural positions those men no longer occupied. Women worked as machinists, miners, assembly-line workers, and in many other traditionally male roles.

Often this is seen as a moment of liberation and progress for women and women's political rights, since prior to this period, women in those societies were generally not employed in such jobs. However, because many of those women lost those jobs, or married and became housewives after the war, it would seem this moment of liberation was only temporary. Also, the following decade, the Fifties, saw a resurgence of strict gender roles for women — especially in the figure of the dutiful suburban housewife, eager to please her work-traumatized husband in every way possible.

In the meantime, technological changes altered domestic work itself. The mass production and increased consumer availability of household domestic appliances such as washing machines, tumble dryers, and dishwashing machines promised to make life easier for women; however, they did not actually change the societal role of housewives as the people responsible for doing that work. Instead, advertising during that period often showed women happy and relieved to have more time to take care of their husbands rather than as being able to pursue their own goals.

One bit of technology did significantly influence the situation of women, however: the pill. Invented in the Fifties and approved for prescription sale by the US Food and Drug Administration in 1960, the pill offered women a technological escape from the inevitability of pregnancy and a degree of control over the decision to raise a child or not.

The introduction of the birth control pill heavily shaped feminist thought in the 1960s,[29] and it is sometimes seen as the true starting point of second-wave feminism. Feminists began to think about pregnancy and motherhood not as natural destinies of women but as just one potential role that they could have. It also meant that pregnancy was less of a risk in sexual relations with men, thus freeing women to explore their sexual desires with fewer economic consequences.

In 1973, the federal decriminalization of abortion through the Supreme Court ruling of *Roe v. Wade* furthered this apparent trajectory towards liberation in the United States. Not only could women choose to avoid conception, they could also choose to terminate a pregnancy after conception.

---

29 The pill was not actually widely available immediately. It wasn't until 1965 that it became legal to prescribe it to any married women in the US. Unmarried women were not guaranteed access to it by law until 1972, the year before *Roe v. Wade*.

Both widespread availability of the birth control pill and then the decriminalization of abortion seemed to give women more control over their reproduction, and yet feminists noticed that society wasn't really becoming more equal. Men still dominated their professional lives and the instruments of political governance, and men continued to physically dominate women. Rape and other sexual assaults continued as they had before: all that had really changed were women's options after such assaults.

The point here is that the technological changes which influenced and shaped feminist thought never fully delivered the liberation they promised. Though machines appeared in almost every home to make work easier for women, those machines never changed the fact that women were expected to do that work. Though women could now mostly control whether or not their bodies would carry a child after sexual relations with a man, their bodies were still subordinate to the bodies of men.

Radical, Eco-, and Marxist Feminisms

This meant that second-wave feminists started looking elsewhere for the roots of the problem. One influential current which arose in response to these observations was called radical feminism. Radical feminism saw inequality between men and women as a "transhistorical phenomenon" arising out of the system they identified as patriarchy. In this framework, men had always arranged societies in such a way that women would be subjugated, inferior, and barred from political and economic access. Thus, the only way for women to achieve liberation and to have equal status with men was through a radical re-ordering of society on all levels.

When we now hear people speaking of "dismantling" or "smashing" the patriarchy, this is why. The influence of radical feminism on the rest of feminism was substantial, and even though radical feminism has now become synonymous with an anti-trans stance (as in "trans-exclusionary radical feminists"), all contemporary feminist thought — as well as queer, anti-racist, and other radical thought — was shaped by radical feminism's framework.

Some radical feminist writers and tendencies were vehemently anti-man in ways that have come to overshadow feminism itself. Lesbianism for some became not just a sexual orientation but rather a radical act, considered the only kind of sexual act that could be free from patriarchal domination. The reasoning behind this idea was that until society itself changed, women would always be in positions of submission to men — even in sex. Some even argued that it was impossible for a woman to have truly consensual sex with a man.

Not all radical feminists saw the patriarchy as the ultimate root of all inequality for women. Some feminists, most notably Silvia Federici, focused instead on the way inequality between men and women was a key feature of capitalism. Using Marxist analyses of historical forces, Federici proposed that the core site of women's exploitation was in their different kind of labor. Silvia Federici names this "reproductive labor," which includes not just child birth but all personal domestic activities (caretaking, cooking, housework, socializing) that both men and women engage in. For her, the role of housewife is a primary site of this exploitation:

This fraud that goes under the name of love and marriage affects all of us, even if we are not married, because once housework was totally naturalised and sexualised, once it became a feminine attribute, all of us as females are characterised by it. If it is natural to do certain things, then all women are expected to do them and even like doing them — even those women who, due to their social position, could escape some of that work or most of it (their husbands can afford maids and shrinks and other forms of relaxation and amusement). We might not serve one man, but we are all in a servant relation with respect to the whole male world.[30]

Marxist feminism and a related tendency, eco-feminism, differ from other feminisms on the question of whether there is anything actually different about women and their labor. Subsequent feminists — especially Judith Butler and those who came after her — reject any sort of natural difference between men and women. For Marxist feminists, women are different from men because of sexual reproduction, while for eco-feminists, women also possess a deeper innate capacity to nurture that men do not. For both, these differences derive from the physical difference between women and men: women have the biological capacity to give birth to children and to feed infants directly from their body, as well as other biological differences (menstruation, the higher presence of estrogen in their bodies, and accompanying differences in perceptions and emotional states).

Marxist Feminism and Eco-Feminism see the difference between men and women as physical and argue that any radical shift towards equal relations needs to accommodate those physical differences. This is an idea that has been discarded by third-wave feminism's framework of gender and sex as constructs or "discursive subjects." In this newer framework, even if there are any real differences between the bodies of women and men, they are irrelevant to the larger issue of patriarchal domination. In fact, it's that patriarchal domination itself which is proposed as

---

30 See Federici, 1975.

the reason we even think of men and women as different categories and therefore mistakenly believe that sex or gender are "real" things.

Enter the Cyborg

To understand how it was that this newer framework of gender — which rejects any natural difference between men and women — became the dominant feminism over other tendencies, we need to meet our first monster: the Cyborg.

Unlike any of the other monsters which arise to show us (*monstrere*) something, the Cyborg is a very new creation. It arose in 1960, the very same year the birth control pill first became approved for prescription in the United States, but it took some time before making its way out of the mind of the men who first identified it into our societal consciousness.

In an article for the journal *Astronautics*, Manfred Clynes and Nathan Kline introduced the Cyborg as the solution to human biological limitations and the slowness of our evolution:

Space travel challenges man not only technologically but also spiritually, in that it invites man to take an active part in his own biological evolution. Scientific advances of the future may thus be utilized to permit man's existence in environments which differ radically from those provided by nature as we know it.

The task of adapting man's body to any environment he may choose will be made easier by increased knowledge of homeostatic functioning, the cybernetic aspects of which are just beginning to be understood and investigated. In the past evolution brought about the altering of bodily functions to suit different environments. Starting as of now, it will be possible to achieve this to some degree without alteration of heredity....

...The purpose of the Cyborg, as well as his own homeostatic systems, is to provide an organizational system in which such robot-like problems are taken care of automatically and unconsciously, leaving man free to explore, to create, to think, and to feel.[31]

For the two authors of that paper, the Cyborg was the solution to the many natural limits which prevented humans from exploring space. This monstrous Cyborg (from "cybernetic organism") would comprise both the human itself as well as all the machines which take over the aspects of that human's survival: eating, breathing, waste elimination, exercise, hygiene, and even the extension of consciousness and his "erotic requirements."

In other words, the Cyborg was an extended human, a hybrid being both natural and mechanical. The mechanical aspects would take care of all the things that Silvia Federici later identified as "reproductive labor." Cybernetics would perform the functions of mother, of wife, and of nurse, dutifully making sure the organism part of the Cyborg was alert, fed, clean, healthy, and had no unmet sexual desire.

It didn't take very long for the Cyborg to appear again in fiction as a creature both of fear and potential. Sci-fi fantasies and horrors of humans augmented by machines became a staple of comics and television series, while philosophers and technological optimists argued the Cyborg was humanity's inevitable future.

Already, medical and scientific advances seemed to point to the Cyborg as our collective destiny. The pill had

---

31 Other benefits, according to the article, include the ability to take care of emotional and sexual satisfaction. See Clynes, M.E. and Kline, N.S., 1960.

proven that the biological processes of conception could be altered and prevented. The first mechanical heart valve transplant in a human occurred six years later. Decades before, machines had already successfully performed external dialysis for failing kidneys. Two years before the Cyborg appeared, wearable artificial pacemakers had been developed, and better designs of artificial respirator machines allowed them to be mass-produced five years before the Cyborg arose. Humans had already begun the process of becoming part machine before 1960, but the pace of these hybridizations accelerated after the monster appeared.

Medical science and technology seemed to blur the distinctions of what was human and what was machine, just as it had changed the relationship women had to sex and reproduction with the advent of the pill. Other advances also blurred those distinctions. Recall that sexologist John Money's first published introduction of the idea of gender as something separate from sexual difference was in 1955. Five years before, the first person in the United States to identify as a trans-sexual had undergone surgery in Denmark. In 1966, John Money opened the first sex-change clinic in the United States through Johns Hopkins University, a practice that involved not just surgery but also the administration of hormones to help the transition.

The Cyborg was everywhere expanding what it meant to be human, taking over bodily functions or even changing them according to its divine objective hidden in the first part of its name. Cybernetics comes from the Greek word *kybernetikos*, meaning "to steer" or "to pilot," as a steersman pilots a ship to its destination. The Cyborg was guiding us, steering us past our natural, biological limits. But where was it taking us?

Twenty-five years after it first appeared, and five years before Judith Butler's publication of *Gender Trouble*, the

Cyborg made its most famous appearance in an influential essay by feminist Donna Haraway. That essay, "A Cyborg Manifesto," was the first significant attempt to wrestle with the consequences of technological change and the growing divorce between the physical and social existence of women.

"A Cyborg Manifesto" was first and foremost a criticism and rejection of feminisms which saw women as physically tied to nature. Throughout the essay, Haraway argues against any sort of naturalization of the idea of women, because technology had already supposedly proven otherwise. However, she is no technological optimist and does not argue that women are actually being liberated by these advances. Instead, she proposes a kind of realist reckoning with the Cyborg. If technological disruption was de-naturalizing women and turning them into hybrid beings — part human, part machine — then women should find ways to liberate themselves through that hybridity.

A significant point Haraway makes is that feminism had already become subject to this hybridity. You couldn't talk about "feminism" as one thing, or even of women as one thing. Everything needed a qualifying adjective to be spoken about, and even then, all those terms were up for debate. These were all effects of technological and societal disruption, and those disruptions had made political organizing among historically recognized groups (race, class, and gender) impossible:

> It has become difficult to name one's feminism by a single adjective — or even to insist in every circumstance on the noun. Consciousness of exclusion through naming is acute. Identities seem contradictory, partial, and strategic. With the hard-won recognition of their social and historical

constitution, gender, race, and class cannot provide the basis for belief in "essential" unity. There is nothing about being "female" that naturally binds women. There is not even such a state as "being" female, itself a highly complex category constructed in contested sexual scientific discourses and other social practices. Gender, race, or class consciousness is an achievement forced on us by the terrible historical experience of the contradictory social realities of patriarchy, colonialism, and capitalism. And who counts as "us" in my own rhetoric? Which identities are available to ground such a potent political myth called "us," and what could motivate enlistment in this collectivity? Painful fragmentation among feminists (not to mention among women) along every possible fault line has made the concept of woman elusive, an excuse for the matrix of women's dominations of each other. For me — and for many who share a similar historical location in white, professional middle-class, female, radical, North American, mid-adult bodies — the sources of a crisis in political identity are legion.[32]

A particular problem for Haraway was the identification of women according to the kind of labor they performed. For "white, professional middle-class" feminists such as herself, it seemed false to identify with the material conditions of lower-class women throughout the world: they did not all share the same material conditions. They were not all housewives, nor were they employed in the domestic, agricultural, or services positions which compose the vast majority of the labor women globally perform.

Haraway particularly struggles over this problem in "A Cyborg Manifesto," repeatedly asserting that it is both impossible and anyway useless to find a common foundation from which women can seek solidarity with each other.

32 See Haraway, 2016.

Her solution is that of hybridity: the Cyborg. Rather than a feminism based upon a natural or physical commonality among women (the "goddess" model proposed by Eco-Feminism), and rather than a solidarity built upon the idea of women's labor (the Marxist Feminist framework), completely new affinities needed to arise.

It's crucial to remember that Haraway — and also subsequent feminists, including Judith Butler — was reacting to a historical moment of technological, social, and economic disruption. The reason Haraway proposes the Cyborg against the more natural or "naturalised" frameworks for feminism is because the sudden prevalence and acceleration of computer (cyber-) technology was transforming labor throughout the world.

"A Cyborg Manifesto" was published in 1985, just at the beginning of the internet technological revolution. Even in those early stages, work and labor had already come to be redefined through technology, changing the way both women and men related to each other, to capital, and to themselves:

Let me summarize the picture of women's historical locations in advanced industrial societies, as these positions have been re-structured partly through the social relations of science and technology. If it was ever possible ideologically to characterize women's lives by the distinction of public and private domains — suggested by images of the division of working-class life into factory and home, of bourgeois life into market and home, and of gender existence into personal and political realms — it is now a totally misleading ideology, even to show how both terms of these dichotomies construct each other in practice and in theory. I prefer a network ideological image, suggesting the profusion of spaces and identities and the permeability of boundaries in the personal body and in the body politic.[33]

Again, Haraway is reacting to societal shifts, shifts in which the category or identity of "woman" is continuously complicated and disrupted by new forms of labor and technology. For her, it makes less and less sense to hold to a natural or naturalized conception of women connected to their bodies, their biological difference from men, or their labor as women since these differences matter very little in the face of technological disruption.

The Cyborg and the Birth of Identity Politics

Haraway also repeatedly criticizes the move towards identity and identity politics: she sees identity itself as a product of the Western conception of the atomized, individual self. Though Haraway never directly references it, a feminist movement originating out of the "Combahee River Collective Statement" six years prior to her initial work on the manuscript for "The Cyborg Manifesto" had already begun to cause significant divisions within feminism and socialism.

Born of a sharp critique of both feminism and Marxism by black women, the "Combahee River Collective Statement" proposed identity itself as the core foundation for all radical politics:

> Focusing upon our own oppression is embodied in the concept of identity politics. We believe that the most profound and potentially most radical politics come directly out of our own identity, as opposed to working to end somebody else's oppression.[34]

---

33 Ibid.

34 See The Combahee River Collective, 1977.

The Combahee River Collective, prior to issuing the statement, had been a significantly active radical group. However, as they admit in their statement, several internal crises had wracked their group (including a "lesbian-straight split" and an exodus by people who, in their words, "did not want to do the political work"), which led them to become instead a very small study group. It was that study group which wrote the statement in 1977.

In the statement, the writers specifically identify white feminism as one of the core reasons for their iteration of a new political framework, since, as they note:

> one issue that is of major concern to us and that we have begun to publicly address is racism in the white women's movement. As Black feminists we are made constantly and painfully aware of how little effort white women have made to understand and combat their racism, which requires among other things that they have a more than superficial comprehension of race, color, and Black history and culture. Eliminating racism in the white women's movement is by definition work for white women to do, but we will continue to speak to and demand accountability on this issue.

The criticism represented by the collective's statement haunts Haraway's "A Cyborg Manifesto" (she dedicates quite a few pages to addressing and praising black women fiction writers), as it further complicates the matter of women as a political class. The problem here is that women can be both oppressed and oppressor. Thus, there is no shared or universal experience of oppression by women, and thus a new understanding of women must be developed.

"A Cyborg Manifesto" can be seen as an attempt to steer both socialism and feminism away from a problem Haraway notes and foresaw as a dead end: the relentless fracturing of radical movements into obsessions with identity. However, not only was Haraway's warning unheeded, her work provided the foundation for an even more fractious kind of politics than she could have anticipated by de-naturalizing women into the technological myth of the Cyborg.

The logic of identity in the "Combahee River Collective Statement" was expanded upon by a legal scholar, Kimberlé Crenshaw, twelve years later. That initial conception of identity politics now had a new name, *intersectionality*. Intersectionality is a both a theory and a framework that proposes to describe how black women can experience multiple oppressions simultaneously along separate axes of their identity. For example, a black woman can face discrimination at work from men because she is a woman, and also experience racism from white people (men and women both) because she is black:

> Consider an analogy to traffic in an intersection, coming and going in all four directions. Discrimination, like traffic through an intersection, may flow in one direction, and it may flow in another. If an accident happens in an intersection, it can be caused by cars traveling from any number of directions and, sometimes, from all of them. Similarly, if a Black woman is harmed because she is in an intersection, her injury could result from sex discrimination or race discrimination.[35]

Few would likely disagree with the core thrust of this argument. However, as intersectional feminism developed alongside the de-naturalization of the category of women, especially through the chaotic alembic of internet culture in the following decades, intersectionality soon became the

---

35 See Crenshaw, 1989.

primary framework by which all identities and oppressions are seen in radical politics. The internet site *Everyday Feminism*,[36] which during its most popular years became a go-to source for any question of identity and oppression, explains the way identity and intersectionality work together this way:

> It makes sense in many ways that those of us with identity privilege would have a harder time including in our feminism those who are oppressed. Privilege conceals itself from those who have it, and it's a lot easier to focus on the ways that we are marginalized or oppressed.
>
> But without an intersectional lens, our movements cannot be truly anti-oppressive because it is not, in fact, possible to tease apart the oppressions that people are experiencing. Racism for women of color cannot be separated from their gendered oppression. A trans person with a disability cannot choose which part of their identity is most in need of liberation....
>
> ...In short, intersectionality is a framework that must be applied to all social justice work, a frame that recognizes the multiple aspects of identity that enrich our lives and experiences and that compound and complicate oppressions and marginalizations.
>
> We cannot separate multiple oppressions, for they are experienced and enacted intersectionally.

---

36 *Everyday Feminism* articles often include multiple bolded and hyperlinked statements, along with other formatting tricks to give articles a sense of meme-worthiness, especially multiple one-sentence paragraphs. I've chosen not to include the emphasis from their native formatting in this quote but preserved their paragraph structure.

Thus, in the words of Flavia Dzodan, "My feminism will be intersectional or it will be bullshit."[37]

From this view of intersectionality, each discrete oppression identity (or oppressed aspect) is compounded and inextricably bound up in the other oppression identities a person has. A black trans woman, for instance, has several identities which all compound oppression: being black and being a trans woman (or "black," "trans," and "woman"). None of the oppressions such a person faces can be talked about singularly or addressed singularly, but rather all must be simultaneously fought and rectified.

This framework, whose original intention was to explain how black women in the United States could experience both misogyny and anti-black racism, is now applied more broadly to every situation in which a person has more than one oppression identity. The result of this — perhaps unintended but regardless now fully manifested — is that compound or hybrid oppression identities have come to constitute a kind of hierarchy of oppression.

The more oppression identities a person has, the more they are oppressed, and consequently, the more deserving they are of social justice and deferential treatment. This is the root of what some critics call "the oppression Olympics," whereby people compare and compete with each other over who is more oppressed. This becomes quite evident when observing conversations between white feminist women and black feminist women: while both groups experience misogyny, only the latter can claim to experience misogynoir.[38]

---

37 See Uwujaren, 2020.

38 A portmanteau of misogyny and the French word for black (*noir*), meaning oppression of black women.

"Cis or Trans?"

These conflicts get even more complicated when rarer or newer oppression identities are claimed. A black feminist woman may experience more oppression than a white feminist woman, but she's got it better than a black trans woman, who, in turn, may still have it better than a disabled black trans woman.

Transgender identity often introduces into these conversations an even more contentious dynamic, because it sometimes can trump racial identity in these hierarchies. For example, consider the significant backlash and "canceling" of Nigerian feminist Chimamanda Ngozi Adichie in 2017 for her statement "Trans women are trans women."[39] On the face of it, at least for those unfamiliar with the many confessional statements that have become a necessity in radical politics, her words might appear completely neutral and rather harmless. After all, it follows the same reflexive semantic logic as "women are women" or "trees are trees." Adichie's sin, however, was that her statement was wrong: the correct formula should be "trans women are women."

"Trans women are women" is a common profession of belief and a political statement found quite often on social media, on protest banners and signs, and also in official speeches and policy statements by activists, politicians, and organizations. It is sometimes also used as a kind of shibboleth or inquisitional challenge to public writers, institutions, and others to verify their adherence to the correct gender framework.[40] The meaning of the statement

---

39 She made this statement during an interview on the British television station Channel 4. See Newman, 2017.

40 I've received several emails over the years asking me to affirm this statement publicly, as have many other leftist writers I

is that trans women should be considered women, rather than men or a fully different category. Whether one believes this statement or not, it glosses over several deep complications and contradictions within this newer gender framework.

Consider one of these complications, the question of "male privilege" as it relates to when a trans woman should be considered a woman rather than a man. Since many trans women transition later in life and are treated by society as men before this point, such individuals would be said to have had male privilege and to have been part of the oppressor category of men. However, transitioning puts the person into the category of women, and women do not possess male privilege. So, when did the person actually lose male privilege and become part of an oppressed identity group?

Adichie's statement was in regards to this apparent contradiction. From such a view, if a man becomes a trans woman, that person does not necessarily or instantly lose all previous male socialization, nor do they gain all the characteristics that put women into an oppressed category (for instance, female socialization in early life, the developmental effects of estrogen rather than testosterone, or physical traits such as menstruation). Thus, feminists such as Adichie propose that trans women be considered a unique category: people who take on the gender roles of woman but who do not retroactively lose their male sexual difference or the benefits of male socialization.

Another contradiction arises from this question of male privilege and transition: At what point is a trans woman actually to be considered a trans woman? As we saw earlier, not all people who identify as trans women medically

---

know. The feminist writer Catherine McKinnon once answered a version of this question with the response, "I am aggressively indifferent to this question."

transition or even take replacement hormones, and some even choose never to adopt "feminine" dress, vocal tones, or affectations. In fact, oftentimes it is argued that mere self-acknowledgment of trans identity is sufficient to make one trans, as this quote from an LGBTQ+ counseling website explains:

> Someone who identifies as *transgender*, simply means the experience of gender and/or personal identity doesn't align with their sex assigned at birth.
>
> So, as we look at the pragmatics of the definitions, yes you can identify as trans without transitioning. Acknowledging that your gender identity is trans does not require anything other than recognizing gender identity from within.[41]

This contradiction leads us back to the strife around Darren Agee Merager and the Wi Spa incident mentioned in the last chapter. Merager claimed to be a trans woman and to be thus owed access to private women-only spaces. The women who encountered Merager saw instead a man in the wrong place. Who was correct?

This same issue arises in legal questions, such as whether or not someone who identifies as a trans woman but who has not medically transitioned should be housed in women-only areas of prisons, domestic abuse shelters, and other places segregated by sex. It's also the question at the heart of protests and anger regarding sporting events. At what point does a trans woman athlete lose male bodily advantage (akin to male privilege) after transition?

The questions posed in these debates and conflicts around gender, sex, and oppression identities all come

---

41 See Archuleta, 2022.

down to the matter of differentiation. Where or when does a "cis-man" stop being man and instead become a woman? Where do we draw the line regarding who belongs in a women-only space? At what point should an oppressed woman be considered an oppressor?

While all deeply contentious questions, we need to keep in mind that they are parts of the larger questions the Cyborg asks. Where is the line between human and machine? At what point do the increasing technological and medical augmentations of our human lives make us less human? And what does it mean to be human in the first place?

Especially, we must remember that Donna Haraway suggested we look to the Cyborg as an antidote to identity politics. The opposite has happened; instead of the dissolution of identity categories towards a politics of ever-shifting hybridity, most radical politics now consist of increasingly fractious and oppositional identity categories. As the naturalistic basis for feminist struggle eroded, being a "feminist woman" no longer meant anything, because one had to identify what kind of a feminist and what kind of a woman one was. This is what has led to the constantly-expanding lists of sexual, racial, gender, and other identity categories. While some might laugh and roll their eyes at such identities, and others might take these all very seriously, the crucial questions the Cyborg asks are still unanswered. Who are we? What makes us human? And where does one category or identity end and another begin?

CHAPTER FOUR: RACE

Europeans are simply a different breed of human. They are socialized to be aggressive people. They are taught to live by the credo, "survival of the fittest." They are raised to be racist.

Caucasians make up only 10 percent of the world's population and that small percentage of people have recessive genes. Therefore they're facing extinction. Whites have tried to level the playing field with the AIDS virus and cloning, but they know these deterrents will only get them so far. This is where the murder, psychological brainwashing and deception comes into play.

Ibram X Kendi (writing as Ibram Rogers),
"Living With the White Race."[42]

For six years, I was a social worker for a large non-profit homelessness agency. That agency was quite progressive, being one of the first in North America to implement the "housing first" model, whereby homeless people with severe addictions, mental illnesses, and other problems are housed in agency-run apartment buildings.

My particular job was one of the lowest in the agency, because I did not have the required university degree for higher-level positions. I was able to secure that job because of "life experience" (I had no university degree at all), because I had been homeless in my early twenties, during which time I sometimes slept in a friend's car or hidden in the bushes in a city park, occasionally on the floor in an

---

42 See Kendi, 2003.

anarchist squat, once in a while in an alley, sometimes on a couch, and quite often in the bed of a random man I'd just met at a bar to trade sex for a warm place to sleep.

This was a very short period of my life, and I was quite lucky. I wasn't addicted to drugs, I wasn't mentally ill, and I actually had a part-time job during that time. Eventually I was able to save up enough money and, through a bit of luck, found a really small room to rent in a house owned by a deadbeat landlord. That was the house I ended up living in for most of my sixteen years in Seattle.

Many other radicals worked for that agency as well, and it was through my co-workers that I first really encountered the beginnings of the shift from older leftist frameworks regarding inequality to these newer identitarian frameworks. In particular, the language which was used to describe homelessness, mental illness, and addiction seemed to constantly shift, first through pressure from younger social workers (many just out of universities) and then through agency policy.

A lot of medical language was applied to homelessness, which may sound at first a bit bizarre, though it had become normal for us. Especially odd in retrospect was the way in which the population we worked with was described as "experiencing chronic homelessness," meaning that they had been homeless multiple times (including continuously) during a period of five or ten years. That is, homelessness was described the way medical problems were described. A person might experience chronic homelessness the same way a patient might experience chronic pain, chronic fatigue, or chronic disease.

This language had several purposes, most of which were of noble intent. Firstly, it served as a way of unlinking a person's identity from their lack of housing, a kind of anti-identity politics. That is, a homeless person was not part of an identity group called "homeless people" but was rather a regular person experiencing a certain condition. This also helped to narrate homelessness as something temporary and as something anyone might experience in their lives.

On the other hand, the medicalization of homelessness made it very difficult to talk about the economic conditions that created it. While we could discuss and ponder the "co-morbidities" of homelessness (mental illness, drug and alcohol addiction, physical disability, and so on), we couldn't point to what a more traditional leftist might identify as economic causes (the extremely high rents in the city, the lack of work available for people without education or trained skills). In other words, homelessness was a condition a person suffered and needed treatment for, rather than a symptom of a much larger economic illness.

Here, it's hard not to notice that the position of the homeless is the inverse of that of other oppression categories. The racism a black person experiences is considered part of a larger system of racist oppression rather than something only a limited number of people might temporarily experience. It is the same for misogyny or transphobia: women and trans people are considered to always face identity-based oppression because the cis-heteropatriarchy reproduces this oppression.

Why the difference, though? After all, homelessness is a measurable state. We can take any person who claims to be homeless and ask an objective question — do they have a home? — and come to an empirical conclusion about the truth of that matter. On the other hand, we cannot easily do the same for a person who claims to experience daily discrimination or micro-aggressions based on their identity. Further, we can we use objective criteria to determine the larger economic conditions in a society related to the condition of homelessness, including the costs of housing, the available number of apartments or houses in an area, the rate of employment and unemployment, and other material factors which contribute to homelessness.

For other oppression identity categories, this can be done only to a limited degree. For instance, we can look at the high unemployment rates of black men in cities or the lower average wages for women and get a sense that there is definitely a problem or injustice occurring. From there, we can then propose theories as to why that is happening (white supremacy, patriarchy, and so forth). But there's a problem here, because the metrics we might use for these latter cases cannot be applied to the issue of homelessness for one very important reason: the majority of homeless people in the United States, the United Kingdom, France, Germany, Canada, and Australia are men, not women.[43]

Social versus Material Conditions

This points to a core problem in the way newer radical frameworks attempt to understand and address injustice. Because they focus primarily on social conditions and social causes, they cannot easily explain the material conditions underlying certain states. This becomes quite evident in two competing models for dealing with homelessness and addiction: harm-reduction and housing first.

Harm-reduction policies and services are focused primarily on the social conditions of homelessness and addiction. Rather than attempting to end drug addiction or homelessness, harm reduction attempts to decrease the social and societal impacts of those problems. Needle

---

43 For U.S. numbers, see National Alliance to End Homelessness, 2019; For Germany, see Wedia, 2019; For France, see Institut National d'Etudes Démographiques; For Canada, see Canadian Observatory on Homelessness; For United Kingdom, see Capon, T., 2021; For Australia, see Capuano, G., 2018.

exchanges and safe injection sites for intravenous drug users (heroin users, for example) are two such harm-reduction solutions, both aimed at reducing the spread of blood-borne contagions (HIV, Hepatitis C) and containing the public effects of such usage in more controllable areas. In many major American cities, sanctioned urban homeless encampments ("tent cities") are manifestations of this same model.

While often seen as similar to harm reduction, the housing-first model goes about things quite differently. In that model, the material conditions of individuals are considered the root cause of their other issues. Rather than attempting to deal with each issue such a person faces separately and reduce the harm of their activities, the policy is to first find housing for them. This is based upon the belief (backed up to some degree with research studies) that a homeless person is likely to fall back into addictions, cause more crime, and decline or be unable to undergo regular treatment when they have no regular address and are too focused on their daily survival.

Both models have quite a lot of things going for them, though their implementation is not always successful. Of the two models, housing first is the closest to what one might consider a Marxist or traditional leftist framework, because of its focus on bettering the material conditions of its "clients."[44] At its core, it inverts the common perception of homelessness as a condition caused by other conditions. For example, while one might suspect that addictions or

---

44 "Client" became the official and politically correct name for the people we worked with, though others such as "consumers of housing services" sometimes were used. The choice of terms involving economic exchange was deliberate, intended to reduce negative stigma towards the homeless while also fitting their policies into larger narratives of capitalist exchange.

mental health issues lead a person to become homeless, housing first points to studies which show that becoming homeless often triggers or worsens such problems. In some research, addiction and mental illness appear to have actually been the result of the stress of being homeless, rather than pre-existing conditions. Therefore, giving people a stable living situation is seen as the first step required before these other conditions can be addressed.

Again, while housing first is often seen as part of the framework of harm reduction, there are some significant differences. Harm reduction seeks specifically to reduce unnecessary or preventable harm caused by homelessness, addictions, and mental illness, while being neutral (or pessimistic) towards the possibility of those situations being successfully changed. That is, instead of trying to change the conditions of the individuals, it seeks to mollify, manage, or control the consequences. For instance, property crime (theft and burglary as well as breaking into automobiles) is a common tactic used by severe addicts in their search for money to support their addictions. A harm-reduction philosophy proposes giving such people access to enough resources (through welfare payments, for example) that they can buy the drugs to which they are addicted without needing to commit crimes.

Harm-reduction policies are often sold to politicians and to business communities on their economic benefits: a cheaper and more efficient way of spending public safety resources. Harm-reduction programs such as needle exchanges reduce the overall cost to police and emergency response services of callouts for overdoses and longer-term public health problems (HIV, Hepatitis, and so on). Increased spending on harm-reduction policies is often justified with studies showing that those it targets often require fewer ambulance rides and are involved in fewer police interventions, thus representing a net savings for the cities and states where they live.

"Good White Men"

The agency I worked for as a social worker focused primarily on the housing-first model, with harm-reduction policies offered after the primary problem (being homeless) was solved. It seemed to work quite well, and working there often felt more fulfilling than any previous jobs I'd held. My role required working rather long days in one of the residential facilities and sometimes in the shelter distributing medications and alcohol to the residents,[45] looking for signs that their mental illness was endangering them or others, calming them down in moments of crisis, finding referrals for services they might need, and also responding to health emergencies as best as I could.

Tragically, I saw a lot of death. Many of the people living at the housing facilities had lived decades on the streets and were in very poor health. Some had severe liver damage from years of alcohol addiction or from hepatitis; others had untreated cancers or other ailments, previously undiagnosed because they couldn't afford doctor visits.

---

45 This is called "alcohol management." Case workers for chronic alcoholic clients purchased a month's supply of alcohol (usually beer, but sometimes wine or vodka) with the client's funds. This was then distributed to them according to a pre-agreed alcohol-management program, ensuring that the client had enough alcohol to avoid withdrawal symptoms and to not to need to commit crimes or drink hand sanitizer to feed their addiction, while hopefully representing a slight reduction in their monthly consumption.

One death was particularly hard for me: a middle-aged woman, a kind and very sweet black woman who often offered us gifts (we refused out of professionalism) as gratitude for helping her get off the streets. Her life previous had been quite hard, with a childhood of severe sexual abuse by her parents, along with many instances of abuse while she was homeless. Getting housing had radically changed her life, and her new situation inspired me and my co-workers, giving us the sense we were truly helping people.

She died of a heart attack trigged by underlying conditions — and she died in front of me. We were all trained in emergency response, including cardiopulmonary resuscitation, and I tried to revive her. The medics who arrived and took over assured me later that I had not failed, that nothing else could have been done, but it's very hard to feel that truth in the moments immediately afterwards.

A few days later, during my lunch break, I went to the nearby cafe where I often sat during my breaks. It was a rather convivial place, in a politically radical neighborhood of Seattle not far from a socialist meeting hall where I'd spent a lot of my younger activist years. I'd often meet interesting people at that cafe, finding myself in political conversations so engaging that I'd have to rush back to work because I'd lost track of time.

That day, just three days after the woman had died, I was drawn into a conversation between two people sitting at the table next to me. They were talking about revolution and anti-capitalist politics, the sort of fascinating conversation which always seemed to last for hours without resolution.

I don't remember exactly the moment that conversation went sour, but I remember why it did. My interlocutors were both younger than I was, and one of them — who was black — had told me he'd just finished his studies at

Evergreen State College. His companion, who was a white woman, had initiated the conversation with me and was working on a higher-level degree.

She asked me what I did for work. I told them both, and then described what had happened to the woman and how I'd tried to save her. Her companion suddenly went quite red in the face and rigid, and I could see — as could she — the veins of his neck and forehead suddenly prominent like steel cables under his skin.

"You think that makes you a good white man?" he said, suddenly shouting at me. The rest of the cafe became very quiet, just as his companion had.

I hadn't understood his reaction, and probably should not have tried to explain. "Uh, no?" I said calmly. "I don't think that has anything to do with being good or bad."

He shouted louder. "The only good white person is the one who knows he should be shot and killed because he is incapable of not harming others."

I sat silently. I didn't know what to say in return, or what had caused his sudden outburst. His companion first glared menacingly at me, then told him they should go to another cafe where there weren't so many "racists." They both stood up and left, and I lingered in shock and confusion before returning to my shift.

It's taken me years to understand that interaction, much longer than it took for me to work through the sadness and feelings of guilt around that woman's death. His statement and accompanying rage were the first such time I'd encountered such a reaction and its underlying ideological framework, though it was hardly the last.

"Antiracist Discrimination"

As with homelessness and gender and sexual differences, there are two distinct frameworks for understanding racism and racial inequality. There are deep disagreements on precisely what can be done to rectify them and whether or not certain aspects are causative or are effects of other causes. As with gender, views on race and racism are not always internally consistent, nor are they held uniformly by all adherents to a given framework.

Also as with gender, many aspects of newer anti-racist frameworks contain deeper and often unexamined beliefs about the nature of race and racism. A helpful place from which to see these beliefs is through the statement of that man in the cafe, that "the only good white man is the one who knows he should be shot and killed because he is incapable of not harming others." Past the deep rage expressed in the words, we can parse out several core beliefs which would lead someone to make such a statement:

- White men are not only inherently harmful to others but are also incapable of not causing harm.
- To be a good person, a white man should know and submit to whatever others do to stop the harm he causes and cannot himself prevent.

These beliefs are not rare. Opening this chapter was a quote from an essay entitled "Living with the White Race." The beliefs expressed in that essay are not very different from the content of the previous statements, though the beliefs of the author of that essay — Ibram Rogers, now named Ibram X. Kendi — have gone on to exert much more political influence than I suspect my interlocutor's have.

Ibram X. Kendi authored that essay when he was twenty-one, years before changing his name, and sixteen years before publishing his most influential book, *How to Be an Anti-Racist*. In that book, Kendi walks back a little the ideas that led him to write the essay, confessing that believing all white people to be part of a monolithic group was itself a racist position he once held.[46] However, despite challenging his previously held beliefs, Kendi develops a framework of understanding race and racism such that they can only be remedied by being actively anti-racist. In one of the most often cited quotations from his book, he states:

> The opposite of racist isn't "not racist." It is "anti-racist." What's the difference? One endorses either the idea of a racial hierarchy as a racist, or racial equality as an anti-racist. One either believes problems are rooted in groups of people, as a racist, or locates the roots of problems in power and policies, as an anti-racist. One either allows racial inequities to persevere, as a racist, or confronts racial inequities, as an anti-racist. There is no in-between safe space of "not racist."[47]

Kendi proposes a hard dichotomy between racist and anti-racist: a behavior, a belief, or a policy is always one or the other, and never part of a third category. In other words, there is no neutral political position to take on the matter: you are either taking a good position or a bad one, a racist stance or an anti-racist stance. This dichotomy manifests in Kendi's most influential political formulation, that of "antiracist discrimination":

> The only remedy to racist discrimination is antiracist discrimination. The only remedy to past discrimination is present discrimination. The only remedy to present discrimination is future discrimination. As President Lyndon B. Johnson said in 1965, "You do not take a person who, for years, has been hobbled by chains and liberate

---

46 I often wonder if the man I met in the cafe came to the same conclusion later in life as well.

47 See Kendi, 2019.

him, bring him up to the starting line of a race and then say, 'You are free to compete with all the others, 'and still justly believe that you have been completely fair." As U.S. Supreme Court Justice Harry Blackmun wrote in 1978, "In order to get beyond racism, we must first take account of race. There is no other way. And in order to treat some persons equally, we must treat them differently." [48]

The quotes Kendi employs are written as part of the legal logic behind affirmative action and desegregation policies, both of which were brought about through the civil rights struggle in the United States. However, this logic has now come to define a much broader program of anti-racism both in the United States and in other countries.

One example of the implementation of this newer anti-racist framework is the move by several local governments in the United States to experiment with race-based basic-income programs inspired by the idea of guaranteed basic income (GBI). GBI is a kind of welfare payment meant to provide a minimum stipend for each individual of an amount sufficient to at least allow them to pay for housing, food, and other basic necessities.[49] The City of Oakland in California, for instance, announced who their program was exclusively for with the following language:

Black, Indigenous, and People of Color (BIPOC) families with low incomes (i.e. groups with the greatest wealth disparities per the Oakland equity index) and at least one child under 18, regardless of documentation status. The term "family" is broadly defined to recognize that families come in all shapes and sizes.[50]

---

48 Ibid.
49 GBI is different from universal basic income (UBI) in that it is not guaranteed to all individuals, only to some.
50 See Oakland, 2021.

Not long after announcing its availability only to people of some races, and subsequently facing both national and international criticism, the City of Oakland quietly removed all racial exclusions from the program language on its website, though it nevertheless reiterated that the income disbursements were meant specifically for BIPOC families:

> "We have not changed the program," said Justin Berton, communications director for Mayor Libby Schaaf. "We have had to clarify that while no family is prohibited from applying, this pilot is intentionally designed to serve and support BIPOC families, who evidence shows suffer the greatest and most disproportionate impacts of poverty."[51]

The design of the GBI experiment in Oakland fits within the larger framework of Kendi's "anti-racist discrimination" in that it favors (or discriminates in favor of) people who are not white over those who are. An obvious question that arises from such attempts is why the race of the poor people in question matters more than the condition of their poverty. In other words, why would an unemployed single mother of three who is white be less deserving of such a program than a black woman in the same condition? Why wouldn't they both be eligible?

The specific defense for favoring BIPOC families (and disfavoring white families) in these disbursements is that BIPOC families "suffer the greatest and most disproportionate impacts of poverty." In other words, according to the city's view, it is better to be poor and white than to be poor and black. This idea is sometimes backed up with a few studies which show that universal programs

---

51 See Marzorati, 2021.

made available for everyone are not always accessed equally by everyone.[52]

Racial minorities in the United States absolutely have higher rates of poverty than other groups. For instance, in 2020 8.2 percent of all white people had incomes below the federal poverty line, compared to 19.5 percent for black people and 17 percent for Hispanic people, while the overall poverty rate in the United States was 11.4 percent.[53] In real numbers, this means the following amounts of people in poverty:

- 16.7 million white people
- 8 million black people
- 10.5 million Hispanic people

Comparing these real numbers to the percentages provides a glimpse at a problem which forms one of the primary critiques of racially exclusive (or in Kendi's words, anti-racist) social programs. Though a black person is much more likely to be poor than to be wealthy, because of their population size they represent only about one-fifth of the 37.2 million poor people in the United States.

To see the problem here, consider the difference between a program that would decrease overall poverty and a program that targets a racial minority. Reducing overall poverty would benefit all the poor, but it would not necessarily change the fact that black people overall are more likely to be poorer than white people. If the ultimate goal is to make all racial groups account for an equal

---

52 For instance, education and housing loan programs offered to military veterans in the United States, which tended to be accessed by or awarded to white veterans more often than black veterans.

53 See Shrider, 2021.

percentage of poor people, then targeting programs to reduce poverty among racial minorities would be required.

Adolph Reed and the Black Marxist Critique

This is where this newer anti-racist framework shows itself to be radically different from a Marxist framework: it is a *race* analysis, rather than a *class* analysis. Anti-racism argues for a racially equal distribution of poverty as the condition of a fair and just society, rather than the elimination of poverty or substantial changes in capitalist class relations. To have a better world, whites should be as poor as blacks, rather than no one being poor.

This problem forms the basis of the Marxist criticisms of social justice identity politics. Many black writers, theorists, and professors who approach race through a Marxist framework have criticized the shift away from class analysis towards anti-racism, including Adolph Reed Jr., Barbara Fields, Cedric Johnson, Kenneth Warren, Touré Reed,[54] and the writers of the black Marxist online journal the *Black Agenda Report*, as well as the popular London-based black writer and podcaster Angie Speaks.

Dr. Adolph Reed's critiques of this newer anti-racism are particularly worth centering for several reasons. First of all, a common response to criticisms of it is that they are "white" critiques, originating from and situated in unexamined white privilege or a kind of mystic state of whiteness (even if the critic is not white). These characterizations ignore the strong tradition of black Marxists rejecting these newer ideas, and despite the constantly uttered refrain that we should all "listen to black voices," when such voices inconveniently criticize the official framework

---

54 Touré is Adolph Reed's son.

of anti-racism, they are often virulently attacked and de-platformed.

This leads to the second reason for my prioritization of Reed's critiques: the intense vitriol aimed at him by what he calls the "identitarian left." These attacks include a highly publicized attempt by a racial-affinity group within the Democratic Socialists of America to silence a public presentation he was scheduled to give. Reed had been invited to speak about the problems of race analysis in building public and socialist responses to COVID-19. The reason he could not be allowed to give this presentation was, according to their statement, that

> the AFROSOCialist and Socialists of Color Caucus opposes Philly DSA and NYC Lower Manhattan branch's decision to organize an event that claims it is good socialist politics to ignore the deadly racist impact COVID 19 is having on Black, Indigenous and People of Color communities (BIPOC)....
>
> ...While working class communities are fighting for our lives, some of our DSA comrades insist we shouldn't focus on racism when it comes to the impact of COVID 19 on working class communities. This attack is reactionary, class reductionist and at best, tone deaf.
>
> We demand the event to be changed to a debate of Adolph Reed's class reductionist analysis versus our intersectional socialist analysis.[55]

Reed could only be allowed to speak, then, if the event were designed as a debate about his larger analysis of race and class and the implications of his "reactionary" ideas. This

---

55 The full statement is available as a Google Document.
See AFROSOCialist and Socialists of Color Caucus, n.d.

led to Reed withdrawing rather than submitting to their demands.

Attacks against Reed's ideas have not been limited to this event, however: he is often held up as a public example of "class reductionism," implying that he and other Marxists, including black Marxists, reduce everything to class analysis and completely ignore race. As such, it's deeply useful to start with Adolph Reed's specific critiques of anti-racism in order to understand the underlying differences between this newer anti-racist framework and a Marxist one.

First of all, Reed asserts that the anti-racist framework essentially reinforces the capitalist, neoliberal order of class relations because it does not actually attempt to deal with the difference between the rich and the poor, but rather with what is often called "horizontal inequality," disparities between groups rather than within them. In his essay "What Materialist Black Political History Actually Looks Like," he states:

> This tendency, which Touré Reed has argued rests on a race-reductionism, has surfaced and spread within the newly revitalized Democratic Socialists of America (DSA), as even many among those who consider themselves socialists object to the organization's selection of Medicare for All as its key political campaign on the ground that pursuit of decommodified health care for all is objectionable because doing so does not sufficiently center antiracist and anti-disparitarian agendas. I submit that there's clearly a problem when anti-socialism is defined as socialism.
>
> ...Not only would pursuit of an agenda focused on addressing "horizontal inequality," if successful, disproportionately benefit upper-status, already well-off people... the reality of a standard of justice based on eliminating group disparities is that a society could be just

if 1% of the population controlled 90% of the resources so long as the one percent featured blacks, Hispanics, women, lesbians and gays, etc. in rough proportion to their representation in the general population; also, advocacy of defining the only meaningful inequality as disparities between groups is itself a career trajectory in the academy, as well as in the corporate, nonprofit and freelance commentary worlds.[56]

Reed's core criticism of the use of race as a primary analysis of social ills — what he and other black Marxist critics have called "race reductionism"[57] — is that race cannot account for larger processes of economic disparity, particularly the growing gap in the United States between the poorest and the richest of each racial group. In fact, while overall black incomes and wealth have increased steadily over the last five decades, that increase has occurred primarily for the richest black people. In an interview regarding his position entitled "The Perils of Race Reductionism," Reed explains:

While from one perspective there is no significant change in the Black-White wealth ratio or Black income as a percentage of White income in the last 50 years, actually, what accounts for the persistence of the aggregate difference, since Black incomes have been rising over the last 50 years in the aggregate, is that rich people's incomes have been rising fastest and that both Black and White people outside of the top 10% have been falling behind.

...To oversimplify it a little bit, it's a rich peoples' wealth gap. You can see the same stuff with even patterns

---

56 See Reed, 2019a.
57 Informing this term is the common dismissal of black and other Marxist critiques as "class-reductionism."

of police killings. The work that race reductionism does is to skewer the actual or the more complex causes of the actual inequality.[58]

In other words, each racial group is experiencing the same problem: the richest within that group concentrate increasingly greater portions of that group's wealth, creating a widening gap between the rich and the poor across all racial groups.

As Reed mentions in that interview, the same analysis can be used to understand the police violence which has triggered the massive Black Lives Matter protests across the United States. Black individuals are killed at a higher rate than all other racial groups except Native Americans, but poor people comprise the vast majority of individuals killed by the police *across every racial group*.

This is because the poor are more likely both to be seen as criminals and also to engage in behaviors considered criminal by the legal regimes where they live. Rich people (black, white, or other) don't normally commit armed burglary, mug strangers on the streets, shoplift, or steal cars. They don't do so because they already have — or can easily purchase — the items sought in such crimes. Poor people, on the other hand, especially the poorest, are more likely to commit such crimes specifically because they don't have wealth:

The problem isn't that police disproportionately kill and maim Black people — that's not good and it's not to be defended — but if the problem is cast that way, then the logical response would be, the structures of policing can be left in place, but that the Black people shouldn't be more than 10% to 12% of the people who are killed or brutalized.

---

58 See Reese, 2021.

...In areas where there are a lot of Black and Brown people, they are overrepresented among the class of people who make people with property feel uncomfortable. Lo and behold, in places like Wyoming, and Montana, and the Dakotas, and places like that where there are virtually no Black and Brown people, there are White people who disproportionately make up the classes of people who make people with property feel uncomfortable. Guess what? Police treat them exactly the same way as they treat Blacks and Hispanics.[59]

"Neo-liberal Social Justice"

Adolph Reed's critique, which is representative of the general Marxist analysis, is that viewing larger economic and societal problems through a framework of race (whether as the primary or the only framework) misses these larger problems and can only ever argue for more equally distributed injustices. Again, as he put it earlier,

if the 1% were [approximately] half women, 12% Black, 14% to 15% Hispanic, et cetera, it would be a just society, even though 90% of the people are getting the short end of the stick. That's the logic of a neoliberal notion of social justice.

Reed's view of this newer framework of anti-racism as "the logic of a neoliberal notion of social justice" is crucial to keep in mind, both because it is common criticism of this framework by black and other Marxists, and also because it points to the class alignment (and allegiances) of those who espouse it. In his essay "Antiracism: A Neoliberal Alternative to a Left," published in the journal *Dialectical Anthropology*

---

59 Ibid.

in 2018, he connects the specific class positions of those who espouse anti-racism to their insistence that race should be primary:

> Antiracist politics is a class politics; it is rooted in the social position and worldview, and material interests of the stratum of race relations engineers and administrators who operate in Democratic party politics and as government functionaries, the punditry and commentariat, education administration and the professoriate, corporate, social service and nonprofit sectors, and the multibillion-dollar diversity industry.... As the society moves farther away from the regime of subordination and exclusion on explicitly racial terms to which race-reductionist explanations were an immediately plausible response, race has become less potent as the dominant metaphor, or blanket shorthand, through which class hierarchy is lived. And as black and white elites increasingly go through the same schools, live in the same neighborhoods, operate as peers in integrated workplaces, share and interact in the same social spaces and consumption practices and preferences, they increasingly share another common sense not only about frameworks of public policy but also about the proper order of things in general.[60]

That is, those who insist that race is at the core of social and economic justice are typically embedded in what Barbara and John Ehrenreich identified as the professional-managerial class: "Elite," highly-educated and comfortably salaried people disconnected from the larger working class.[61] One need only consider the economic positions

---

60 See Reed, 2018b.

61 We'll look deeper into the professional-managerial class later in this book.

of the most prominent theorists and activists of anti-racism — Ibram X. Kendi, Kimberlé Crenshaw, Ta-Nehisi Coates, Patrisse Cullors, Rachel Cargle, Ijeoma Oluo, and Nikole Hannah-Jones — to note this connection.

Reed extends this class analysis beyond merely the personal and class position of anti-racist theorists to the larger industry of anti-racism which now exists to help politicians, governments, and corporations implement it:

> Like any ideology that gains traction, race reductionism also has a material foundation. Black ethnic politics consolidated around exponential growth of a stratum of office holders and public functionaries, and it has encouraged and reinforced development of what might be called a political economy of race-relations or diversity management. That includes a burgeoning, multibillion dollar diversity industry that extends to corporations and universities, where pursuit and monitoring of diversity is woven into human resource functions and overseen by in-house diversity professionals and administrators and freelance consultants....
>
> ...The political economy of race relations management has grown symbiotically with neoliberalism. The symbiosis may be clearest in the privatization, outsourcing, and overall retraction of social services, as claims to authentic representation of "community" voices and perspectives factor into criteria for awarding contracts and standing in policy processes that are increasingly insulated from democratic oversight and accountability.... The symbiotic relationship shows up also in the ways that a politics grounded on identity can obfuscate dynamics of economic inequality and dispossession by rendering them in cultural terms.[62]

---

62 See Reed, 2018a.

The Mysticism of Race

Reed makes one other crucial point throughout his critiques which will become important when we look at other questions of identity as well. He asserts that race and racism have both taken on a kind of mystical or esoteric quality disconnected from material reality or practical discourse:

> Racism and white supremacy don't really explain how anything happens. They're at best shorthand characterizations of more complex, or at least discrete, actions taken by people in social contexts; at worst, and, alas, more often in our political moment, they're invoked as alternatives to explanation. In that sense they function, like the Nation of Islam's Yacub story, as a devil theory: racism and white supremacy are represented as capable of making things happen in the world independently, i.e. magically. This is the fantasy expressed in formulations like racism is America's "national disease" or "Original Sin."[63]

We often hear race and racism spoken about as if they are themselves explanations. This can be seen easily when we consider how race is offered as the primary explanation for social and economic problems which cannot easily be reduced to racism.

For example, consider the introduction of the concept of "multi-racial whiteness" to explain why many black and Hispanic people voted for Trump or joined anti-immigrant political movements.[64] In a framework in which such

---

63 See Reed, 2020
64 This concept, introduced by New York University professor Cristina Beltran, was disseminated widely in progressive media stories. See Garcia-Navarro, 2021.

support is considered inherently racist, the minority racial status of those people must be translated or transformed into a kind of whiteness so that the framework is not undermined.

This is one part of the mysticism of race and racism which Reed critiques. However, it has even more obvious manifestations. Consider, for example, Ta-Nehisi Coates' description in his famous essay for *The Atlantic* "The First White President," of "the passive power of whiteness — that bloody heirloom which cannot ensure mastery of all events but can conjure a tailwind for most of them," as well as Coates' description of Donald Trump: "Whereas his forebears carried whiteness like an ancestral talisman, Trump cracked the glowing amulet open, releasing its eldritch energies."[65]

While Coates' descriptions of race as a magical power might be dismissed as mere metaphor, more complex, quasi-theological discussions about race and racism form core arguments within anti-racist theory. In countless articles on social justice sites, in many books, and in the more casual discussions of activists, we see and hear how all white people have "inherent privilege" regardless of their actions or material conditions, or how all white people "benefit from" or "uphold" white supremacy. We also read that the matter of privilege also exists for lighter-skinned black people: though they have less privilege than white people, they nevertheless have more than darker-skinned people.[66]

These kinds of contortions are a result of race and racism being seen as the primary cause of social or economic inequalities. They are the proverbial hammer for which every problem is a nail: even non-white people can have

---

65 See Coates, 2017.

66 See Simeon, 2019.

"whiteness," since whiteness (and white supremacy, and so forth) are stand-ins for the notion of sin:

> Because it is an evanescent Evil that is disconnected from specific human purposes and patterns of social relations, racism, again like "terrorism," can exist anywhere at any time under any manifest conditions and is a cause that needs no causes or explanation.[67]

Reed's point about race and racism being an "evanescent Evil," a "devil theory," and functioning similar to the Catholic notion of Original Sin are particularly important, because they will help us understand our next monster, the Zombie.

---

67 See Reese, 2021.

CHAPTER FIVE: THE ZOMBIE

Perhaps you've already noticed some parallels between the esoteric nature of racism within anti-racist theory and the question of gender in radical politics. After sex as a description of physical differences became secondary to the social and psychological sense of gender, many of the conflicts about sex and gender within feminism and in larger society hinge on where one thinks gender is actually located. In other words, the current gender framework suggests you can be a woman or man socially and psychologically (that is, internally) regardless of genitals, secondary sexual characteristics, or any other physical markers of womanhood. Gender is, as many definitions now put it, a "felt sense," rather than a physical category.

Whether you consider this true or not, it's important to remember this framework is historically new. This isn't how anyone thought of sex and gender seven decades ago: sex and gender weren't even different things until John Money, and then second wave feminists, began thinking of them as different. It's a new framework, but it also borrows from something very old, which we'll see when we look at one more argument from Adolph Reed about the problems of neoliberal anti-racist politics.

The Recent Origins of Race

What makes a person black? What makes them white? These are questions that parallel the questions of gender and sex now, though race is an older idea. Older, but not ancient: race as a form of division among humans has only really been around for about four hundred years.

It can be very difficult to conceive of this, but the idea of humans having or being a race was an after-effect of the transatlantic slave trade, rather than its cause. Portuguese, Spanish, Dutch, and English traders in slaves often called the people they sold "black" or "negro," but they didn't see these words as meaning that those people were actually a different race of human from them. This idea came later through colonial administration. Colonial governors desperately needed to create legal definitions to distinguish between the lower class of European workers who lived in the colonies and the slaves and indigenous people there.

One of the reasons for their desperation was that those three different groups kept intermixing. As Peter Linebaugh has shown in his research on early relations between displaced European (mostly English and Irish) workers, indigenous peoples, and African slaves in the American colonies, all three groups tended to befriend each other, share knowledge with each other, intermarry, and rise up against their leaders together.[68]

It's easy to forget this, but the vast majority of Europeans in those colonies didn't own slaves. Instead, it was the upper classes, the merchants, the large landowners, the colonial administrators, and the rest of the early capitalist class who claimed humans as their property. Just as easy to forget is the reason why many of the lower-class Europeans were in the colonies. They had been displaced from their homes and villages through Enclosure, the process of selling off and turning into private property land once seen as common.

Enclosures displaced millions of peasants in Britain, making it impossible for them to grow their own food

---

68 See Linebaugh and Rediker, 2012.

and raise their own livestock to support themselves. Such peasants had a bitter choice to make: they could either move to the already crowded cities to try to find work, or they could get on a ship headed to one of the new British colonies to work there. Those who took the second option didn't have it much better than those who took the first. They arrived in colonial settlements and found their lives not much different from what they had been under Feudalism. When they got there, they also encountered other people who'd been brought over in ships to work in the colonies: slaves from Africa.

While this was not always the case, very often the displaced Europeans and the enslaved Africans noticed they had a similar enemy (and it wasn't each other). The people who had enslaved the Africans were the very same class of people — and sometimes the very same people themselves — who had forced European peasants into extreme poverty. Because of this recognition and the constant intermixing (culturally, socially, and also sexually) of the two groups, colonial administrators needed to create legal barriers and boundaries to keep them separated.

The Africans had to become one legal category of person, the European workers another, and thus "white" and "black" were born into law. It took a while for these ideas to be expanded elsewhere. In the 1700s, Enlightenment and Age of Reason philosophers and scientists began to treat these legal fictions as scientific categories. This was the birth of "race science" and all the horrors it entailed: the classification of skulls, the vivisection of Africans and indigenous Americans, and all the theories about racial difference which still persist today.

Race has no biological or physical basis. It's a political construct, created through legal fictions and enforcement of those fictions. It then became a social construct: people began to see themselves as "white" or "black," and to see others this way, too. Newer radical frameworks generally concede this point. However, in many radical arguments, race is still treated as something that cannot be transcended or switched, as if it is nevertheless an inherent thing.

The Problem of Transracialism

The persistence of race considered as an essential or inherent trait in radical anti-racist politics is seen best in the matter of Rachel Dolezal, a self-identified "transracial" woman who was outed by her parents as being white in 2015. At that time, Dolezal was the president of the Spokane, Washington, chapter of the National Association for the Advancement of Colored People (NAACP), and had been living as a black woman for over five years. Outrage over Dolezal's actions took several forms, including accusations that she culturally appropriated blackness and that, by taking on the role of chapter president of a black organization, she had stolen a job from a deserving black person.[69] As the revelations about her occurred at roughly the same time that several celebrities publicly identified themselves as trans women (most notably Caitlyn Jenner), Dolezal's claim to be transracial initiated a contentious popular and academic debate about transgender identity and transracial identity.

These debates occurred at a particularly contentious political moment in the United States, a time when social justice, intersectional feminism, police killings of black people, and the alt-right were constant discussion topics

---

69 After her outing, the national body of the NAACP wrote in support of Dolezal, and she was noted by others as having revitalized the otherwise moribund Spokane chapter. Spokane's black population at the time of Dolezal's tenure was 3 percent, translating to about 6,000 people. See Tognotti, 2015.

on social media. That moment saw the sudden popularity of sites like *Everyday Feminism*, relentless media attention given to alt-right figures such as Milo Yiannopoulos and Richard Spencer, and aggressive Antifa protests. Black Lives Matter protests had also just begun the year before, and 2015 was the beginning of the extreme rhetorical conflicts in the presidential contest between Hillary Clinton and Donald Trump.

Rachel Dolezal's making a claim to transracialism during such a time should thus be seen as a politically important event. Transracialism represented a threat to the foundations of the new gender framework, and especially to the early unification of anti-racist politics with the new conceptions of gender and identity. The doctrinal threat can be summarised quite simply (as was the common response by many to the matter): *"If a person can change their gender, why can they not change their race?"* The corollary to that question was also asked: *"If you cannot change your race, doesn't that mean you cannot change your gender?"*

What was really at stake was the matter of identity — and especially of declarative gender, which we saw in Chapter Three. According to the logic of declarative gender, not only can individuals define for themselves their gender identity, society is then obligated to accept and acknowledge their declarations. In other words, if a person was born a man, has male and even very masculine features, yet says "I am a woman," then this person therefore really is, and it is bigoted and oppressive ("transphobic" and even "fascist") to act or think otherwise.

By this same logic, however, if a woman who was born to white parents and lived most of her life appearing as a white woman then claims to be a black woman, she would also need to be accepted as such. Of course, the really severe backlash against Dolezal's claim to transracialism revealed that most people were quite unwilling to accept this.

Many black activists and media figures were particularly vociferous in their attacks on her and on transracialism in general. Several noted in particular that transracialism could not easily occur in both directions: that is, though it might be possible for a white person to "pass" successfully as a black person, a black person with particularly dark skin would not be so successful.

Particularly representative of these arguments was Ijeoma Oluo, a Seattle digital marketer turned anti-racist activist and author. In a self-described antagonistic interview with Rachel Dolezal at the request of the journal *the Stranger,* Oluo wrote:

> The degree to which you are excluded from white privilege is largely dependent on the degree to which your appearance deviates from whiteness. You can be extremely light-skinned and still be black, but you cannot be extremely or even moderately dark-skinned and be treated as white — ever.
>
> By turning herself into a very, very, very, very light-skinned black woman, Dolezal opens herself up to be treated as black by white society only to the extent that they can visually identify her as such, and no amount of visual change would provide Dolezal with the inherited trauma and socioeconomic disadvantage of racial oppression in this country.
>
> ...I try one more time to get an answer to this question, but from a different angle: "Where does the function of privilege of still appearing to the world as a white person play into this and into your identity as affiliating with black culture?"
>
> Dolezal seems to struggle for a moment before answering: "I don't know. I guess I do have light skin, but I don't know that I necessarily appear to the world as a white person. I think that since the white parents did

their TV tour on every national network, some people will forever see me as my birth category, as a white woman. But people who see me as that don't see me really for who I am and probably are not seeing me as a white woman in some kind of a privileged sense. If that makes sense."[70]

The argument by black anti-racist activists and theorists that the shade of Dolezal's skin made her still appear as a white person led to unintended contradictions with the logic of transgender identity, since "passing" as the opposite gender is not considered a pre-requisite to actually being trans. In fact, the idea that a trans person should successfully appear or even try to appear as their declared gender is considered by many trans activists to be transphobic and a bigoted enforcement of patriarchal gender norms.

What arose from these contradictions can be seen as a dialectical conclusion which, like most such conclusions, created a new contradiction. Importantly, that conclusion resulted in a rather metaphysical and esoteric conception of identity closely resembling the idea of a soul. This can be seen best in the most definitive response to conflict between transgender identity and transracial identity, an explanation by two academics published in the *Boston Review* several years later:

Being Black isn't simply a matter of internal identification; it is also a matter of how your community and ancestors have been treated by other people, institutions, and governments. Given this, we think that race classification should (continue to) track — as accurately as possible — intergenerationally inherited inequalities.

...Notice that this argument does not apply in the

---

70 See Oluo, 2017.

case of gender and gender inequality. Gender inequality, unlike racial inequality, does not primarily accumulate intergenerationally, if only for the obvious reason that the vast majority of households are multi-gendered. While parents often are responsible for ingraining patriarchal ideas and rigid gender norms in their children (it is extremely difficult to avoid!), this is not a "passing down" of socioeconomic inequality itself but, rather, of a socialization that perpetuates gender inequality.

We think that the reasons in favor of trans-inclusive gender classification outweigh the reasons against it, and that the reasons against transracial-inclusive race classification outweigh the reasons for it.

...Someone cannot make themself more likely to experience the intergenerational health and economic impact of systemic racism simply by identifying as Black (much less, as philosopher Kwame Anthony Appiah observes, simply by refusing the word "white"). This intergenerational inequality is inherited independently of what persons might hope, believe, or desire about themselves, or even how they present themselves.... Moreover, this logic cannot be wielded against transgender-inclusive gender classification for the simple reason that gender inequality is not accrued intergenerationally and that it affects both transgender and cisgender women. Put simply, then, we think that transracial-inclusive race classification would undermine our ability to track racial inequality, and for reasons that are irrelevant in the case of transgender-inclusive gender classification.[71]

In other words, though there may be no genetic or biological traits that form the basis of race, racial inequality is an inherited trait, something that "accrues

71 See Dembroff and Payton, 2020.

intergenerationally." A black person inherits racial inequality, while a woman does not inherit gender inequality. Racial inequality, then, is something transmitted or inherited, something a person is born with or into, and thus it cannot be transcended by choice.[72]

Adolph Reed's observation that anti-racism poses racism and white privilege as a kind of animate force or Original Sin is instructive here. Teasing out the consequences of "intergenerationally-inherited" inequality, we see that it mirrors the belief that a white person is born into privilege and also cannot fully transcend whiteness. Thus, race in this framework functions as an essential or inherent feature, one that bears with it inviolable traits. Simultaneously, though it is an inherited feature, its intergenerational transmission is not related to the physical body of the person (race as an essential or biological trait) at all.

Again, Adolph Reed offers a profound insight into the problem here, pointing to the mystical nature of identity in the debates over Rachel Dolezal:

The fundamental contradiction that has impelled the debate and required the flight into often idiotic sophistry is that racial identitarians assume... that race is a thing, an essence that lives within us. If pushed, they will offer any of a range of more or less mystical, formulaic, breezy, or neo-Lamarckian faux explanations of how it can be both an essential ground of our being and a social construct, and most people are willing not to pay close attention to the justificatory patter.... Nevertheless, for identitarians, to paraphrase Michaels, we aren't, for instance, black because

---

72 As can be seen in Ijeoma Oluo's insistence in their interview that "no amount of visual change would provide Dolezal with the inherited trauma and socioeconomic disadvantage of racial oppression in this country."

we do black things; that seems to have been Dolezal's mistaken wish.... That, indeed, is also the essence of essentialism.[73]

In other words, race is treated as a really existing thing which resides somewhere in the person as part of their essence. To sound a bit like a medieval theologian for a moment, where, then, does race actually reside if not in the body? The answer appears to be: within a non-physical body both external and internal to the individual, occupying a social role through its intangible yet really existing social (or "intergenerational") reality. In other words, a soul.

A white person, therefore, cannot become a black person because they bear the indelible mark of whiteness (privilege that always operates and benefits them), just as a black person bears the indelible mark of blackness (inequality they inherit intergenerationally that will always disfavor them in social, economic, and political relations). But because race has no basis in physical reality (it is a constructed/made-up category created during the Enlightenment and the birth of capitalism), it is located outside physical reality just as the soul is seen to be in Christian theology.

The soul plays out also in the intersectional framework of gender, but in a slightly different way. Gender, like race, is seen as an indelible and inviolable part of a person irrespective of physical reality (sex), and is described as an internal sense:

Gender identity refers to one's internal sense of feeling masculine, feminine, both, somewhere in between, or neither. Like many things that people experience internally, there is also a desire to express that outwardly, which is why

<hr>

73 See Reed, 2015.

gender identity can influence gender expression....

...Similar to sexual orientation, gender identity is generally viewed by therapists as something that people are born with, and not something they "choose."[74]

Thus, a trans person was born trans but mistakenly "assigned" the wrong gender or sex at birth. One doesn't become trans, then, but rather brings their outward gender expression (and optionally, through hormones or surgery, their body) in line with their actual gender identity. That identity, as with race, is located somewhere outside of the physical characteristics of the person yet simultaneously felt "inside," just as the eternal soul was described as both external yet internally animating the physical flesh.

Thus, radicals — probably without ever realizing they have done so — have recreated the metaphysical category of a soul in order to allow for transgender identity and exclude transracial identity. That soul is both raced and gendered, but it derives its race from generational inheritance (Original Sin) while deriving its gender from something fully transcendent to and independent of the flesh.

This leads to the fragile contradictions between the "sins" of white privilege and male privilege, another dialectical conflict awaiting resolution. Rachel Dolezal could not be allowed to claim transracial identity because she cannot be allowed to escape her white privilege. On the other hand, a male immediately loses his male privilege when recognized as trans because, as in the evangelical conversion moment, he becomes always-already a trans woman and is retroactively forgiven of all sins through

---

74 See Blake Psychology, n.d. This definition is typical of other offerings, including those using the "Genderbread Person" model.

transfiguration of the body into the qualities and nature of the true, eternal soul.

What's in Your Head?

We've already looked at how the Cyborg presents a challenge to understanding where a human ends and a machine begins, as well as where male or man ends and female or woman begins. The Cyborg also demonstrates (another word derived from the Latin root that became "monster") the difficulty of defining what it really means to be one race or another. As we saw with the matter of "multi-racial whiteness," some propose that a person can be not-white and yet still nevertheless be white; on the other hand, while a person can have a female body but be a man; a person born "white" can never be truly "black," no matter their social or psychological reality.

The root of the word psychology is *psyche*, the Greek word for "soul." Though most psychology and most radical politics are explicitly secular, the soul still haunts them as a kind of container into which inherent traits or the "felt sense" of inner life are placed. In other words, even if one doesn't believe there is such a thing as a soul separate from the physical body, we speak, act, and think as if there really is one.

If gender is a "felt sense" or internal reality, then it exists separate from or transcendent to the physical body. If racial oppression and white privilege are "intergenerationally inherited" even though race is not a biological reality, then oppression is transmitted through a transcendent, esoteric mechanism which has no physical location.

One of the most significant legacies of the European Enlightenment in our modern ways of understanding the world, ourselves, and each other is what is called Cartesian dualism. This is the idea that the mind and the body are separate things altogether, that the realm of thought and inner reality is separate from our existence as physical beings. Cartesian dualism asserts that we are not bodies who think, we are instead minds inside bodies.

This idea of mind is actually a continuation of Christian dualism, as seen in the words attributed to Jesus: "The spirit is willing but the flesh is weak." Within Christianity, which dominated Europe for much of the last two millennia, there is a spirit or soul that exists separate from the physical body. In fact, it wasn't even Christianity that came up with the idea: Plato insisted that the spirit and flesh were separate things altogether long before Christianity arose.

This kind of dualism has several consequences that are most easily seen when compared to other kinds of dualism and non-dualistic frameworks. Animist frameworks, for example, also involve the concept of spirit or soul, but rather than bodies being inhabited by spirits, spirits arise out of the physical existence of the thing. For example, the spirit of a tree and the tree itself are not two different things. Instead, they are facets of the very same thing, and they each arise together from the existence of the tree. A spirit can be separated from a body, but the spirit is also a kind of body, so in death we don't "leave" our bodies, we continue on as a body in a different form.

In Platonic and Christian dualism, the spirit or soul is merely living inside of a body, inhabiting it as if it is a house. When a person dies, the spirit is "freed" from the body and goes on into a transcendent (non-physical) eternity. Cartesian dualism substitutes the mind for the soul or spirit, but the results are the same in this respect. While Christians believe there is an eternal soul that directs the actions of the body, Cartesian dualism proposes a mind that does the same thing.

Soul Dualism and the Zombie

Like other animist frameworks, many African animisms see the soul and the body as two different souls living together. There is a body-soul which returns to the earth after the death of the body (and becomes another body-soul), and then another soul (sometimes called the "wandering soul" or "free soul"), which can leave the body. Neither of these souls "die" when the body dies; they both continue on in the lives of other people, animals, plants, or even forces such as wind, rain, and natural processes.

In these kinds of frameworks, called "soul dualist" or "dualistic pluralist," the wandering, free soul — which is able to leave the body in dream or trance — can sometimes be trapped. Some shamanic traditions practice "soul retrieval" for people who have gotten very ill or experienced deep trauma. The underlying belief here is that the wandering or free soul has become trapped or lost and is unable to rejoin its body-soul companion. The person whose wandering soul is missing can become very sick or mentally disturbed and even violent, showing symptoms modern psychology might classify as schizophrenia, depression, or other related mental illnesses.

These animist ideas birthed what is perhaps the most famous of the monsters that show us something profound about our current situation, the Zombie. The Zombie first became known outside of Africa through Haitian voodou, which is a syncretic religion mixing West African and indigenous Caribbean (Taíno) animisms with Christianity.

First recorded in English in 1819, the Zombie has a much older history rooted in Central African beliefs. Its name likely derives from the Kongo words for spirit (*nzambi*) and fetish (*zumbi*). A fetish in animist frameworks is anything normally "inanimate" (that is, without spirit) that nevertheless happens to have a spirit, usually through magical means. An object, a carving, a statue, or even a piece of clothing can become a fetish if a spirit that was not born from its existence enters it. Even a living thing can become a fetish if some other spirit than that which was already part of it enters and lives there.

If this idea seems a bit "primitive" or ridiculous compared to our modern way of seeing the world, it's helpful to remember that we do some apparently ridiculous or at least "unscientific" things as well. We collect souvenirs and items touched by famous people as valuable, "sacred" things, name objects like cars and speak to them as if they are people, treat favourite T-shirts or stuffed animals as if they are part of us, become emotional about flags or the latest iPhone, and in many other ways treat objects as sacred and as "fetishes" the way pagan and animist peoples do.

The Zombie is a human without a wandering soul. In Haitian belief, that wandering soul could be trapped by a *caplata* or a *bokor*, a female or male sorcerer who makes deals with divine beings for their own personal gain rather than on behalf of the community (as opposed to a *mambo* or a *houngan*, a priestess or a priest). Why would a sorcerer choose to do such a thing? There are several reasons. First of all, the resulting Zombie has no will of their own. Without their wandering or free soul, the body-soul of the Zombie can be compelled to do whatever the sorcerer demands of them, assuming the Zombie has the energy to do so. The problem with Zombies is that, without their wandering soul, they tend instead to shamble around in a catatonic state, acting listless, depressed, and in all other ways like a defeated slave.

The other reason a sorcerer might create a Zombie was actually the primary reason in most cases. Remembering one of the Kongo roots of its name means "spirit," the wandering soul of the victim can be used to create a powerful fetish. Trapping that soul within an object gives the sorcerer power not just over the body-soul but over the wandering soul, which can empower items with magical essence.

In other words, the sorcerer gained two souls in the process. The first was the body-soul, which could be enslaved and made to perform work (albeit rather ineffective work) for the sorcerer. The second soul, the wandering soul, could then be used to increase the power of the sorcerer through creation of magical items.

What the Zombie Shows Us

When we think of the Zombie now, we generally conjure in our heads shambling, rotting corpses dressed in rags and feasting on the flesh of humans. Modern film depictions of the Zombie postulate infectious diseases or viruses as its origin: a mistake in a lab spreading through the population, turning each new victim into a ravenous killer. In most portrayals, they are mindless beings, either risen from the dead and thus no longer really able to die, or diseased humans who cannot be cured, only killed.

Zombies have been used as metaphors in criticisms of all manner of behaviors. Gluttonous consumers of television programs have been called zombies, as have those who stare at their smartphones in public without any awareness of their surroundings ("smombies," from "smartphone zombie"). People who appear to follow political demagogues unthinkingly often get called zombies. Political critics of extreme European lockdowns during the initial wave of COVID-19 infections referred to those who didn't question such measures as zombies, while at the same time, some who embraced these policies used the metaphor of a zombie apocalypse to illustrate their necessity.

It's not difficult to notice that film depictions of zombies often reflect the way societies look at supposedly mindless masses. Their torn clothing and their dirty and diseased or rotten appearance, for instance, mirror the way homeless and immigrant populations are viewed by the urban and upper classes. Some directors have purposefully highlighted these similarities as political and social commentary. The film *28 Weeks Later*, for instance, names the quarantined or safe area of England "the Green Zone," which was also the name of the occupied area of Bagdad where international occupiers lived, operated, and governed Iraq. Outside that zone was danger, unnamed throngs of people seen as dangerous enemies "mindlessly" seeking to kill those inside.

These contemporary depictions stray quite far from the traditional animist understanding of the Zombie. In animist cultures, the Zombie is missing a part of itself that can be gotten back. It can be healed, made whole again, but only if its trapped wandering or free soul is released.

It's important to remember that the Zombie arises not out of Christian or Western cosmologies but rather from animist ones. In the Western view, the soul or (particularly for the secular Western view) the mind is separate from the body and superior to it. What a person thinks or believes is therefore their "true" self, their true essence.

The anti-racist framework — as iterated by Ibram X. Kendi and other non-Marxists — argues that there is an essential and inherent trait of humans called race, similar to the Christian view of an essential or inherent soul. Race and racial oppression are "intergenerationally-inherited," existing not in the body but in the "true self," the psyche or soul. This is the inviolable or unchangeable part of a human, and their race then determines how they will always act with others. Thus, a white person is born with the "bloody talisman" of white supremacy and dominance, and only those who live a life of constant penance (through anti-racist actions) might be able to remove that eternal stain.

The Zombie and the animist framework from which it arises point to a different potential political framework, one much closer to the black Marxist position. Rather than being the root of all racist problems, the wandering or free soul has been trapped by the belief in race as a really existing thing. As though a sorcerer, race imprisons a part of us, turning us into zombies constantly seeking some sort of resolution to a past wrong that cannot be resolved until the sorcery is broken.

The true sorcery, as Adolph Reed and others would argue, is capitalism. Capitalist social relations are founded upon the enforcement of class divisions: the lower classes must see themselves as enemies of each other rather than as a singular group exploited by the capitalists. Not only must they see each other as enemies, but they also must never fully understand the nature of that exploitation. They must not see class exploitation at all, or the sorcery behind their material conditions; they must not see why we have all become zombies.

The Zombie has more to show us, however. The persistence of a metaphysical or esoteric "sense" of identity in gender in radical politics now points to something we are missing — or unable to speak about — in our Western frameworks. Feeling like our true essence exists in a state of contradiction with our physical selves is hardly an unusual state or condition. What is unusual is that we insist we can only be one thing, that the "spirit" or the interior sense must make the physical self conform to its beliefs.

In other words, many of our conflicts around identity derive from the limits of our Western cultural legacy, which holds that there is a "true self" or soul that is merely living in a body. Animist frameworks instead see multiple "true" selves who are companions to each other; none of these selves are superior to another, none of them are the "real" self, but rather all inform and co-create each other. When one is missing, the person becomes ill, beset by sorrow or trauma, or is easily pushed around and manipulated by others. The person may even try to replace the missing soul with something else, a borrowed or external identity. Such an identity might suffice for a little while, but the only cure for a Zombie is for them to be made whole again.

The Zombie reveals yet one more thing, a matter which will become important in the next chapter and its following interlude. Humans can become zombified, but so too can concepts. Many times, especially through the mechanisms of capitalist alienation, ideas that once held great power and the potential to liberate become separated from the material realities and contexts which birthed them.

Like lost or trapped wandering souls, ideas such as mutual aid, reparations, solidarity, and class consciousness can become fetishized as if by sorcerors, trapped and wielded as weapons against the very movements from which they derive. The damage done by these zombified ideas can be quite severe, especially in the hands of grifters, the professional-managerial class, and capitalists themselves.

CHAPTER SIX: THE PROBLEM OF CLASS

I love the way you hate cis-men.[75]

I haven't the faintest notion what possible revolutionary role white heterosexual men could fulfill, since they are the very embodiment of reactionary-vested-interest-power.[76]

A little more than twenty years ago, I visited my father and my birth town in Ohio. I was living in Seattle at the time, blissfully enveloped in the gay and radical bubble of Capitol Hill, the "gay ghetto," as it was sometimes called.

It had been years since I'd been back to the land that birthed me, and I wasn't really thrilled to be there. I'd left when I was twelve, after my father had divorced my schizophrenic and developmentally disabled mother. We then moved to southern Florida, so all my teenage years — as well as early twenties — had been lived far from that bizarre "backwards" world of Appalachia and its inhabitants.

I had developed an intellectual distance from that particular culture and the people there. I considered them stupid and uneducated, and I believed I was better than them, an arrogance which I could not easily hide when I went for the visit. I was twenty-four, had already lived

---

75 From a viral social media list of queer compliments proposed as an alternative to compliments directed at a person's body.

76 Robin Morgan, as quoted in the second-to-last paragraph of the Combahee River Collective Statement.

in several cities, and styled myself an anarchist and leftist radical. My father was a factory worker who had never lived in a city and had most definitely never read Judith Butler. He was married to a deeply religious woman who had never finished high school. We didn't get along so well, as she thought I was a Satanist and I just thought she was really, really dumb.

I stayed with them in their house in a run-down former factory town utterly destroyed by the North American Free Trade Agreement (NAFTA). Half the people there had no work, while the others were driving sixty miles to work in one of the few factories still running. Despite its poverty, there was a small branch library in the town, staffed almost entirely by women without college degrees. Because of Bill Clinton's "welfare-to-work" policies in the late 1990s, they had to get jobs in order to keep receiving welfare benefits.

I was initially quite excited to visit that library, and then became completely depressed to see how very few adult books it actually had on its shelves. Most of the books were children's books, but there was also a very long shelf of Christian fiction and Christian romance, with a few "secular" crime and mystery titles. The reference shelves looked like despair itself: mostly cookbooks, two atlases, and a handful of dictionaries and books on Ohio state law.

I asked the woman working at the desk for the title I'd been hoping to borrow: *To The Lighthouse* by Virginia Woolf. It had been assigned for a class when I was in school, but I had never gotten around to reading it, and for some reason really wanted to now.

"You want three books?"

I shook my head in confusion. "No, just one."

"I don't reckon we got a book about lighthouses and wolves in Virginia. You know what it's called?"

It all really could have been a comedy script. Eventually, I did get the book. The actual librarian, who floated between several different branch libraries, was in the next day and told me she would order a copy for the library.

As I mentioned, my father's then wife was deeply religious and not very well educated. In fact, she'd never lived anywhere else except that very small town. She was deeply against alcohol, and I wasn't allowed to have any in the house while I stayed with them. That was fine for me — there were only three or four beers you could buy at the small grocery story in the town, and they all tasted like diluted urine.

My twenty-fifth birthday occurred while I was visiting them, and my father drove the three of us to the fanciest restaurant within a thirty-mile radius, an Olive Garden. For those unfamiliar with the wasteland of American corporate chain restaurants, it's an Italian restaurant where they give you free salad and bread sticks: that's a really, really, really big deal if you're poor. Also, for those unfamiliar with the hinterlands, it's worth knowing something else that's crucial to this story. At that time, at least, there were only really two different brands of coffee you could purchase in most grocery stores: Folgers or Maxwell House. Both are awful, though you wouldn't know that if they were the only ones you'd encountered. I did, unfortunately, as I'd been living in Seattle.

So, during three months of staying with my father, I'd had nothing approximating what I considered "real" coffee. One of the first things I noticed when we entered the restaurant was an espresso machine. This moment felt like a gift from the gods, or a love letter from urban civilization. When the waiter arrived, I ordered a cappuccino, the only espresso drink on their menu. Extremely excited, and it anyway being my birthday, before he left the table I then asked if it were possible to have two espresso shots in the drink, rather than one. "It's been a really long time, man,"

I said, as if I were a straight male prisoner propositioning a cell mate.

As I waited, I suddenly noticed my father's wife's knuckles had gone completely white. She was gripping the edge of the table as if a storm were blowing through, ready to sweep her away.

"What's wrong?" my father asked her.

She answered through clenched teeth. "I said no alcohol while he stays here."

My father looked as confused as I did, and it wasn't until my cappuccino arrived that we figured out what had made her so angry. "He ordered two shots," she said, gesturing towards it. And even after I explained that they were shots of espresso, she was still angry, because she had assumed espresso was an alcohol she had never heard of.

I only stayed another month there before traveling again, and my father only stayed another year with her. Towards the end of my trip, he'd offered to drive me to the nearest college town because I was really miserable. There was an actual coffee shop there, and also an Amish grocery where we could get "some of that organic food you keep complaining you can't find here." He was right, and it was a good day with him, but there's something I remember particularly during that long drive which really made me understand the condition of people there.

We had passed a billboard along the way, a colorful one depicting Jesus with a quote from the Gospel of Matthew. Jesus is holding his hands out while floating in the clouds, and he looks kind and caring, while in large white letters enclosed in quotation marks are his words "Come unto me, all ye that labor and are heavy laden, and I will give you rest."

I asked my dad about it, and he told me those billboards were very common. They were part of an anti-union campaign that had started right around the time the factories had begun to lay off large numbers of workers due to NAFTA.

My intellectual distancing from the people there had only gotten worse during my stay. The woman working at the library who didn't know who Virginia Woolf was, my father's wife and her ignorance about espresso, and countless other incidents all contributed to a larger narrative about myself and the idiocy of others. These people were all backwards and stupid, while those of us in the cities, or at least those in the cities who were similar to me, were part of a different order of human beings, enlightened, progressive, "radical."

Encountering that billboard suddenly forced me to question all that. It was clear propaganda, and extremely subtle. It was an "innocent" quote from the Bible operating on a level of symbolic meaning that few except poets usually access. My dad only knew it was anti-union propaganda because he was working a union job: the shop stewards had talked about it. Most wouldn't have caught on to it or noticed the subtle statement, "You don't need a labor union, you just need Jesus."

Thus, there I was, a young radical, certain that revolution was just around the corner, yet belittling and judging all these "backwards" and "ignorant" working-class people.

The Fear of the Rural

Unfortunately, the arrogance I showed then isn't rare at all. In fact, it's a core feature of radical politics in the United States. This "liberal" or "urban" elitism paints entire groups of people as lesser than others, too stupid to know the difference between a shot of vodka and a shot of espresso, too imbecilic to know that Virginia Woolf is an author, and too primitive to ever question their religious beliefs. Those people are "hicks" living in "flyover" states, and it's safer to keep such people contained and entertained rather than ever let them have any political power.

In fact, radical politics thrives on and enforces a fear, distrust, and often outright hatred of the rural poor. For many radicals, such people — especially whites, but also devout Catholic Hispanics and devout Pentecostal blacks — represent an amorphous, faceless enemy that will vote for fascism if they're not stopped. After all, it was such people — and not the supposedly enlightened urbanites — who voted for Trump rather than Hillary in 2016 or for Brexit in the United Kingdom. They are also the ones who vote for politicians who vow to stop the teaching of critical race theory in schools and to limit participation in women's sports based on biological sex rather than declared gender.

This condescending divide isn't new. It's a holdover from older leftist movements, especially anarchism and utopian socialism, both of which inherited bourgeois protestant moral constellations. In those constellations, people in the cities saw themselves as enlightened, while the peasants farming outside the towns were dirty and stupid, still eating roots and baking with unrefined flour. Such people couldn't read, while the town dwellers were doing accounting, practicing law and medicine, buying imported spices and teas arriving from the colonies, and no longer believing in "superstitious" religious ideas.

This tension between a "civilized" urban population and the "uncivilized" peasants continued into anarchism and utopian socialism, because both of those movements were primarily urban. Utopian socialism especially — which argues more equal and just societies can be created through mass education — saw the ignorance of the poor as the primary barrier to their enlightenment.

We see this continue in progressive attempts to introduce gender and critical race theories into early education. The logic here is that if young children learn about pronouns and white privilege, a future society will have less racism and transphobia. The strongest resistance to such radical educational policies has been from parents in rural school districts, a fact that only serves as more apparent evidence that the rural poor are backwards, superstitious, and inherently racist or transphobic.

On the other hand, it's not hard to understand why those rural parents might feel an "elitist urban" agenda is being forced upon their children. No small part of that sentiment derives from right-wing media, of course, but the sense that urban areas have more political power and that politicians make decisions based upon allegiances to political ideologies which benefit the rich is also a significant factor. NAFTA, and the neoliberal political ideologies which justified it, wrought significantly more economic damage in rural areas than it did in the cities; it affected manual and industrial workers much more than urban office professionals or service workers.

While Marx and subsequent theorists using Marx often showed a distrust and sometimes condescending view of the rural poor, the class analysis that Marx proposed undermines this urban/rural divide. The rural worker and the urban worker are both part of the same class and are both in exploitative relationships with their bosses. This understanding is what led to many successes in labor movements for agricultural workers — immigrant and otherwise — especially for figures such as Cesar Chavez, a labor organizer who was also a Catholic. Rather than seeing rural workers as hopeless and superstitious reactionaries, and instead of assuming they were too ignorant or stupid to understand class analysis, such unionizers spoke directly to their material conditions (poverty, long hours of work, low wages) and organized them along those lines.

Exactly this sort of legacy was why my own father was part of a union in Appalachia, as were his father and most of his friends. Union work was the best work you could find, and getting a union job meant you could actually support a family rather than having to wait for monthly trucks to deliver government food and fuel aid. While I would hardly call my father educated or even very literate, he had a concrete understanding of how capitalism worked, how the labor he performed translated into profit for the bosses, and why it made more sense to co-operate with his co-workers — white, Hispanic, and black — for better wages and working conditions.

This more basic understanding of solidarity and class relations runs counter to urban distrust and fear of the rural poor (and especially of the rural white male). Particularly in the political rhetoric of Democratic politicians such as Hillary Clinton, such people are described as racist and sexist "deplorables," as being impossible to change, and as hostile to the utopian visions of equal and fair capitalist societies such politicians present.

The White Male Apex-Oppressor

Current radical frameworks solidify this view through the hierarchical constellation of oppression identities. Consider the apex-oppressor class within intersectional feminism: the "white, heterosexual, able-bodied cis-man." Within this cosmology, it is he for whom all the world has been made, all institutions founded, all laws designed, all wealth accumulated, and all exploitation effected; just as the wolf is the apex-predator in an ecosystem, he preys on others while being uniquely "privileged" to fear no predation himself. Yet unlike the wolf and other natural apex-predators, all of whom have an overall balancing and positive effect on the ecosystem (keeping herbivore populations in check and thus benefiting the survival and growth of forests), the social justice framework often sees the white, heterosexual, able-bodied cis-man as having no purpose within the social order except to dominate.

Do such men actually exist? Perhaps, but their physical reality is less relevant to the identity hierarchy than what they stand for symbolically. The white, heterosexual able-bodied cis-man is a created category, in the same way that the proletariat and the bourgeoisie were creations of capitalist modes of production and the Christian and the heathen were creations of the Catholic Church. That is, he is a symbolic construction crafted through ideological pastiche and bricolage, sewn together from loose historical and mythological threads according to a pattern that maps him onto physical reality only through collective belief.

Many radicals correctly understand that there are social relations and disparities underpinning economic and societal oppressions. Some people have more wealth than others, and the people who compose those groups engage in social and political struggle to maintain that wealth and also to guarantee their continued access to further wealth creation. The pre-capitalist aristocracy in Europe employed physical and social (or symbolic) violence to ensure their large landholdings were secure, and to make sure they had a continued supply of landless peasants who could be compelled to labor on their land. Trade guilds restricted access to specialized crafting skills to guarantee higher wages and continued demand for the labor of their members. Protestant town-dwellers employed in specialized labor (medicine, law, academia, and accounting) adopted and propagated specific social codes and signifiers to ensure the new professions they quickly dominated would not be open to those outside their religious and political sensibilities. The early "captains" of capitalist industrial production likewise learned quickly to accumulate not just economic capital but symbolic capital, influencing the legislative politics which formed our still current forms of private property and wage labor.

Every group which finds a way to accumulate wealth finds ways to hold onto it and to increase it. Radicals who focus on social oppression rather than capitalist exploitation, however, treat the white, heterosexual, able-bodied cis-man as a transcendent oppressor category who is the true cause of all suffering.

In a way, the fixation on social justice has merely retooled the formula from *The Communist Manifesto* with different actors. Rather than "the history of all hitherto existing society" being "the history of class struggles," it is the history of race struggles, or gender struggles, or struggles of sexuality, or of ability. In the intersectional social justice cosmology, it is not the limited bourgeois class against the innumerable proletariat, but rather the white, heterosexual, able-bodied cis-man against everyone else in the world.

The economic, political, and social system that the bourgeoisie class created has a name: capitalism. The white, heterosexual, able-bodied cis-man is likewise said to have created systems: white supremacy, cis-heteropatriarchy, toxic masculinity, and countless other sub-systems (homophobia, ableism, and so on). He has constellated a symbolic order at the top of which he alone sits, accumulating wealth and preventing all others from accessing his proprietary secrets. His systems are the reason why black people are poor, why trans people commit suicide, why people with invisible disabilities struggle to hold regular jobs, and why many gay teenagers struggle with meth addiction or are bullied at school.

Intersectional social justice politics engages in the very same symbolic ordering in which Marx and Engels engaged, but towards different ends. Whether or not there is "such a thing" as the white, heterosexual, able-bodied cis-man is just as irrelevant as the question of whether or not the world can be divided between bourgeoisie and proletariat. What is important here is that the white, heterosexual, able-bodied cis-man is a *symbolic category* that this political framework attempts to manifest as a physical reality.

In other's words — specifically in the words of French sociologist Pierre Bourdieu — the white, heterosexual, able-bodied cis-man is being *instituted* into the constellation of radical political struggle:

> The act of institution is thus an act of communication, but of a particular kind: it signifies to someone what his identity is, but in a way that both expresses it to him and imposes it on him by expressing it in front of everyone (*kategorein*, meaning originally, to accuse publicly) and thus informing him in an authoritative manner of what he is and what he must be. This is clearly evident in the insult, a kind of curse (*sacer* also signifies cursed) which attempts to imprison its victim in an accusation which also depicts his destiny. But this is even truer of an investiture or an act of naming, a specifically social judgement of attribution which assigns to the person involved everything that is inscribed in a social definition.[77]

Bourdieu's framework proposes that the core goal of acts of institution is *division*. A category is named in order to divide the people within it from other categories to which they might otherwise belong. "Bourgeois," for example, institutes a categorical division between the group of people named the bourgeoisie and all the other people in the world: the proletariat.

The white, heterosexual, able-bodied cis-man is also a category of division. He must be identified, categorized, and

77 See Bourdieu, 1992.

ultimately instituted so that all other identity categories can be defined by their lack of his traits. However, unlike the single binary division between the proletariat and the bourgeoisie, whose primary definitional distinction is material and functional (one owns or has access to the means of production, the other must sell their labor in order to engage in production), the white, heterosexual, able-bodied cis-man is constructed through a series of binaries.

Each of these binaries are binaries of oppressor/oppressed. His race (white) sets him apart as the oppressor of all people who are not white; his sexuality (heterosexual) makes him the dominator of all homosexuals, bisexuals, and asexuals. His lack of disability allows him to dominate all those with disabilities. And his sex/gender is not only male/man (thus dominating women) but also unchanged since birth, thus making him the oppressor also of trans and non-binary people.

The hierarchy can be drawn out as a pyramid with him at the top. At the very bottom is his supposed opposite, the black, disabled, queer trans woman, and between them are all the other people in the world holding intersecting oppression identities. Each of those people experiences domination, but they can also potentially dominate those below them because of vestiges of privilege remaining in any traits shared with the apex-oppressor.

This is the reason for the common social justice slogan "Listen to black trans women" (or another variant, sometimes used as an addendum to other slogans, "...especially trans women of color"). The white, heterosexual, able-bodied cis-woman may feel she suffers societal oppression, and she may be correct, but ultimately any oppression she suffers pales in comparison to those below her in the hierarchy. The white, gay cis-man, even if he has disabilities, still possesses unfathomable and unforgivable privileges that the black, disabled, trans woman will never experience.

What About Class?

The identity hierarchy created though these theories obviously lacks one category: class. In fact, class cannot be introduced within these categories without undermining the entire framework. Consider: What does a jobless and homeless white, heterosexual, able-bodied cis-man really have in common with a CEO who possesses all those same identity traits? Or for that matter, what do certain among a CEO's employees have in common with him except for those identity markers?

We might also ask, what does a black woman millionaire entrepreneur (such as Oprah) really have in common with a single black woman holding down two jobs yet who is barely able to afford rent and feed her children? And more so, is their shared racial identification actually stronger and more relevant than the shared class identifications between such a woman and a white woman in the same economic situation?

This is the reason any Marxist (including a black Marxist such as Adolph Reed) who attempts to reintroduce class as a framework and foundation for solidarity or radical organizing is typically smeared as a "class reductionist." Class destabilizes the entire discourse by looking for commonalities and differences along a fully different set of co-ordinates which cut across all the other identity categories. It divides every supposedly unitary oppression grouping by asking a simple question: Do you have access to wealth and the creation of more of it? Or must you sell your time, your body, and your labor for even the minimal means of your survival?

The question of class also threatens the stability and position of those who argue most on behalf of identity politics. Consider a short list of such theorists: Rachel Cargle, famous for her statement, "I refuse to listen to white women cry," owns several businesses and has a net worth estimated at three million US dollars. Judith Butler is reported to have about nine million US dollars in wealth. Robin DiAngelo, who runs a consulting business for corporate diversity programs and is the author of *White Fragility*, is also a millionaire, as are Ta-Nehisi Coates, Ibram X. Kendi, and Kimberlé Crenshaw.

In other words, they're all much better off than the "marginalized" people for whom they position themselves to speak. The problem for such theorists is that in a class framework they have much more in common with the capitalists than they do with the poor. As we saw in the analysis of Adolph Reed, the class identity of these theorists would distance them from the groups for whom they position themselves to speak, while also giving the lie to the idea that the white, heterosexual, able-bodied cisman is a homogenous category.

The Professional-Managerial Class

In fact, the class positions of these theorists are likely the primary explanation for the complete absence of class analysis within their criticisms of race and gender. Consider again how Donna Haraway's "A Cyborg Manifesto" explained the need to redefine "woman":

> For me — and for many who share a similar historical location in white, professional middle-class, female, radical, North American, mid-adult bodies — the sources of a crisis in political identity are legion."

Haraway was writing after the "Combahee River Collective Statement,"[78] the assertion of which that identity needed to be a primary foundation for all political struggle significantly shook the left's understanding of class and sex. However, there was also another influential essay published a few years before to which Haraway was also reacting. That essay, written by Barbara and John Ehrenreich and published in 1977 in the journal *Radical America*, offered a completely different framework for understanding the failures of leftist organizing in the United States.

For the Ehrenreichs, the core issue was not the difficulty of defining women or the need to better understand identities, but rather the ascendancy and dominance of the professional-managerial class (PMC) to which not only the authors but also Haraway, the members of the Combahee River Collective, Judith Butler, and all the dominant theorists of identity politics belong.

The Ehrenreichs defined this PMC as follows:

> We define the Professional-Managerial Class as consisting of salaried mental workers who do not own the means of production and whose major function in the social division of labor may be described broadly as the reproduction of capitalist culture and capitalist class relations.
>
> Their roles in the process of reproduction may be more or less explicit, as with workers who are directly concerned with social control or with the production of propagation of ideology (e.g.; teachers, social workers, psychologists, entertainers, writers of advertising copy and TV scripts, etc.). Or it may be hidden within the process of production, as is the case with the middle-level administrators whose functions... are essentially argued by the need to preserve

---

78 A statement, incidentally, composed by black, professional, middle-class females.

capitalist relations of production. Thus we assert that these occupational groups — cultural workers, managers, engineers and scientists, etc. — share a common function in the broad social division of labor and a common relation to the economic foundations of society.[79]

The PMC roughly translates into the idea of "white-collar workers," those who work in offices rather than in service, factory, or manual labor jobs. The Ehrenreichs' definition is broader, however, in that it includes people who work in ideological professions which do not have a specific administrative role, including artists, writers, entertainers, professors and other educators, psychologists, and social workers. As ideological workers, their function is not physical production but rather the "reproduction of capitalist cultural and class relationships."

Key to understanding the PMC is that they are a small subsection of the working class itself, meaning they do not possess their own means of production and must sell their labor. That is, they are not actually part of the capitalist class, but nevertheless share and reproduce the cultural values of the capitalists. Barbara and John Ehrenreich describe them as a "derivative class," a class derived from the masses of the proletariat to support the capitalist order.

The very definition of the PMC — as a class concerned with the reproduction of capitalist cultural and class relationships — precludes treating it as a separable sociological entity. It is in a sense a derivative class; its existence presupposes: (1) that the social surplus has developed to the point sufficient to sustain the PMC in addition to the bourgeoisie, for the PMC is essentially nonproductive; and (2) that the relationship between the bourgeoisie and the proletariat

79 See Ehrenreich and Ehrenreich, 1977.

has developed to the point that a class specialising in the reproduction of capitalist class relationships becomes a necessity to the capitalist class. That is, the maintenance of order can no longer be left to episodic police violence.[80]

In other words, the PMC is a highly paid subset of the proletariat whose salaries and lifestyles derive from their role as reproducers and guardians of the social order. This work exists so that the capitalists do not need to use relentless, naked violence to keep workers in line. They create the cultural forms — the structures of domination — which ensure the rest of the working class remains content with their economic situations. They train, civilize, supervise, treat, and amuse the producing classes — the factory and service workers, the manual and agricultural workers, the "blue-collar" sorts — and by doing so smooth over and mollify class tensions so to ensure the perpetuation of the capitalist order.

The PMC is also what has been called by conservative critics the "liberal latté-drinking urban elite," since their values, professions, and lifestyles — even among those who hold to leftist political frameworks — are heavily aligned with an urban (bourgeois) cultural sensibility. Demographic polling on political issues supports this critique — those with higher degrees and higher incomes who live in urban and suburban areas show higher support for liberal or progressive policies and candidates than those with lower incomes, less education, and those of their cohort living in rural areas.

In this way, the PMC also maps closely to the older Marxist analysis of the *petite bourgeoisie* (the "little urban class"). These were the small shop owners, doctors, lawyers, and people in other highly specialized and rare professions

---

80 Ibid., p. 15.

who did not work for a wage but were nevertheless not true capitalists (because they did not exploit the labor of others to increase their capital). Despite not actually being engaged in capitalist exploitation, their cultural and political values aligned with the capitalist class, and they strongly supported political repression of the lower classes.

The PMC, then, is an evolution or expansion of the petite bourgeoisie, with the important distinction that they are often also salaried.

The PMC versus the Rest of the Working Class

The observation that the PMC is not actually engaged in physical production is deeply important for understanding the tensions and diverging concerns between them and the rest of the working class. We can easily sense a vast difference in values and economic concerns between a woman working in a meatpacking plant in Des Moines, Iowa, and a woman running a yoga studio in Portland, Oregon. We can sense this same difference when we consider other comparisons:

- A black trans woman working for an investment bank versus a black trans woman working at McDonald's
- A Hispanic woman cleaning houses through a maid service versus one teaching gender studies at UCLA.
- A black male sanitation worker versus a black male editorialist for *The Atlantic*
- A white male construction worker versus a white male database administrator

Besides deep differences in compensation and standards of living, not to mention the vast disparity in the physical effects of their labor on their bodies, the relationship between the PMC and the rest of the working class is one of unequal consumption. That is, the rest of the working class is producing the physical goods and services (housecleaning, food and food service, construction, sanitation, dry cleaning) which the PMC rely upon for their elevated standards of living.

This tension inevitably creates a deep difference in values and cultural worldviews, one which especially manifests in leftist political organizing. In a 2019 interview for *Dissent Magazine*, Barbara Ehrenreich elaborated on some of the personal experiences which had led her and her former husband John Ehrenreich to develop their analysis of the PMC. After recounting a story in which a leftist professor and his wife accusingly read aloud quotes from Mao at her because of her working-class sensibilities, she then explained:

> There were fights that would break out in food co-ops — they were called the "Twinkie wars." People wanted the food co-op to carry the highly processed, no-doubt-bad-for-you foods that they could get in the supermarket, and the more PMC types did not want that.
>
> So, there was a lot of empirical data that went into this essay. There was a real difference between people who worked essentially telling other people what to do — and teachers get included in that — and people who do the work that other people tell them to do. It becomes a difference between manual and mental labor, but it carries with it a shitload of weight — I see it all the time, the contempt for especially white working-class people among leftists of college backgrounds.

While these experiences occurred before "The Professional-Managerial Class" was written, they could just have easily occurred today. In fact, Barbara later recounts in that same interview a more recent experience which elucidates this divide succinctly:

In 2009, there was an event — part of an international series of socialist gatherings — in Detroit. There was a workshop at this conference, and I had invited a group of working-class people from Fort Wayne, Indiana, who I had become close to. About six or seven of them drove from Fort Wayne to Detroit, and they were mostly laid-off foundry workers: stereotypical white men — though, actually, not all of them were white. I was closest with one of them, Tom Lewandowski, who created a workers' organization and was the head of the Central Labor Council in the Fort Wayne area. [At the event], they talked about what they were facing in the recession. And then some woman in the room who was an adjunct professor suddenly says, "I'm tired of listening to white men talk."

I was so aghast. Of course, it was a big setback for my friends from Fort Wayne, who were humiliated. I advised Tom not to get into settings where he would be subjected to that ever again. There has to be a way to say to such people, look, we know you probably aren't doing great as an adjunct, but have some respect for other people's work and their experience, and recognize that they are different from you in some way. I've just had too many encounters like that, which are kind of heartbreaking.[81]

In the woman's statement, "I'm tired of listening to white men talk," which has become somewhat of a rallying cry for some radicals, we can begin to detect the reason for the existence of the "white, heterosexual, able-bodied cis-man"

---

81 See Press, 2022.

as the alpha-oppressor category. He is a symbol for the entire working class, the uncultured manual worker who doesn't use the right words, who eats processed foods, and who has never read Judith Butler. This is all regardless of the fact that he isn't actually representative of the working class, a class which is composed also of black and Hispanic people and women as well. Despite the true diversity of the working class, he functions as its symbol specifically because he isn't oppressed on account of his identity, only on account of his class.

The problem here is that he functions as the symbolic container for everything the PMC is not, both below their economic status and also above. He is not only an angry, brutish, cheap-beer drinking, working-class and especially rural threat, he is also the capitalist for whom those in the PMC ultimately work. The rich who own the banks, the newspapers, the media and internet technology corporations, and who fund the non-profit organizations and educational institutions from which the PMC derive their high salaries and standards of living share the same identity categories (white, cis, able-bodied, heterosexual, male) as the car mechanic who shops at Walmart, lives in a trailer, listens to country music, and watches Fox News.

Of course, there is another buried contradiction here, as the PMC is itself also mostly white, even after years of pressure to implement corporate diversity, equity, and inclusion policies. Here, though, the point of such policies is always to improve the racial and gender diversity of the PMC, rather than to improve the material conditions of the more traditional working class. None of these theorists are arguing for more inclusive, equitable, and diverse hiring policies for the masses of laborers in construction, manufacturing, janitorial, hospitality, agriculture, or retail work, only for those who head those industries and manage those workers.

Professional-Managerial Class "Leftism"

This contradiction derives from the complete disconnect between the PMC and the rest of the working class, and it is sustained by the complete avoidance of class analysis. When such workers are even treated in any political discourse, they are caricatured through the symbolic container of the white, heterosexual, able-bodied cis-male. Again we must ask what objectively binds such men together, and we will each time come up lacking. The farmhand who works the fields near my home has little in common with the farmer who owns those lands. The white male delivery driver for Amazon has little in common with the white male CEO of Amazon. Yet each of these men, according to the intersectional social justice framework, benefits from and maintains esoteric systems of domination: white supremacy, cis-heteropatriarchy, toxic masculinity, global anti-blackness, and so on.

This is how the PMC is able to categorize them as a unified group, dissolving all differences — *especially their unequal material conditions* — into a monolithic force. This is also why there's so little adoption of the social justice framework among the rest of the working class except in their most populist forms, forms which they encounter primarily through cultural entertainment and social media. It's also why there is such a backlash against identity discourse in the United States, the United Kingdom, and in France, from the "reactionary" movements that oppose the teaching of declarative gender theory, critical race theory, or *le wokisme* in early education, as well as increasing anger towards liberal or left-identified politicians and activists who dismiss such concerns as coming from "deplorables" or "fascists."

The problem is that the PMC cannot actually speak for the rest of the working class, because although they hold cultural and political positions which give them the influence to actually change and shape society, their material conditions, lifestyles, and values are closer to the capitalist class. What they imagine as a march towards progress and equality, what for them looks like liberation, appears not only out of touch but also dictatorial to the rest of the working class. This is because the concerns of the working class are more practical, and are related to their actual economic situations rather than esoteric categories.

This difference is particularly sharp when it comes to PMC "leftist" analysis of the family and traditional cultural values. A migrant agricultural worker is much less likely to see their calls to "abolish the family"[82] or challenge binary gender roles as helpful or even good, especially because their families are often the only refuges they have against the alienation and exploitation of capitalism. But we must also ask, why would a construction worker really care that facial feminization surgery is not always fully covered by medical insurance companies when he doesn't even have medical insurance? And what relevance are any of the discourses about white privilege, cis-heteronormativity, or the gender pay gap in Silicon Valley tech companies to a minimum-waged retail clerk (of any gender or racial group) at Walmart?

What we once conceived of as "the left," before it became dominated and transformed by the PMC and their theories, proposes different co-ordinates and different lines

---

82 The title of a book by one such PMC writer, Sophie Lewis. In her works, she argues for the abolition of the nuclear family to be replaced by amorphous communal relations. See Wildermuth, 2022 for my review of her book. Also see Wildermuth, 2020 for a longer discussion of the tensions between Marxist Feminism and Lewis's techno-utopian socialism.

of solidarity: ones based in class. In a class framework, the rural working class and the urban working class naturally have much more in common with each other than either group has with the capitalists. They have a shared interest in getting fair returns on their labor and gaining greater access to their own production.

Unfortunately, because of the proximity of the PMC's cultural values to the capitalists', as well as their role as reproducers and sustainers of capitalist social relations (as managers, educators, entertainers, and so on), the PMC currently functions much more like the religious clergy often did in early industrial Europe. Rather than using their relatively protected positions and increased influence to oppose the capitalists, they instead placate, police, and discipline the working classes. In lieu of preaching class consciousness against the exploitative actions of the capitalists, they subject the poor to sermons warning them to seek forgiveness from their inherent privilege, internalized patriarchal gender norms, and their deplorable, oppressive natures. Only by acknowledging these sins and following the one true path can the working class then find salvation from the misery of capitalism.

In case such a comparison to religion seems flippant or unsubstantiated, we should look once again at the core difference between the categories of divisions instituted by intersectional social justice and Marxist class analysis.

Both institute categories of division, but each attempts to do so based on entirely separate premises. Intersectional social justice creates the division among mostly static — and often essentialist — identity markers that defines and determines their relationship to other such markers. A person cannot change their race (just ask Rachel Dolezal), nor can they — without self-mutilation or significant corrective medical procedures — switch between the categories of "abled" and "disabled." Despite talk of sexuality and gender being "fluid," this framework also posits these as inherent things a person does not really change: the trans person is said to have retroactively always been the gender they later identify as, not the gender they were "assigned." Likewise, what is changeable about a gay man or lesbian woman's sexuality is not their desire for men or for women but rather their understanding of what constitutes the men and women they desire.

Marxist class analysis, on the other hand, draws no such hard boundaries between the workers and the owners. There is no essence or immutable trait which creates the bourgeoisie or the proletariat, because they are categories of function. To put it more plainly, though in the framework of intersectional social justice a white woman can never become a black woman, in class analysis a capitalist may become a wage laborer merely through a bit of economic misfortune. Likewise, though a black street-gang member can never become a white street-gang member, through force or luck he can find himself later employing scores of others in capitalist enterprise.

That is, class is not an immutable or essential trait, though of course there are countless barriers to transcending it. Wealth has its own logic, and those who hold it tend to desire to continue holding it, employing soldiers, lawyers, and politicians to keep social conditions most amenable to its continued accumulation. These are the "systems" and "structural oppressions" which many radicals accurately sense yet wrongly attribute to race, gender, sexuality, and ability.

There are superstitious aspects of these misidentifications. Seeing that many of the richest capitalists are white, and heterosexual, and male, intersectional social justice makes the wrong connection between those identity markers and the massive wealth they possess. Much like the Calvinist bourgeoisie in Europe attributed their own wealth and success to God's grace and their status as part of the "elect," radicals treat the white, heterosexual, able-bodied cis-man as a kind of divine figure possessing puissant traits which cannot be attained, only undermined through cultural change, "anti-racist discrimination," educational programs, and relentless privilege checking.

INTERLUDE: THE GRIFT

We've already met the Cyborg and the Zombie. We'll meet a third monster, the Vampire, in the next chapter. Before then, however, we need to look at how the current iterations of radical politics, the framework of intersectional social justice (or what some call "woke ideology"), affects everyday interactions between people. We also need to give our attention to several well-intentioned yet disastrous political attempts to implement this framework. As elsewhere, I'll begin with my own experience.

For the majority of my sixteen years of life in Seattle, I rented a dilapidated house in a rapidly gentrifying neighborhood of the city with multiple others. We called it an anarchist commune, and sometimes also the "Pirate House" on account of the Jolly Roger we flew from the railing of the large, rotten wooden balcony outside my bedroom.

We referred to the actual owner of the house, the man to whom we paid rent each month, as our "slumlord," but we meant this in the kindest way possible. There was black mold in one of the bathrooms, the staircase to the second floor was crooked and one of its steps was loose enough to cause many guests to trip, and we had to heat the house with electric heaters and the oven during the winter. But we had an agreement: the landlord charged us very little for rent and didn't come by the house to see what kinds of illegal or political acts we engaged in; in exchange, we didn't report the countless violations of city housing and health codes in the house he rented to us.

Altogether, I and the other six to eight roommates[83] paid less in rent for a four-bedroom home than the average price of a no-bedroom studio apartment in the same area, and despite all its problems we adored the place. Living so cheaply in an expensive city meant we had enough money to work the only sporadic jobs any of us were able to find or keep (line cook, server, retail clerk, nightclub doorman, barista, entry-level social worker) and still have enough money to survive, to throw large parties, and to squander away anything left over for books, games, computers, and failed artistic projects.

There were several ways to get a room in the house whenever one was vacated. I had found my "in" to the house by crashing on the floor occasionally. I had been the homeless punk friend of one of the people already there; when one of the other roommates decided to move out and there was a room open, they offered it to me. Others became part of the house by being the girlfriend or boyfriend of one the roommates, and others still by being friends in desperate need of housing just at the moment someone moved out. It was all usually luck, and rarely a formal process, and our landlord didn't care who we moved in — provided the rent was always paid.

One time, however, a roommate needed to leave suddenly because she was moving back in with her ex-boyfriend. We didn't know anyone who needed a room, so we posted an advertisement on Craigslist: "Tiny room in a queer punk co-op house, 200/month, no pets, smoking okay, view of mountains and Lake Washington." Someone answered, and we invited her over for tea, and then she moved in the next week.

---

83 This living arrangement was often in constant flux. Once we had ten people living there, but two were sleeping on couches and one was sleeping in a bedroom closet.

That didn't go so well. For the first month things were mostly fine. She'd not told us before moving in that she was a sex worker and would be hosting her clients in the house, but since I had prostituted myself several times while I had been homeless, and because we considered ourselves a sex-positive house, we were quite willing to accept this.

"Just let us know when a guy's coming over so we're not surprised," I had asked her.

"That's an invasion of my privacy," she had spat back.

"Oh, sorry," I replied. "You're right, sorry."

That had felt a little weird, but we went with it. She was trans (and reminded us very often, especially when we asked her to please wash her dishes), and we were all queer anarchists and were committed to "anti-oppression work," so of course we didn't want to violate her privacy. But another problem became much more difficult to negotiate through our anti-oppression politics.

Each month, we paid our rent by writing individual checks to the landlord and dropping them off in a remote mailbox. The month after the new roommate had moved in, the landlord called us to say that one of those checks had bounced: hers. The other roommates appointed me to handle the situation.

"Hey," I said. "The landlord said your check bounced."

"Not possible. There's enough money in my account."

I really didn't know what to say. "Uh, could you call him and tell him that?"

"I'm busy," she'd said, then slammed her bedroom door.

I covered her rent that first month. It was only $200, which was only two overtime shifts at the homeless shelter where I was currently working. So it was no big deal. No big deal except that it happened the next month, too. She slammed the door on me again when I told her, and then shouted at me when I said I couldn't afford to cover her rent that month.

"I'll have to find more tricks," she spat back. "The last one tried to choke me and you guys didn't come help."

I was genuinely mortified. "Oh my gods, I didn't know."

"No one cares about trans people," she said, looking hurt.

"Look. I can cover it again. But I can't next month. And this would be easier if you let me know ahead of time that you need help."

It happened again. The third month of unpaid rent, I refused to pay. She then called me a transphobe and wrote social media posts about her transphobic housemates. The more I tried to explain that I wasn't, that this wasn't about her being trans but about her not paying the rent, the more proof I seemed to be offering her that I actually hated trans people.

Something had changed in my head during that conversation, though. The way she said something, something I don't remember, felt uncomfortably familiar. It felt less like a memory and more like an echo. As she berated me from the other side of a closed door, I suddenly understood what she was doing, *because I had done it, too.*

When I first came out as gay, along with the relief of no longer needing to hide "who I was" came a really useful and utterly invisible pass for some really awful behavior. I could shut down arguments with friends or co-workers really quickly by reminding them they were straight, that the whole world was built around them, and that they would never understand how hard it was to be gay. Whether they were asking me to pay back the ten dollars I owed from dinner a few weeks before, or to replace the CD they'd lent me that I scratched beyond use, or just asking me to not be such an asshole sometimes, my gayness became a trump card that could end any conversation.

It took me too long to notice that it also ended friendships. Of course, it only really worked on friends, or on people sympathetic to me. I tried reminding a boss about my sexuality when I'd showed up late one too many times, and that got me nowhere. It also didn't work with bill collectors, or with the bouncer who threw me out of a bar for being too drunk, or really anyone else with power. In fact, it only worked on people who liked me, on people who really wanted to be "good" or "sensitive" and didn't want to hurt anyone. And that felt awful, because I was bullying people who just wanted to be nice. I realized in that moment my roommate was doing the same to me.

"You need to find another place," I suddenly said, surprising myself. "I can't pay your rent again."

"You can't make me leave!" she replied, swinging the door open. "This is transphobic discrimination."

I shook my head. "No. This is me choosing not to pay your rent for you."

She eventually moved out, though not without a few fruitless phone calls to trans rights groups and the city's tenants' union, as well as months of really awful social media posts. And though I was glad to find a new roommate who would actually pay rent on time to replace her, I did still feel rather awful about it for a while.

I guess that is inevitable, though. I imagine the former friends who finally stood up to my own bullying of them probably felt a tinge of regret as well. Perhaps it all could have gone better between me and them, or between me and her. And I wonder if they had lingering doubts long after, just as I did after asking that roommate to leave. "Am I homophobic and don't realize it?" perhaps they asked themselves, just as I sometimes asked myself, "Do I unconsciously hate trans people?"

Regardless, this was no way to keep friendships or relationships, nor did such manipulation actually stop homophobia, or transphobia, or any oppression or injustice. For me as for her, identity had become a weapon, not against people who wielded actual power over my life (landlords, bosses, the capitalists), but a crude bludgeon with which to manipulate people not much better off than myself.

You Owe Me

In almost two decades of being in radical spaces I've seen this pattern repeated relentlessly. One such example occurred at Occupy Seattle during a general assembly. It ground to a halt because of a speaker who decried the crowd's refusal to acknowledge how traumatic and oppressed her life as a trans black woman had been.[84] I've already mentioned the time I watched a friend berated for asking his roommates to replace food of his that they'd eaten. He wasn't BIPOC like they were, he was a settler-colonist and living on stolen lands, so how dare he demand they replace the food they'd eaten? It was he that *owed* them.

The internet makes this behavior even easier. For years there have been thriving online forums devoted to it, including one called "Anarcho-Communism: Radical Communal Learning Space." In that forum, non-white people post payment and personal fundraiser links with explanations that they are opportunities for "yt"[85] members to pay reparations and learn about mutual aid. It's difficult not to notice that these function much like indulgences in the Catholic Church did, a method of absolving yourself of the sin of white-skin privilege by paying someone's cell phone bill, funding their gender surgeries, or buying things

---

84 I personally knew this person, and I was one of the people who tried to help afterwards. I still receive emails and direct messages containing "reparations" requests (money for groceries, mostly) from this person to this day.

85 A shorthand for "white" often in use on such forums.

for them off their Amazon wish lists. Of course, if you are not part of one of those forums, you can use your own social media accounts to sell these indulgences, as occurred over ninety thousand times on Twitter alone from 1 January to 23 June 2021:

> There have been more than 91,000 tweets which mention "cashapp reparations," "venmo reparations," or "venmo cashapp reparations," according to an Axios analysis of data from Keyhole, since the start of the year.[86]

This sort of behavior functions as a kind of opportunism or grift. Participants wield zombified leftist concepts as a bludgeon against others. Reparations, for example, were once understood to mean specific payments to black slaves or their descendants to compensate for their stolen labor, with the funds for such payments derived specifically from former slaveholders or from the estates and states which accumulated wealth from their labor. In these online demands, however, reparations have come to mean something quite divorced from this original framework. Reparations have become instead a collective debt owed by all white people to any black person demanding they pay up.

This form of individual reparations is also divorced from collective black organizations' iterations of reparations, as per this statement by the Movement 4 Black Lives (M4BL):

> We demand reparations for past and continuing harms. The government, responsible corporations and other institutions that have profited off of the harm they have inflicted on Black people — from colonialism to slavery through food and housing redlining, mass incarceration,

---

86 See King, 2021.

and surveillance — must repair the harm done. This includes:

1. Reparations for the systemic denial of access to high quality educational opportunities in the form of full and free access for all Black people....
2. Reparations for the continued divestment from, discrimination toward and exploitation of our communities in the form of a guaranteed minimum livable income for all Black people, with clearly articulated corporate regulations.
3. Reparations for the wealth extracted from our communities through environmental racism, slavery, food apartheid, housing discrimination and racialized capitalism in the form of corporate and government reparations focused on healing ongoing physical and mental trauma, and ensuring our access and control of food sources, housing and land.
4. Reparations for the cultural and educational exploitation, erasure, and extraction of our communities in the form of mandated public school curriculums that critically examine the political, economic, and social impacts of colonialism and slavery, and funding to support, build, preserve, and restore cultural assets and sacred sites to ensure the recognition and honoring of our collective struggles and triumphs.
5. Legislation at the federal and state level that requires the United States to acknowledge the lasting impacts of slavery, establish and execute a plan to address those impacts...[87]

---

87 See M4BL, n.d.

M4BL's reparations program is built primarily upon the redistribution of wealth towards black people as a collective group, rather than towards individuals. It's also worth noting that none of the reparations proposals are directed at individuals, nor do they even use the term "white" in describing who is responsible for ameliorating systematic barriers to material wealth for black people. On the other hand, high-profile individuals and groups have argued for "individual" reparations, including most notoriously Marissa Jenae Johnson and Leslie Mac's now-apparently defunct Safety Pin Box subscription service. As detailed in an article by the BBC, the service was for "white people striving to be allies in the fight for Black Liberation":

> For between $25 (for an electronic membership) and $100 (for a physical box mailed to subscribers) (£19.75 to £78.99) a month, subscription members are sent a set of tasks that will help them "do tangible ally work and support black women in both power and deed." Johnson says that the target customer is a white person who already recognizes his white privilege but "wants to learn, who believes in giving back to black people, is humble and willing to make mistakes."
>
> "This [is a] huge group of white folks," says Mac. "They've gone and read Ta-Nehisi Coates' book, they have a good understanding of this puzzle of white supremacy and racial injustice, and they're at a moment where they don't know where to go with that."
>
> The first sample task, for example, helps users chart the ways in which they wield power in everyday life — whether it is how they spend money, or in their jobs or their church — and how to redirect it to benefit people of colour.[88]

88 See Lussenhop, 2016.

While such for-profit reparations schemes (Safety Pin Box was a commercial enterprise, though part of the profits were claimed to be redistributed to unnamed "black femme" activists) may seem extreme, in my own experience I've seen many examples of businesses and artists' fundraisers marketed to funders and customers as ways of paying reparations or supporting trans and non-binary youth. Making reparations for white or cis privilege becomes an added value to a product or service, an extra (and intangible) perk for a Kickstarter or GoFundMe campaign.

Such schemes are not limited to the internet, and the logic of reparations and Ibram X. Kendi's formula for anti-racist discrimination have been increasingly implemented in businesses and restaurants (for instance, increased fees for white customers), organizations, and notoriously in some recent large political events. During the Gay Pride celebrations in the summer of 2021 in Seattle, Washington, an event called Taking B(l)ack Pride charged a reparations entrance fee for white people, while non-white people were allowed in for free. As the official event information stated:

> All are free to attend HOWEVER this is a BLACK AND BROWN QUEER TRANS CENTERED, PRIORITIZED, VALUED, EVENT. White allies and accomplices are welcome to attend but will be charged a $10 to $50 reparations fee that will be used to keep this event free of cost for BLACK AND BROWN Trans and Queer COMMUNITY.[89]

The year before in Seattle, during the Capitol Hill Autonomous Zone (CHAZ, later renamed CHOP),[90] areas,

---

89 Their peculiar formatting preserved.
90 Capitol Hill Organized Protest. The reasons given for the changed name vary, though some who were part of the events have told me it was to move away from the "white"

meetings, and activities (including a community garden and artistic events) were designated as only for trans, non-binary, and POC participants. More famously, one participant gave a speech to loud applause, demanding white participants pay individual reparations to black participants:

I want you to give $10 to one African American person from this autonomous zone. And if you find that's difficult, if you find that's hard for you to give $10 to people of color, to black people especially, you have to think really critically about, in the future, are you actually going to give up power, and land and capital when you have it? If you have a hard time giving $10, you got to think are you really down with this struggle, are you really down with the movement? Because if that is a challenge for you, I'm not sure you are in the right place.

So find an African-American person — white people, I see you, I see every single one of you, and I remember your faces — you find that African-American person, and you give them $10."[91]

Separate but Equitable

The more common implementations of this ideological framework in the previous decade began primarily in activist spaces, universities, and privately-organized events, taking the form of exclusionary "safe space" policies.

---

legacy of Hakim Bey, the originator of the term Temporary Autonomous Zone. Other explanations online cite an internal conflict between anarchist-aligned and non-anarchist-aligned leadership, and some explain that it was so as to appear less threatening to the city and to local businesses.

91 Transcription mine. See Vincent, 2020.

The most well-known and internationally publicized instance of this was the event I mentioned in the first chapter, the "Day of Absence" and subsequent protests at the Evergreen State University in 2017. Other events at universities have included the establishment of POC-only dining halls and dormitories, while privately organized events including comic and fantasy fiction conventions, esoteric and herbalist conferences, and other gatherings usually considered apolitical have been pressured to create spaces exclusively for BIPOC, trans, and non-binary attendees—lest they face protests and organized campaigns to scare off participants, vendors, and advertisers.[92]

The primary justification for these kinds of separate safe spaces is based upon the principle of equity, as opposed to equality. While equality refers to equal treatment, equity insists that equality can only occur when disadvantaged or oppressed peoples are given extra privileges or resources in order to ameliorate the effects of injustice. Reparations operate upon this principle, as does Kendi's "anti-racist discrimination" framing. "Safe" or exclusionary spaces are justified by the principle of equity in that, in order to compete equally with others, some people need the right to exclude others. This logic extends even between groups of oppressed minorities, for instance in black-only spaces that exclude even other people of color, as explained in this *Everyday Feminism* article cited by the organizers of Taking B(l)ack Pride in their defense:

---

92 I've been a part of several such events, including one I organized. One of these, the longest-running and largest conference on paganism in the United States, no longer exists due to the organizer's eventual exhaustion with each subsequent year's escalating demands for more BIPOC- or trans/non-binary-only programming and spaces.

We Need Our Own Space — Yes, Even from Other People of Color and White Allies

Occasionally, in response to "POC-only" or "Black-only" events and spaces, non-Black folks will express confusion or frustration. Many well-meaning allies want to show support and understand the issues that are impacting Black people. In instances that call for solidarity and building a wider movement, this support is increasingly important. But when explicitly asked to "move back" as white or non-Black people, the best way to support us is to respect that demand. There is a set of shared experiences within Blackness that are not shared by all people of color. There's a difference between having an understanding of racism in America and living that experience.[93]

The same article explains that such exclusion can only go one direction if it is to be equitable. A white-only space would be inherently racist because whites are seen as already wielding significantly more social power than non-white people. Being the dominant and oppressor group within social relations, in order to be anti-racist white people must make every effort to be inclusive of non-white people in their groups. A separate standard, that of exclusion for the sake of equity, must be encouraged to operate within non-white communities.

This logic has been formalized within the burgeoning corporate consulting field called diversity, equity, and inclusion (DEI). DEI advisors and consulting firms advise corporations, universities, and institutions on how to implement policies and hiring practices that create more

---

93 See Jones, 2015, cited in the "Why Reparations" section on the Taking B(l)ack Pride website. Original formatting has been truncated.

equitable, diverse, and inclusive staffing. Per the description of one such consulting company:

> The workplace is changing in profound ways. From the ways we communicate, to corporate culture and how we do our jobs on a daily basis; the pace of change can be dizzying. Add to the mix new technologies and the permanent marks of a global pandemic. It's easy to see why companies must constantly innovate their Diversity, Equity, and Inclusion policies.
>
> This is especially true for talent acquisition and hiring, where the competition for top people is as steep as ever. As is the incentive for building workplaces around diversity, equity, and inclusion. After all, it's people at the core of innovation and inclusive groups tend to yield better results.[94]

DEI consulting is also a rather profitable economic activity. According to one market study by Global Industry Analysts, Inc., in October of 2021, such consulting was worth 7.5 billion US dollars in 2020, and is predicted to be worth 15.4 billion US dollars by 2026.[95] One of the largest corporations implementing DEI policies is the financial investment firm Goldman Sachs. Goldman Sachs, which at the end of 2021 held 1.5 trillion US dollars in assets, is better known for its role in the 2007–2008 housing and financial collapse which sparked Occupy and the 2010 sovereign debt crisis in Europe, as well as its use of offshoring to hide wealth from taxes. It was also a favorite private speech stop for presidential candidate Hillary Clinton in the lead up to the elections in 2016.

---

94 See Ideal, n.d.
95 See Global Industry Analysts, 2021.

Goldman Sachs explains their deep commitment to DEI on their website this way:

> At Goldman Sachs, we believe in the power of Black voices and in committing capital towards creating change. Where those come together is where we can make progress towards racial equity. That's why we are investing in the power of Black communities. Supporting the power of Black businesses. Recognizing the power of an inclusive workforce.
>
> As a firm focused on sustainable and inclusive growth, we are channeling the power of capital to drive economic prosperity for more people. We have long been committed to promoting inclusion, diversity and equity within our own firm, throughout our industry, and in the communities in which we live and work. We believe the effort needed to truly bridge gaps in inequality is ongoing — we know there is more to be done, and we continue to aim higher.[96]

"Intersectional Imperialism"

The corporate trend of adopting equity and related principles into business models has been described by some as a form of "elite capture" or recuperation of more authentic anti-racist and gender activism. This goes beyond corporations: the Central Intelligence Agency and the US Military have created recruitment advertisements narrated with direct reference to social justice identity politics. For instance, in one US army recruiting advertisement, a female soldier states the following:

> This is the story of a soldier who operates your nation's Patriot missile defense systems. It begins in California,

---

96 See Goldman Sachs, n.d.

with a little girl raised by two moms. Although I had a fairly typical childhood, took ballet, played violin, I also marched for equality. I like to think I've been defending freedom from an early age....

...With such powerful role models, I finished high school at the top of my class and then attended UC Davis, where I joined a sorority full of other strong women. But as graduation approached, I began feeling like I'd been handed so much in life. A sorority girl stereotype. Sure, I'd spent my life around inspiring women, but what had I really achieved on my own?

I needed my own adventures, my own challenge. And after meeting with an army recruiter, I found it, a way to prove my inner strength and maybe shatter some stereotypes along the way.[97]

A CIA recruitment video makes even more use of these themes:

When I was seventeen I quoted Zora Neale Hurston's "How it Feels to Be Colored Me" in my college application essay....

...I'm a woman of color, I am a mom, I am a cisgender millennial who's been diagnosed with generalized anxiety disorder. I am intersectional, but my existence is not a box-checking exercise. I am a walking declaration, a woman whose inflection does not rise at the end of her sentences suggesting that a question has been asked... I used to struggle with imposter syndrome, but at thirty-six I refuse to internalize misguided patriarchal ideas of what a woman can or should be. I am tired of feeling like I'm supposed to apologize for the space I occupy, rather than intoxicate people with my effort and my brilliance....

I stand here today a proud first-generation Latina and

---

97 Transcription mine. See US Army, 2021.

officer at the CIA. I am unapologetically me. I want you to be unapologetically you. Whoever you are: know your worth, command your space. *Mija*, you're worth it."[98]

Examples of such apparent "misuses" of identity politics and social justice themes abound throughout corporate advertising and political speech, including US vice-president Kamala Harris's inclusion of her pronouns (she/her) on her personal Twitter bio. But are these really misuses?

Often citing the concept of recuperation as first iterated by the Situationist International, some radical theorists insist that the use of identity politics and cultural-political forms by the powerful are merely cynical attempts to strip a liberation theory of its power. Such an idea seems to have merit on its face, until we again remember the economic and social status of those who originated these ideas. That is, rather than an organic and lower-class revolutionary politics, the foundational theories of this framework all originate within the PMC.

A deeper analysis is needed here, as the adoption of this framework by the powerful is precisely what has helped give it the political clout to displace and suppress class analysis. Neither Goldman Sachs, the United States Army, nor most definitely the CIA can be said to have a particular desire to see a massive redistribution of wealth along the lines of Marxist class revolt in the US. In fact, we might be forgiven for suspecting such institutions are deeply interested in making sure such a thing never happens.

On the other hand, nothing within the framework of intersectional social justice is incompatible with the continuation of capitalism or of the United States' military policies. A non-binary or a trans soldier is just as capable of enforcing the will of the capitalist class upon the people

---

98 Transcription mine. See Central Intelligence Agency, 2021.

of other nations as a cisgendered one. Investing in black-owned businesses and hiring more black woman bankers, stock brokers, mortgage lenders, or corporate board members and CEOs would not actually alter capitalism itself, only the aesthetic of capitalism and the skin color of capitalism's managers.

This observation is the inverse of a rather famous speech made by Hillary Clinton to a private, union-organized rally in 2016, during a time when her leading rival for the Democratic National Convention nomination was senator Bernie Sanders. Sanders' campaign platform, while not explicitly Marxist, included many reform proposals directed at the working class and employed a popular critique of the financial institutions from whom Clinton was known to derive significant funding and support. According to the *Washington Post*'s account of her speech:

> "Not everything is about an economic theory, right?" Clinton asked her audience of a few hundred activists, most of them wearing T-shirts from the unions that had promoted the rally. "If we broke up the big banks tomorrow — and I will, if they deserve it, if they pose a systemic risk, I will — would that end racism?"
>
> "No!" shouted her audience.

In her speech, she then continues with the call-and-response, asking if such an action would end "sexism," "discrimination against the LGBT community," "make people feel more welcoming to immigrants overnight," or "solve our problem with voting rights" before finishing with:

> "Would that give us a real shot at ensuring our political system works better because we get rid of gerrymandering and redistricting and all of these gimmicks Republicans use

to give themselves safe seats, so they can undo the progress we have made?"

"No!"[99]

I was still living in the United States during this time, and my own experience was that Clinton's candidacy and her subsequent failure to win the presidential election in 2016 triggered the conditions that made identity politics fully displace class analysis. During that time, it was impossible to be on social media as a leftist without encountering *Everyday Feminism* articles, memes arguing against class reductionism, and a deeply polarizing narrative that asserted that anyone who didn't vote for Hillary Clinton — even if they also did not vote for Trump — was an enemy of black and trans people. After Trump's election, it was also common to see emotional posts by activists and others declaring that trans and black people were in both physical danger and deep states of trauma, as well as many posts urging people to completely disassociate from family members and friends who had voted for Trump.

It was not just on social media that such a conflation of support for a presidential candidate and outright hatred of people with oppressed identities occurred. A popular book published during the first year of Trump's presidency, *Antifa: An Antifascist Handbook*, made the same argument:

> While one should always be wary about painting large groups of people with a broad brush, it is clear that ardent Trump supporters voted for their candidate either because of or despite his misogyny, racism, ableism, Islamophobia, and many more hateful traits. There is certainly a significant difference between "because of" and "despite" in this context, and sensitivity to the difference should attune us

---

99 See Weigel, 2016.

to the importance of mass organizing, which can divert potential fascist-sympathizers away from the Far Right. It is always important to distinguish between ideologues and their capricious followers, yet we cannot overlook how these popular bases of support create the foundations for fascism to manifest itself....

Any time someone takes action against transphobic, racist bigots — from calling them out, to boycotting their business, to shaming them for their oppressive beliefs, to ending a friendship unless someone shapes up — they are putting an anti-fascist outlook into practice that contributes to a broader everyday anti-fascism that pushes back the tide against the alt-right, Trump, and his loyal supporters. Our goal should be that in twenty years those who voted for Trump are too uncomfortable to share that fact in public. We may not always be able to change someone's beliefs, but we sure as hell can make it politically, socially, economically, and sometimes physically costly to articulate them.[100]

A significant point in many of these analyses was that Trump's election was driven by white, working-class anger towards minority groups. Citing exit polls which showed that large majorities of white people in lower economic brackets and without college degrees had voted for Trump over Clinton,[101] "white working class" became code for misogynist, transphobic, racist, and fascist. This narrative dominated and still dominates, despite polls showing that in many voting districts throughout the United States — and especially in economically depressed areas in the Midwest — large percentages of those supposedly racist white workers had voted for Barack Obama in previous elections.

---

100 See Bray, 2017.
101 See Agiesta, 2016.

Evergreen State College history professor Stephanie Coontz was one of the few authors at that time to push back against this analysis:

> Trump's dog-whistle appeals to racism were not the only reason Clinton failed among white voters without a college education. The last time around, these voters comprised more than one third of the Americans who voted for Obama.
>
> But Clinton failed to duplicate that success in any state that was up for grabs in this election. In one Ohio county where President Obama won by a 22-point margin just four years ago, Trump defeated Clinton by six points.
>
> So what's going on with these voters?
>
> As a recent CNN poll shows, white working-class and rural voters without a college degree are not the poorest of Americans, but they are the most pessimistic about their future prospects. A full half expect their children's lives will be worse than their own, and less than a quarter expect their children to do better.[102]

Despite polling and analysis showing that economic prospects were a primary concern of the working class — white and otherwise — the narrative that a racist, transphobic, nationalist, and fascist insurgency was occurring in the United States persisted throughout the rest of the decade, and still persists

Let's step back for a moment to consider the larger political narrative which arose during these years, one which now fully dominates radical politics in the United States. Trans people, black people, and all others with oppression identities became a collective political category victimized by Trump and all those who either voted him

---

102 See Coontz , 2016.

or didn't vote for Hillary Clinton. Clinton's failure to win the election signaled not just the success of Trump's political campaign but also an ascendancy of whiteness, transphobia, and bigotry that needed to be stopped.

While for Antifa, stopping this rising fascist tide would require social, economic, and physical violence, more broadly the belief was that a focus on justice divorced from class analysis was needed. As Clinton asserted, "economic theory" and attacking the financial investment system would not stop racism, sexism, and homophobia. With the media maintaining the narrative that those same people who cared about their economic situation were themselves racist, homophobic, and sexist, social justice and identity politics became, by default, opposed to those concerns.

Again, from a class analysis, this dichotomy is an obviously false one. Raising the standard of living for the working class by increasing the minimum wage, creating stronger worker protections and job security, funding education and job training, making housing affordable, and socializing healthcare would benefit the entire working class, which includes racial minorities, women, gay, and trans people. However, such policies would provide much less benefit to the PMC, who can already afford those things due to their significantly higher salaries and greater degree of education. For them, such "economic theory" is irrelevant and unable to provide what they are most concerned about: equitable and inclusive access to the higher tiers of salaried positions.

To put this in a more direct way, the PMC stands to gain very little from political movements and reforms that target the poor and the non-salaried working class. On the other hand, they are much more likely to benefit from racial and gender reforms, as well as from cultural movements which favor their lifestyles and political fashions over those of rural and non-urban people. Professionals who work in technology, finance, and in management greatly benefit from globalization and the trade policies (such as NAFTA) which harmed lower-class workers. As such, it's not difficult to understand why they might resist all efforts to discuss class and instead favor a political framework built upon identity.

CHAPTER SEVEN: THE VAMPIRE

Over the last twenty years, I've noticed a pattern in my many friends and acquaintances who have styled themselves as "activists." You know the sort, I'm sure. They're the ones who position themselves as a voice speaking on behalf of a nebulous and constantly shifting group of the "oppressed," while themselves possessing many of the traits we'd otherwise consider "privileged." They're often middle class, or from more elite families, with parents they don't really like but who have nevertheless funded their travel, their education, and their healthcare.

Whether you define yourself as a leftist or not, a particular person (or maybe several) probably appeared in your mind as you read that previous paragraph. I'm sure you've known them, encountered them, perhaps were friends with them, maybe even once looked up to them, and maybe even still do.

These sorts of people always have an "oppressive behavior" to point out, and a host of articles from *Everyday Feminism* or *Teen Vogue* to send to you about the topic, or a list of academic theorists you should already have deeply studied. They're really good at all this, and their knowledge is one of the reasons everyone respects them — or comes to fear them.

Let me tell you about one such person. We'll call her Karen. Karen was a friend of mine for almost two decades. We met at a radical event; both of us were anarchists, and both recognised a natural affinity for each others' ideas. Karen could be a lot of fun to be around, though even back then she seemed to always find a moment to bring any party to a halt with discussions about systemic oppression.

I liked Karen a lot, and it seemed like everyone else did, too. But then one friend made clear she didn't want to have anything to do with Karen any longer. She told me, "I don't think you should stop being friends with Karen, but what she did to me was really awful," and she would say no more. Karen, on the other hand, had lots to say about how oppressive that friend was and how I shouldn't talk to her anymore. Karen also made sure other people knew they shouldn't talk to that woman, either. That friend eventually disappeared out of the lives of anyone who knew Karen, eventually leaving the city altogether.

This happened later to other people, people Karen made sure we knew were not "good" people.

Karen had a long series of failed relationships with activist men, each of whom turned out to be horrific abusers. We were always shocked by these revelations, and though it was difficult for us at the beginning to accept how awful these men were, we soon did what we knew was "right." We knew that to be good radicals, we needed to believe victims, and we needed to show patriarchal men that they were not welcome in our spaces or our lives.

We knew this, of course, because Karen made sure we knew this.

Karen didn't just help us root out the bad men in our lives, but also and especially the women. Though those women were not "abusive," we learned that they were very manipulative. They were backstabbers, or had internalized their misogyny, or were really just "not good for you to be around." And you could tell which of these women were the "not good for you to be around" sorts, because they were the ones with the most personality, the sorts who immediately attracted the attention of everyone — especially of men.

Karen would bristle when they were around and then talk privately to me later, asking if I had noticed certain oppressive qualities in those women. I always had to admit that I hadn't noticed, because they seemed like fascinating and intelligent people to me. Karen would look disappointed at this, so I'd add, "But maybe I missed something?" Fortunately, Karen was always ready to educate me on what I'd not seen about them. Often, I'd go along with all this, though I secretly kept up friendships with some of these women that Karen had identified as bad people. I just never told Karen that.

Karen moved away for a while to do activist work in other cities. I'd receive occasional updates from her, detailing first how incredible the community solidarity was in her new milieu (there was a time she said "milieu" a lot, because it was a super important word to use). But then would soon come the tragic stories about activists in those places who just refused to really live up to their values. So Karen was off to a new milieu, a new city, and eventually new disappointments.

She eventually returned, and we took up our friendship again. By then, I had started working on some projects that she offered to help me with, help that would best use her university training. She was really proud of that training, but also deeply frustrated that the massive amounts of money she'd had to borrow had not yet resulted in the kind of income she should be earning with that degree.

She explained that the reason for her lack of work was patriarchy. Men were always being hired for the positions she wanted, and when women were hired instead of her, it was also because of the patriarchy. I never really understood this part, but since I was a man (she reminded me of this all the time), I would *never* be able to understand this stuff. So it was better to just nod my head and offer her "emotional labor" as repayment for all the emotional labor she'd given me.

This bit — the bit about emotional labor — never really made sense to me, no matter how many times she explained it. I understood the concept, at least through Marxist Feminism. But Karen's version of emotional labor was completely different from that framework. You see, it turned out that all the men in her life, including me, had been constantly demanding emotional labor from her, which was also why she was unsuccessful in finding the work she deserved. We were all draining her of the energy she needed to use for her own success, and it was really time for us to give it back to her.

This sounded good at first, but I was honestly a little confused, because I never asked her to do any emotional labor for me. In fact, I was known for often being too quiet about my personal crises, rarely even letting my closest friends or partners know when there was something I could use help talking through. Whenever Karen and I would meet for coffee or dinner, the conversations were quite one-sided. But I was a good listener and enjoyed her company, so I never complained.

Still, I read all the *Everyday Feminism* articles she sent to me about it and tried my best to make sure I was never demanding such labor from her. At the same time, I became a kind of free therapist for Karen, especially when she needed to talk about how her partner was too masculine, too independent, and too afraid of commitment. He never understood what she needed, especially how she needed him to change his career choices and the friends — especially the female friends — he chose to be around.

I held my tongue. Honestly, I started to feel a bit bad for her partner. She was making some really intense demands on him and it didn't seem fair. But Karen had also told me that men "always" take the side of other men, no matter how abusive they clearly are being, and so I kept quiet.

I left the United States after that, but we kept in touch. Things were often going poorly for her, and I did my best to listen to her when she needed to discuss these things. She was particularly frustrated that she'd been turned down for a high-paid position in a radical organization that she "obviously" had deserved. Instead, a man had been chosen. She was also frustrated that her partner seemed disinclined to leave everyone he knew and loved to move to a new city for her. But then Karen was soon relieved: he finally decided to "love her more than he loved those friends" and relocate with her.

Around that time, Karen and I began to have some weird disputes that always resulted in streams of texts with links to more *Everyday Feminism* articles. They became political disputes, but were also again about emotional labor, and about my unaddressed toxic masculinity. But I kept up the friendship as best I could and kept keeping space for Karen's criticisms about my life and behavior and trying to conform to her expectations.

The moment I realized this wasn't really a friendship at all came when I finally broke down and asked her for some emotional labor, too. I was in an abusive relationship at the time. Karen had been in abusive relationships, and I thought maybe she could help me understand what was happening. The man I was with had physically attacked me a few times, something which really should have made me leave. But I stuck around, thinking maybe it was all just temporary.

When I told her about this, Karen sent me some more *Everyday Feminism* articles and explained that *my* toxic masculinity was causing my partner to abuse me. She related it to the situation with her current partner, how sometimes she had to physically lash out at him because he wasn't doing enough work to make her feel secure, self-confident, and emotionally stable. It was *his* fault that she reacted like that, just like it was *my* fault that the man I was with "needed" to be violent to me.

I'm embarrassed to say that I accepted all of this and tried her advice. As she suggested, I tried to make that man feel more secure, emotionally stable, and self-confident. And I kept trying until he hit me again, and then I finally decided to leave.[103]

Of course, things got even worse between us after that. She started making demands, including trying to force me to publish something she had written. When I declined, she tried to triangulate, to draw other people in to force me to accede to her demands. And of course, at that point it was all about social justice now: I was oppressive, and she needed to make sure everyone knew it.

Siphoning Power from Radical Movements

Looking back now at everything I knew about Karen, about all the patterns of the accusations she made at others in radical communities, about all the people she successfully turned into pariahs and expelled from groups, as well as about her constant flight from one city to the next to find a new radical utopia, only to leave soon after, nothing of what she said to me when I was being abused is surprising. Nor was her subsequent turn from friend to would-be saboteur.

What is surprising, however, is how long it took me to understand how many of my own political ideas were

---

103 To be clear, I don't *blame* Karen for this. If there was any fault at all, it was mine for refusing ever to question the kinds of narratives that people like Karen not only propagate but survive by.

shaped by people like her. Karen was the ideal social justice warrior, the paragon of the anti-oppression activist. She was part of the PMC, from a stable yet "problematic" family, highly educated, and brilliantly adept at the use of political theory and social manipulation.

Happiness and success seemed constantly to elude Karen and other activists like her. Despite the abundance of wealth and opportunities they enjoy, it's never enough. Someone is always oppressing them by getting something they deserved instead, and there's always an esoteric political framework at hand to explain why that happened. Such people are particularly good at triangulating, at drawing unrelated people into personal conflicts and turning those people against someone. They're masters of the "callout," deftly directing social pressure against someone who has personally offended them with the ultimate goal not of righting some wrong but of exiling that person completely.

I've met many versions of them, of all identities. Whatever that identity is, they find a way to weaponize it, and have a particular fondness for going after people with the exact same identity as theirs. They are the trans activists who seem particularly fond of silencing other trans people, women who go out of their way to isolate and smear other women, and the black social justice activists who never seem to be able to maintain friendships with other black activists for very long. That's because they need to position themselves as *the* representative of their identity group. If you are going to call out someone's oppressive behavior towards your identity group, the worst thing that could possibly happen is another person of that same identity saying, "No, that wasn't oppressive."

Another thing you'll notice about such people is that they don't usually start organizations or projects: they join them. They'll tell you that they have great ideas, but of course some sort of systemic injustice or barrier always gets in the way. Instead, they devote their radical energy to existing movements and organizations to help make them better, less oppressive, and more radical. Once they join, however, the organization often starts to implode, especially if the group has no clear leadership structure. Non-hierarchical organizations are where they thrive best, because when there are no clear leaders or power structure, there are no processes for confronting their destructive behavior. If the group does have leaders, however, you can be assured there will soon be some leadership crisis after this person has joined.

While these people exist in every sort of community, leftist and radical communities seem especially ideal ecosystems for them. That's because most people who are drawn to these movements have a deep desire to do good, to address suffering and exploitation. That means, unfortunately, that we tend to be much more naive about human nature than right-aligned groups are.

As one leftist writer described the problem in his essay, "A Ring around Utopia:"

> The understandings of hierarchy as something desirable or abhorrent exhibited by theorists on the left and right are abstractions. Failures to understand power on its own terms can lead to it becoming twisted and perverted. Coercion, in effect, is the perversion of power....
>
> Hierarchy is an abstraction, so can be abolished. Power, on the other hand, is real, and power dynamics will not just disappear even if you believe you have abolished them. A reluctance to address this issue unfortunately gives clout to the oft heard right wing critique of the left that "if you try to abolish hierarchy, it will only result in a new one forming in its stead."
>
> Power dynamics are ever present and power itself cannot be "abolished," but that does not mean the dynamic

has to be oppressive or twisted into one of coercion. It is arguably healthier to calmly and patiently observe the way power flows rather than attempt to pretend — under the guise of "abolishing hierarchy" — that it does not exist.[104]

The right has always understood something that the left continuously fails to grasp: people enjoy power and will try to accumulate it whether they are conscious of it or not. Thus, instead of pretending it is possible to eradicate power, the right insists it is best to formalize those power structures, to have clear lines and hierarchies through which power runs. Leftist groups, instead, often deny that the "oppressed" also accumulate power, and thus become victims of people like Karen.

I suspect this is why the American left has accomplished absolutely nothing for decades. Groups that might otherwise have been able to organize people into general strikes or other labor actions implode the moment activists like Karen accumulate enough power. Suddenly, the leaders are all oppressive, every potential action is "problematic," and what is really needed is not collective action but more self-reflection.

Elite Overproduction and Elite Capture

Occasionally, radicals might suspect or even accuse these destructive activists of being government saboteurs. While they certainly do have disruptive and often crippling effects on groups and movements, and though governments absolutely do use infiltrators to monitor and sometimes entrap radical groups, activists such as Karen are products of a larger mechanism at play within capitalism.

---

104 See Elm, 2021.

We've already encountered the concept of the PMC, a kind of elite subset of the working class whose ideas and labor help sustain the capitalist class system. "Elite" is another word for such people, used more often by those approaching their existence from a non-Marxist perspective.

One such non-Marxist perspective is that of the writer Peter Turchin, who introduced the idea of "elite overproduction" as a cyclical feature of civilizational collapse. Briefly stated, his idea is that societies always train a certain group of youths as potential elites. Those elites are not only highly educated, but also told throughout their entire childhood that they are destined for an elite role in society, whether it is in politics, government, or upper management, or just a role of intellectual or creative importance.

According to Turchin, societies eventually hit a point where the number of elites they have produced is much higher than the number of elite positions for them. People who were raised with the belief that their ideas or work are more important than others', that they are somehow unique and set apart from the masses, then find in such situations a deep abyss between that belief and the reality of the world. Having too many elites and not enough positions to distract them with is much like a society having too many men and not enough work to employ them with. At best, these surplus elites turn to reckless adventurism or self-destruction through drugs; at worst, they amass power for themselves and enlist others in crusades to get what is "rightly theirs."

Turchin's theory does offer some potential insight into the problems caused by the influence of PMC activists on larger leftist movements. Here we can recall Adolph Reed's earlier analysis that "diversity" and other anti-racist ideas propagated by non-Marxist theorists reflect the PMC position of those theorists:

> Diversity as a norm of fairness pervades the professional-managerial strata and ratifies an ideal of social justice that harmonizes seamlessly with market-driven neoliberalism because it combines celebration of difference and aggressive pursuit of equality of opportunity, to the exclusion of economic redistribution.[105]

Reed's larger point is that social justice, anti-racist politics specifically rule out class politics because of the very class position of those who hold these views. In other words, the radicalism of elite theorists such as Ibram X. Kendi does not and cannot argue for an end to capitalism because this would threaten their status as elite.

Another view on the influence of the elite on radical movements comes from Olúfẹ́mi O. Táíwò in his book *Elite Capture: How the Powerful Took Over Identity Politics (and Everything Else)*. Táíwò insists that the core framework of intersectional social justice politics is sound and should be kept; the problem, in his view, is that the (primarily white) elite keep turning it towards their own ends instead of revolutionary change.

> Critics and detractors of these political commitments claim that they reflect the social preoccupations of "rich white people" or the "professional-managerial class." And they're not completely wrong. But that fact is just something that identity politics, wokeness, and the like have in common with everything else in our lives: the increasing domination of elite interests and control over aspects of our social system. That's because almost everything in our social

---

105 Reed, A., 2018a.

world has a tendency to fall prey to elite capture. In other words, it's not just that wokeness is too white. It's that everything is.

True, whiteness and eliteness are two very different things. For our purposes, though, this is a fair dig because they have gone hand in hand in many parts of the world for the past few hundred years, with consequences that have shaped everything around us."[106]

In other words, Táíwò at least acknowledges that there is a large gap between what radical identity politics claims to want to create in the world and what is actually being created by it. He also acknowledges that such politics are heavily influenced (or in his words, "captured") by an elite class who bend these ideas towards their own end. However, he gives very little attention to class itself and even suggests that class analysis has a racist element to it:

Instead of broadening the context we look for elite capture within, we could maintain the same scale but reverse the identities. That is: instead of thinking about the class politics of racial studies, one could describe the race politics of class activism, where we might find that whites (racial elites) tend to capture the decision-making process of socialist organizations, labor unions, and the like.[107]

Táíwò's solutions to the problem of elite capture come off just as esoteric as many of the radical anti-racist theories he claims we must salvage from the elites. For instance, he suggests a new kind of politics, "constructive" rather than "deferential," as the key to combatting elite capture of social justice politics:

---

106 See Táíwò, 2022.
107 Ibid.

I am arguing here for another approach — one that concedes that we have to start with the interactions that we have most control over, but that keeps in view the point of changing how those interactions go: to rebuild the whole of society, not just our interactions. Rooting ourselves here thus gives us a constructive politics.

A constructive politics pursues specific goals or end results, rather than aiming to avoid "complicity" in injustices that we assume will mostly persist anyway. If it's "epistemology" or knowledge practices we're concerned about, then a constructive politics focuses on institutions and practices of information gathering that are strategically useful for challenging social injustices themselves, not just the symptoms manifest in the room we happen to be in today.

In general, a constructive politics is one that engages directly in the task of redistributing social resources and power, rather than pursuing intermediary goals cashed out in symbols."[108]

In other words, he advocates focusing not on economic issues or the material conditions of lower classes, but rather on "redistributing social resources and power." This insistence on social justice rather than economic justice — as well as his conflation of "white" and "elite" throughout his book — seems to help explain why the very first advanced praise introducing the book is from none other than Ibram X. Kendi himself.

Regardless of his failure to connect the class position of anti-racist theorists to the limits of the theories they argue for, Táíwò nonetheless notices that the influence of the elite seems to be affecting radical politics. Elite capture is a concept older than his analysis: it's a term used to

---

108 Ibid.

explain what happens when international monetary and development aid that is sent to struggling nations gets instead "captured" or siphoned off by local elites (business owners, politicians, and even social aid organizations) instead of arriving at its intended target. In other words, the elites act as a kind of parasite on the system, sucking out the life of development programs and radical political frameworks.

The Vampire

And so we meet our next monster, the Vampire.

Of all the monsters in this book, the Vampire is the oldest and the most global. While generally thought of as originating in medieval Eastern Europe, the Greeks and the Romans both recognized undead beings who could drain the life or the blood from living victims. Asian religious beliefs — including Hindu and Shinto beliefs — and Aztec, African, and even Jewish and Islamic folklore warn of revenant spirits, and prescribe funeral rites and protection rituals against such beings. Hundreds of ancient cultures have known of the Vampire, calling it by countless names for much, much longer than it has existed in Western consciousness.

Because there have been so many kinds of Vampire, it's not easy to reduce its existence to a short definition. In many cases, the Vampire is a dead human returned from the grave. However, in just as many stories the Vampire never died, but rather was possessed by an evil wandering spirit. In many stories, the Vampire is visible and corporeal, while in others he or she can never be seen.

The drinking of blood is one of the most commonly agreed-upon attributes of the Vampire, but there is far from a consensus. In some instances, the Vampire steals semen, phlegm, entrails, or unborn children, while in others the

Vampire steals soul essence, vitality, or even parts of a human's shadow. In all these cases though, the Vampire steals something from a human.

Theft of something from the living is therefore one of the only commonalities we can find in these stories, though there is another near universal trait the Vampire possesses which is even more relevant. In almost all stories, a Vampire is created through some sort of trauma, lack, bitterness, or a desire for revenge. In many cultures, a woman who died in childbirth or who could not otherwise bear a child was at risk of becoming a Vampire. Other cultures warned of disinherited children or men betrayed by their friends or family rising from the dead to steal from the living. Paupers and orphans were often susceptible to becoming Vampires, as were those who'd lived deeply envious lives leading them to work black magic to gain wealth, love, or longer lives.

The idea of the Vampire being a lord or ruler who sucks the life from peasants (as in popular tales about Vlad the Impaler) is actually quite a new idea, and is very rare in global myths, though in the eighteenth and nineteenth centuries this version became quite common. Depicting the elites or the aristocracy as parasites on the people even became a popular leftist trope, and Karl Marx describes capital itself as a kind of Vampire:

> Capital is dead labor, which, vampire-like, lives only by sucking living labor, and lives the more, the more labor it sucks.[109]

Later leftists, on the other hand, have even invoked the Vampire as a symbol for the excesses of social justice identity politics and especially the way the focus on identity has had a vampiric effect on leftist movements. The most

---

109 See Marx, K., 1996.

famous of these invocations was in Mark Fisher's essay "Exiting the Vampire Castle," published in late November 2013. Fisher was responding specifically to attempts to "deplatform" other leftists in the United Kingdom for not being of the right ethnicity or gender to speak on radical issues, and saw this as representing a larger shift from the pursuit of economic justice to nebulous social justice identity concerns:

> Rather than seeking a world in which everyone achieves freedom from identitarian classification, the Vampires' Castle seeks to corral people back into identi-camps, where they are forever defined in the terms set by dominant power, crippled by self-consciousness and isolated by a logic of solipsism which insists that we cannot understand one another unless we belong to the same identity group.

In other words, the Vampires' Castle is a kind of ideological system which constantly traps people within it. It does so not just to those already within its identity framework, but also attempts to pull other people in through those it has already captured. Once within the vampiric ideology of identity, it becomes impossible not only to escape but even to oppose its framework:

> The Vampires' Castle specializes in propagating guilt. It is driven by a priest's desire to excommunicate and condemn, an academic-pedant's desire to be the first to be seen to spot a mistake, and a hipster's desire to be one of the in-crowd. The danger in attacking the Vampires' Castle is that it can look as if — and it will do everything it can to reinforce this thought — one is also attacking the struggles against racism, sexism, heterosexism. But, far from being the only legitimate expression of such struggles, the Vampires' Castle is best understood as a bourgeois-liberal perversion

and appropriation of the energy of these movements. The Vampires' Castle was born the moment when the struggle not to be defined by identitarian categories became the quest to have "identities" recognised by a bourgeois big Other....

...The problem that the Vampires' Castle was set up to solve is this: how do you hold immense wealth and power while also appearing as a victim, marginal and oppositional? The solution was already there — in the Christian Church. So the VC has recourse to all the infernal strategies, dark pathologies and psychological torture instruments Christianity invented, and which Nietzsche described in *The Genealogy of Morals*. This priesthood of bad conscience, this nest of pious guilt-mongers, is exactly what Nietzsche predicted when he said that something worse than Christianity was already on the way. Now, here it is....

The Vampires' Castle feeds on the energy and anxieties and vulnerabilities of young students, but most of all it lives by converting the suffering of particular groups — the more "marginal" the better — into academic capital. The most lauded figures in the Vampires' Castle are those who have spotted a new market in suffering — those who can find a group more oppressed and subjugated than any previously exploited will find themselves promoted through the ranks very quickly.[110]

In case Fisher's reference to religion and psychological torture seem a bit overblown from a "cis white man," it's helpful to note that others with "marginalized identities" share his view. Another essay, "Excommunicate Me from the Church of Social Justice," written by Frances Lee (a self-identified queer, trans person of color), is written from

---

110 See Fisher, 2013.

a position even more embedded in the framework Fisher described:

When I was a Christian, all I could think about was being good, showing goodness, and proving to my parents and my spiritual leaders that I was on the right path to God. All the while, I believed I would never be good enough, so I had to strain for the rest of my life towards an impossible destination of perfection.

I feel compelled to do the same things as an activist a decade later. I self-police what I say in activist spaces. I stopped commenting on social media with questions or pushback on leftist opinions for fear of being called out.... I'm exhausted, and I'm not even doing the real work I am committed to do. It is a terrible thing to be afraid of my own community members, and know they're probably just as afraid of me. Ultimately, the quest for political purity is a treacherous distraction for well-intentioned activists...

...Telling people what to do and how to live out their lives is endemic to dogmatic religion and activism. It's not that my comrades are the bosses of me, but that dogmatic activism creates an environment that encourages people to tell other people what to do. This is especially prominent on Facebook. Scrolling through my news feed sometimes feels like sliding into a pew to be blasted by a fragmented, frenzied sermon. I know that much of the media posted there means to discipline me to be a better activist and community member. But when dictates aren't followed, a common procedure of punishment ensues. Punishments for saying/doing/believing the wrong thing include shaming, scolding, calling out, isolating, or eviscerating someone's social standing. Discipline and punishment has been used for all of history to control and destroy people. Why is it being used in movements meant to liberate all of us?... Why do we position ourselves as morally superior to the un-woke? Who of us came into the world fully awake?[111]

Though Lee does not directly link the problem to the displacement of class analysis as Fisher does, Lee comes to a similar conclusion about the role of guilt as Fisher does in his description of his "third law:"

> The third law of the Vampires' Castle is: propagate as much guilt as you can. The more guilt the better. People must feel bad: it is a sign that they understand the gravity of things. It's OK to be class-privileged if you feel guilty about privilege and make others in a subordinate class position to you feel guilty too.[112]

For both writers, and for others, the mechanisms of guilt and shaming appear to be the primary drive causing the inner chaos and self-destruction of radical movements. In Fisher's essay, however, his reference to Nietzsche's warning that "something worse than Christianity was on its way" points us to an even deeper principle related to guilt and shame which neither he nor Lee named: *ressentiment*, a philosophical and psychological concept which closely mirrors a much older animist belief in a kind of vampirism.

The Vampiric Gaze

To understand the concept of *ressentiment*, let's return to Karen again, my pseudonymous former friend. Many times, Karen expressed a belief that she was owed something:

---

111 See Lee, 2017. Note also that this is one of many examples of "woke" being used by social justice activists to describe their own movement before right-wing commenters described them this way.

112 See Fisher, 2013.

emotional labor, positions of authority or creative influence, and more recognition in social groups. To me, it often felt as if she kept a constantly unsettled and ever-lengthening balance sheet of personal and societal injustices. Every position she failed to get, every recognition she felt she deserved but which was "stolen" from her, every moment when others failed to see her importance, and every moment someone failed to give her what she merited drove Karen deeper and deeper into a state of bitterness. As the bitterness increased, so too did her activism and her drive to change the world around her to finally get the justice that she felt she lacked.

Karen, like many other radical activists, had succumbed to *ressentiment*. In a state of *ressentiment*, a sense of hurt begins to define the person such that everything reminds them of that hurt. This can be real physical abuse or just a sense of disappointment: it doesn't matter. What matters is that the person then begins to resent others who seem to not experience this sense of hurt. They also feel that the success, joy, contentment, popularity, beauty, or other positive traits of others represent a direct insult to them.

People caught in *ressentiment* start to look for external causes for their internal sense of hurt, and they then develop worldviews that help sustain them. The "incel,"[113] for example, is a man in a state of *ressentiment* who soon begins to believe that women themselves are the cause of his internal sense of hurt. These explanations then become sustaining fantasies which allow him to continue in this state and see himself as a righteous victim, rather than as just some guy who doesn't have a girlfriend.

Social justice identity politics, feminism, critical race theory, and even Marxism to some degree are all easily retooled as sustaining fantasies for those in a state of

---

113 From "involuntary celibate."

ressentiment. It is especially destructive when those experiencing *ressentiment* are a "frustrated elite," as in Peter Turchin's framework of elite overproduction. People who believe they are naturally or morally better than others, or those who felt they were promised a life of leadership and influence which never actually manifested, can find in such political frameworks a readily available "other" who is the cause of their suffering.

Of course, we can truthfully state that none of these frameworks have *ressentiment* at their core. In the hands of a disappointed, disinherited, frustrated elite, however, they serve as perfect ready-made explanations for their *ressentiment*. All they need to do is study them, learn all the right words and phrases, and apply their "elite" understanding of how to manipulate human social relationships within established groups and movements to accumulate some semblance of the power they believe they deserve.

That is, they become vampires. However, vampirism does not only infect the elite and radicals; anyone whose sense of hurt and injustice turns into *ressentiment* can find themselves becoming unwittingly destructive of their families, friendships, communities, and even society itself. As we've seen, the Vampire has been a widely known monster throughout many societies across time and the world. *Ressentiment* was even more prevalently understood throughout many cultures and many historical periods, though it was regarded not as a philosophical or psychological concept but rather as an almost universal magical idea: the Evil Eye.

The near universality of this idea can be readily seen in the preponderance of localized names for it across completely unrelated languages: *malocchio*, in Italian; עַיִן הָרַע , in Hebrew; *kem göz*, in Turkish; عين الحسو د in Arabic; 邪視, in Japanese; and μάτιασμα, in Greek. While specific variants of the concept (and what to do about it) differ in each culture, the core belief is relatively the same: a person, possessed of resentment or jealousy at the good things in another person's life, has the power to destroy those things through their envious gaze.

This mechanism is written about most by the ancient Greeks, for whom there was a scientific explanation for its power. For instance, Helidorus explained, "When anyone looks at what is excellent with an envious eye he fills the surrounding atmosphere with a pernicious quality, and transmits his own envenomed exhalations into whatever is nearest to him." Plutarch defined its mechanism this way:

> Envy, ensconced by nature in the mind more than any other passion also fills the body with evil.... When, therefore, individuals under envy's sway direct their glance at others, their eyes, which are close to the mind and draw from it envy's evil, then attack these other persons as if with poisoned arrow.

Children (especially boys) were widely thought to be the most vulnerable to it, especially envy from barren women or women whose children were not considered beautiful, talented, or strong. But while the victims of the Evil Eye were frequently thought to be more often male, those who possessed or used the Evil Eye were not assumed to be primarily female. There are countless stories of men using the Evil Eye, especially those possessing certain physical features. For instance, in Italy, the *jettatore* (throwers of the Evil Eye) were thought to be mostly men who had high eyebrows, striking facial features, and intense stares. In other cultures, the Evil Eye was more likely to come from a person (of either sex) with blue eyes (thus the common blue color of talismans against the Evil Eye, though in much of India the color black is used). Again regarding sexual difference, in India crossdressing during a wedding is still sometimes performed as a way of warding off the eye, so that the envious cannot tell who is male and who is female.

Though in Western secular culture the Evil Eye is no longer widely acknowledged as a magical force, the practice of warding it off still continues. For instance, in many places in Europe is it thought that talking too openly about good things that have come to you (especially if you have been poor) will cause you to lose them. Medieval Christian practices of warding against the Evil Eye (attributing good things that happen to you to God instead of to luck or your own actions — which persists still in Islam as well) continue even in American society. In my own childhood in Appalachia, for example, I often heard my grandmother and other older relatives speak of how it's best to get rid of any unexpected amounts of wealth (especially gambling winnings) and to not talk too much about good things because someone might get jealous and, anyway, "the Lord giveth and the Lord taketh away."

Though Western secular culture appears to have widely abandoned belief in magic or the Evil Eye, nevertheless modern folk conceptions continue under different names. For instance, the concept of the "psychic vampire" mostly describes the same thing, as does to some degree the psychological condition of the narcissistic personality disorder.

The Evil Eye is also accurately described by the psychological and philosophical concept of *ressentiment*, popularized most notably by Nietzsche. While the word *ressentiment* in French translates directly to "resentment," it is often left in French to signify difference from its more simple English equivalent. That is to say, *ressentiment* is not just resentment; rather, it is an entire psychological or spiritual state which acts as a force on social relations. In a state of *ressentiment*, a person does not just envy the success, wealth, beauty, or good luck of another person but also builds an ideology and moral framework around the belief that others should not have those things, with explanations founded upon the idea that we are "good" and those we resent are "evil."

In one of Friedrich Nietzsche's most well-known discussions of *ressentiment*, he describes the state through a story about lambs being attacked and killed by large predator birds:

> But let us return: the problem of the other origin of the "good," of the good conceived by the man of *ressentiment*, demands its solution.
>
> That lambs dislike great birds of prey does not seem strange: only it gives no ground for reproaching these birds of prey for bearing off little lambs. And if the lambs say among themselves: "these birds of prey are evil; and whoever is least like a bird of prey, but rather its opposite, a lamb — would he not be good?" there is no reason to find fault with this institution of an ideal, except perhaps that the birds of prey might view it a little ironically and say: "we don't dislike them at all, these good little lambs; we even love them: nothing is more tasty than a tender lamb."[114]

In Nietzsche's understanding of *ressentiment*, those who experience bad things develop a morality not just about those who cause bad things to happen but also about themselves. As victims of the birds of prey, the lambs are good because the birds of prey are evil.

Nietzsche specifically uses the example of lambs and birds to make the point that there is no real basis for the moral calculations the person in a state of *ressentiment* makes. The lambs and the birds are acting according to their

---

114 See Nietzsche, 1923.

nature: carnivores eat flesh, herbivores do not. A moral framework as to why the lambs are being eaten is useless (the birds will not stop eating the lambs just because the lambs judge them to be evil), and more so, the lamb cannot be said to be more moral or more good than the birds, because there is no moral choice being made. That is, the lambs do not make a moral choice to not eat animals, they just do not. The birds do not make a moral choice to eat animals, they just do.

Thus, if lambs experienced *ressentiment*, they might build an entire morality around not eating flesh. The logic here would be that, because they do not eat flesh, and because they are the victims of those who do, no one should eat flesh. To eat flesh is to be evil, to not eat flesh is to be good. But, of course, the core problem with this moral framework is that the lambs are not actually choosing to not eat flesh: they cannot digest it. That is, they are not refraining from anything, but they then expect all others to make the same choice (which is not a choice for them at all) in order to be moral.

The Clinging Dampness

Ressentiment has two core features that are both based on moralizations. The first is that it creates a morality in which victims are "good" because they are victims, and those who are not victims are evil because they are not victims. That is, it is moral to suffer, and suffering is proof of being good. More importantly, *ressentiment* creates a morality around refraining from an action that we were not going to do or are not capable of doing anyway. It creates a "good" out of passivity and non-action, while those who are active and who act are "evil."

Together, these two aspects set into motion a process within the person experiencing *ressentiment* which traps them in a state of being unable to act and being unable to experience joy. We all have encountered people in our lives who are trapped in this state. The friend who seems to never be happy, no matter what happens to them; the relative who is constantly bitter about their own experiences and cannot help but discuss them at every opportunity; the co-worker who complains they will "never find love" because no one will ever truly understand them; or the lover for whom nothing we do is good enough and who constantly moves the goalposts regarding what it means to truly love them.

Each of these sorts of people is trapped in *ressentiment*, incapable of ever being happy or satisfied. Those of us who know and love them, who see their potential and the good things that already exist for them, are often left perplexed by their constant state of misery. We might explain it as depression, or try repeatedly to help them through their pain and trauma, but ultimately nothing ever truly works.

Worst of all, our interactions with them feel like a constant drain on our own joy. Not only do the discussions seem to go nowhere, but they are always one-sided and always seem to return to the same problems, the same misery, the same suffering. We become afraid of telling them about the good things in our lives for fear of exacerbating their own sense of lack. When we do speak of good things (a new lover, an opportunity for a new job, an upcoming vacation), they will often say they are happy for us, but then add, "I wish nice things like that happened for me, too."

Even the best interactions with people trapped in *ressentiment* will feel tiring, but the more common ones tend to bleach the color from our own lives. They may convince us that the good things in our life are not as good as we think they are, that they are stained or tainted with negatives that we failed to notice. Such interactions occur even more so with the politically inclined, who might remind you that bad things are happening in the world, or trace for you the chains of exploitation that created the gift you just received, or tell you that the international plane trip you are about to take will add more carbon dioxide into the atmosphere, or how the film or work of literature you enjoyed was oppressive to others. And while each of these things may indeed be true, their introduction of these facts into your moment of joy and happiness will seem willfully timed to dim the sunlight in which you dance.

In English, people like this are often called "wet blankets" and are said to "dampen" a mood, which parallels an observation about people in this state found in traditional Chinese medicine. A person in a state of "dampness" has over-extended or depleted yin energy, which blocks *yang* and *qi* (life force) energies. Such a dampness gives them a blocked, constipated personality, by virtue of which nothing really seems to move for them in their life. They are like a stagnant muddy pool which entraps others, reminding us of the other English idiom for such people: "stick-in-the-mud."

"It is your fault I am miserable"

Everyone probably experiences these moments occasionally in their lives. I have. In such times, everyone around us seems to have a life better than ours, with more success, better health, or better looks. We resent them for their happiness, wish they would shut up about their amazing lover or exciting job, because it feels like they are rubbing salt into our invisible wounds. For most of us, these are only ever temporary moments. The wheel turns and we are happy again, we get our verve or spark back, life returns and feels full again. When the muck is gone, we might look back and feel a little embarrassed at how overdramatic we were being, apologize for our foul temper, and move on.

Those more permanently in a state of *ressentiment* do not have such returns to joy and life, and through an internal process they come to hate both the good and beautiful moments as well as the bad. When good things happen to them, they quickly find the bad therein, the cloud in each silver lining, the tree in the way of each view of the forest. The mental process by which this occurs takes multiple forms, but they all are ultimately founded upon an ideological process with certain negative beliefs. "Good things don't happen to me" is one of those beliefs, and "I don't deserve good things" is another; "The world is against me" is yet a third. These beliefs filter each new experience in a way that narrates them as only temporary moments of respite from an otherwise uninterrupted progression of misery.

Crucially, these beliefs come to form not just a personal ideological framework but also a morality that externalizes the *ressentiment* onto others. Think of the well-known trope of the mother who constantly reminds her adult children each time they call her that they "never call, never write," that she was "sick with worry," and that she is alone now that they have moved out; or the incel who blames feminism as the reason he cannot find a girlfriend; or the woman who blames the patriarchy for the fact that none of her relationships with men are ever stable; or the person who blames immigrants or "the system" for their inability to find a job.

Ressentiment displaces and projects personal suffering onto "the other," whether that is a friend, a family member, a lover, or a symbolic group or system. The person in a state of *ressentiment* does this in order to sustain the *ressentiment*, to avoid ever looking at the terrible possibility that they are also actors in their own life, because agency is the opposite of and antidote for *ressentiment*.

As Gilles Deleuze puts it in his discussion of Nietzsche:

"It is your fault if no one loves me, it is your fault if I've failed in life and also your fault if you fail in yours, your misfortunes and mine are equally your fault." Here we rediscover the dreadful feminine power of *ressentiment*: it is not content to denounce crimes and criminals, it wants sinners, people who are responsible. We can guess what the creature of *ressentiment* wants: he wants others to be evil, he needs others to be evil in order to be able to consider himself good. You are evil, therefore I am good; this is the slave's fundamental formula."[115]

A reader steeped in the Western secular tradition and its social justice co-ordinates might bristle at the mention of "feminine" power and especially at the reference to slave morality. Here we need to remember that "feminine" in many alchemical, philosophical, and healing traditions is a co-creative principle within each person, a necessary "cooling" force which sustains life, too much of which leads to the "dampness," which Chinese traditional medicine identifies with this state of *ressentiment*. In other words, *ressentiment* isn't a female or male trait.

As for the reference to the slave, in Nietzsche and elsewhere "slave morality" is not the morality of people in slavery but rather of people who choose to avoid or relinquish agency. The slave for Nietzsche is the person who sees themselves always as a passive object, a person incapable or unwilling to take risks or even to act at all. They are those who obey orders unthinkingly because they have no will of their own. Slave morality is the sustaining morality of the person in *ressentiment*. Seeing themselves constantly as victims of others, they create moral co-ordinates according to which their suffering is proof of their righteousness. They feel other people have harmed

---

115 See Deleuze, 1983, p.119.

them (which may be true, but need not be for *ressentiment* to occur); therefore, those people are evil. And if they are evil for harming them, that means the person they harm must be good, specifically because they suffer harm from those they see as evil.

These harms and this suffering can be real or imagined, it does not matter. Deleuze points out that the process occurs in the mind irrespective of the actual conditions the person has been in. The person in a state of *ressentiment* is reacting to "traces," which is to say memories of the feeling of harm:

> There is therefore no need for him to have experienced an excessive excitation. This may happen, but it is not necessary. He does not need to generalise in order to see the whole world as the object of his *ressentiment*. As a result of his type the man of *ressentiment* does not "react": his reaction is endless, it is felt instead of being acted. This reaction therefore blames its object, whatever it is, as an object on which revenge must be taken, which must be made to pay for this infinite delay. Excitation can be beautiful and good and the man of *ressentiment* can experience it as such; it can be less than the force of the man of *ressentiment* and he can possess an abstract quantity of force as great as that of anyone else. He will none the less feel the corresponding object as a personal offence and affront because he makes the object responsible for his own powerlessness to invest anything but the trace–a qualitative or typical powerlessness.[116]

This reaction (felt, rather than acted out) is not a reaction to actual experiences but rather to a feeling of being wronged. Also, the sense that one is wronged (and therefore

---

116 Ibid., p.115.

"good") infects every experience the person has. This is how *ressentiment* sustains itself, eventually creating the conditions that keep the person always feeling harmed.

So, to return to the previous examples I offered, we could see how a bitter mother who constantly complains to her children that they don't call enough would make it so that her children actually call her less. They might avoid calling her specifically because they do not want to be subject to her attempts to make them feel guilty. A man who believes feminism is why he cannot get a girlfriend will act towards women in a way that makes clear his hatred for feminism; this could lead any potential girlfriend to avoid him, thus sustaining his *ressentiment*. A woman who believes all men are patriarchal pigs is likely to treat every man in her life as if he is oppressing her; any prospective lover would then be likely to withdraw the first moment her *ressentiment* surfaces, which in turn would seem to her like more evidence that she is correct.

The Narcissistic Personality Disorder and Mass Politics

The modern diagnosis of narcissistic personality disorder (NPD) parallels this process. The person with NPD constantly believes they are a victim of others yet simultaneously believes they are unique and superior. They have a sense that good things should always happen to them yet never do, and thus present themselves in all their relationships as someone who is owed everyone's attention, affection, care, and often obedience. They do this through manipulation, using guilt, shame, and gaslighting to convince those around them they have harmed the person with NPD and therefore need to make amends.

Constantly casting themselves as the passive victim of life, circumstances, systems, or just bad luck allows the person experiencing *ressentiment* to avoid looking too closely at their own life. Often, a simple change of perspective would be enough to alter these patterns, but with that change comes something much harder for the person to grasp: that they are not "good" and others are not "evil." That is, they would need to let go of their most cherished belief, that they are a sacred victim, and instead acknowledge they were also active participants in many of the bad things that have happened in their life, and that only they are responsible for how their life is going. Unfortunately, for the person experiencing *ressentiment* this truth is unbearable. As the people around them withdraw in order to protect themselves, the person suffering *ressentiment* must then expand their social and ideological framework to include more people.

Here is where *ressentiment* begins to have larger societal effects, because more and more people are required to be labeled "evil" in order to sate the desire of those with *ressentiment* to see themselves as "good." Mass populist movements are often born from this expansion when particularly charismatic people find ways to spread their ideological theories as to why they are constantly being harmed. Antisemitic movements are one of the most obvious that come to mind, positing a secret cabal of "evil" Jews as the reason for mass suffering. Eruptions of anti-immigrant sentiment, or of nationalism during times of war, are also obvious examples of *ressentiment* played out in larger theaters of the absurd.

But other less violent — yet still destructive — outbreaks of *ressentiment* occur in society. Because *ressentiment* is ultimately a passive principle, the person experiencing *ressentiment* needs to remove agency not just from themselves but also from others in order to maintain their own fantasies of victimhood. We see this particularly in NPD psychological abuse, in which the abusive person convinces their victim that they cannot survive without their abuser. To do this, they must remove from the victim their sense of self and agency, convince them that they are really "nothing," that they are not special or unique, and remove from them their sense of individuality.

On a larger scale, this is the process that Soren Kierkegaard called "leveling":

> The *ressentiment* which is establishing itself is the process of leveling, and while a passionate age storms ahead setting up new things and tearing down old, raising and demolishing as it goes, a reflective and passionless age does exactly the contrary; it hinders and stifles all action; it levels. Leveling is a silent, mathematical, and abstract occupation which shuns upheavals. In a burst of momentary enthusiasm people might, in their despondency, even long for a misfortune in order to feel the powers of life, but the apathy which follows is no more helped by a disturbance than an engineer leveling a piece of land. At its most violent a rebellion is like a volcanic eruption and drowns every other sound. At its maximum the leveling process is a deathly silence in which one can hear one's own heart beat, a silence which nothing can pierce, in which everything is engulfed, powerless to resist.[117]

Ressentiment, when it becomes leveling, is ultimately the unbalanced *yin* principle spread throughout society, a constant wet blanket cast upon every fiery manifestation of difference, uniqueness, individuality, and distinction. Perhaps the most common manifestation of this leveling in radical politics is the phenomenon of the "cancellation," whereby a particular person is brought down to a given level through public criticism and accompanying harassment for

---

117 See Kierkegaard, 2010.

"problematic" behavior or speech. It is rarely unknown or insignificant people who become the target of cancellations, but rather those who have accumulated some degree of influence. Regardless of the criticism's actual content — whether justified or not — the mass politics of cancellation functions as a way of pulling the target back down to everyone else's level — if not lower.

Identitarianism and *Mauvaise Foi*

Leveling *ressentiment* also propagates "slave morality" the same way that slave owners degraded the sense of self of their slaves. Instead of being individuals with agency, they became objects that existed only as part of a category or role (slave). *Ressentiment* reduces people, turning them from individuals with the agency to choose their own life into members of larger identity categories which define them. All men, all black people, all disabled people, all heterosexuals: individuals become subsumed into these larger categories and are judged by them.

In social justice identity politics, this manifests in the condition that Jean-Paul Sartre called *mauvaise foi* (bad faith). *Mauvaise foi* is the abandonment of freedom and agency at the feet of an external. For Sartre, while the barriers some people face can absolutely be crushingly difficult to overcome, agency can never be truly abdicated. A black person who believes that white supremacy is everywhere "keeping him down," or a trans person who believes the "cis-heteropatriarchy" is preventing him or her from being their true self, is in a state of *mauvaise foi*. For them, the external categorization — the identity hierarchy — already defines what is possible and what is not, who is the victimizer (the other) and who is victim (themselves).

When an external entity, system, structure, or amorphous other is responsible for your own suffering, then only some action or change in that external source can fix it. It's the other's fault, so they must fix it, regardless if they even know they are to blame or that they had anything to do with it. Demanding an end to cultural hegemony, or white supremacy, or patriarchy, or ableism — mere names for esoteric, imagined systems without material basis — certainly feels like a political act, but it also functions as a way of displacing agency onto something wholly external.

Social justice identity politics is not the only framework to rely upon such an externalization, nor does it necessarily have a monopoly on the politics of identity. Reducing the external "other" to a mere identity category is the core mechanism of nationalist and racist identitarian movements as well (as, for example, the actually existing but relatively small white supremacist movements in the United States, or the far-right European identity movements attacking immigrants). For such groups, the blame for personal or societal problems rests fully on black people or Muslims, and those problems can only be resolved once that external other is made to pay.

Social justice identitarianism is founded upon this same process, though with different groups identified as the external cause. White people, or cis people, or able-bodied people, or heterosexuals: they are the root and agents of oppression and suffering, and only once they "acknowledge their privilege" can those suffering oppression finally find justice.

In both these forms, *ressentiment* functions as a vampiric thirst. An injustice (perceived or real) has occurred, leaving a traumatic "trace" within the victim. This trace festers and grows until the person is overcome with the sense that they cannot experience happiness, success, fulfillment, or any other goal because an "other" possesses a vital essence the person does not.

The Vampire demonstrates to us *ressentiment* in its most extreme form. As with ancient conceptions of the Evil Eye, the person experiencing *ressentiment* drains the joy and vitality of others in the mistaken belief that this might finally end their bitterness and envy. *Ressentiment* causes the person to suck the life of the living in search of satiation for a hunger that can never be fully filled. As with Marx's formulation of capital as "dead labor," the more the Vampire sucks, the longer it lives on to drain others.

While some still argue that radical identity politics have been hijacked or "captured" by an elite, the Vampire shows us that any one of us — elite or otherwise — can become so filled with *ressentiment* that we sabotage and destroy even what we love. The Vampire's warning to us, and its challenge, is thus similar to that of the Cyborg: not understanding where we end and others begin, and abandoning our personal agency at the altar of impersonal systems, turns us into monsters ourselves.

CHAPTER EIGHT: "CULTURAL MARXISM" AND THE SPECTER OF FASCISM

How does one keep from being fascist, even (especially) when one believes oneself to be a revolutionary militant? How do we rid our speech and our acts, our hearts and our pleasures, of fascism? How do we ferret out the fascism that is ingrained in our behaviour?[118]

For seven months, I lived with two anarchists and their children in Seattle. Our apartment was just around the block, perhaps one hundred meters, from one of the last remaining historic black bars in the city, in a high-crime neighborhood. Our next-door neighbor, a very old black woman, had installed iron grating over her windows and sometimes sat outside with a shotgun.

I remember one specific summer evening in our apartment, hanging out with friends. We heard a shout from the front yard of our home, so I leaned out the window to see what was happening. I saw a woman squatting on the grass, her skirt hiked up, and she shouted again at me: "Hey, throw me down some toilet paper." I didn't. Perhaps you can understand my reasoning for denying the woman her request. Seeing as I would need to clean up human defecation the next morning, I reasoned that I would prefer to not also need to clean up used toilet paper, as well.

---

118 From Michel Foucault's preface to *Anti-Oedipus: Capitalism and Schizophrenia*. See Deleuze and Guattari, 2019, p. xiii.

A few months later, I was alone in the apartment and heard gunshots. Minutes later there was a knock on my door, and when I answered it, there was a man standing in front of me. His hand was pressed against his stomach, trying to staunch a massive flow of blood, and he asked me to help him. I was an anarchist at the time and believed that the police were absolutely an evil force which should never be relied upon for anything. However, I also didn't know how to save a man dying from a gunshot wound.

"I'll call the medics for you," I offered, panicked.

The man became really agitated at this. "No, don't call the cops, you have to help me." Because I told him that I needed to call them to at least get an ambulance for him, he ran away. The police arrived at my home some minutes later, and I explained that the man looked like he was dying. They searched for him afterwards, but it wasn't until the next morning that his dead body was found. He'd hidden in one of our neighbor's bushes and bled out during the night.

These are not the only stories that haunt me from my time in that place. The others involve my roommates, their children, and their larger social group of radical activists. They organized a radical-parents meetup every month to create a solidarity network for other anarchist, vegan parents. Such meetings often occurred at our apartment, meaning that I'd sometimes return home after work to find the place full of naked children running about while their parents smoked marijuana and talked about revolution.

The naked children parties were honestly a bit weird for me, and I really preferred not to be at home when they were happening and to be alerted beforehand in case I had planned to invite friends over. Weirder, however, were some the political ideas some of the other parents had about veganism and child-rearing, especially certain beliefs about sexual liberation and children. I saw nothing that approximated child abuse or anything that should probably have been reported to a child protection officer or the police, but the ideas themselves were often enough for me to worry for the children. Some expressed beliefs that children should be able to explore their sexuality with adults in a playful manner as a way of avoiding future psychoses, an idea I'd heard expressed in many other radical spaces as well. Years later, in other radical groups, I encountered those beliefs again and saw incidents that did really concern me, including encouraging early adolescent children to sexually flirt with adult friends of their parents. One mother of such a child explained that she encouraged such things because to do otherwise would be to repress her child. Regardless, her explanation still didn't sit well with me or another adult to whom the child was being sexually "assertive."

The Tragedy of the *Kinderläden*

What I witnessed might have been rare or exceptional, though the ideas these adults were expressing are rooted in a particular form of radical theory that inspired a historical experiment decades before these parents were even born: the *Kinderläden*.[119]

Kinderläden — "children shops" — were anti-authoritarian day care programs started by anarchists and other leftists in West Germany during the 1960s. Founded upon the anti-authoritarian and sexual repression theories of Theodor Adorno, Jürgen Habermas, and Wilhelm Reich, *Kinderläden* were an attempt to implement many of the radical ideas that have become core features of left-utopian beliefs. These ideas included communal child-raising,

---

119 *Kinderläden* is the plural of *Kinderladen*.

autonomous and local control, and a focus on raising children to be independent thinkers, unashamed of their bodies and free of patriarchal and capitalist indoctrination. On the other hand, these ideas and the experiment of the *Kinderläden* also represent a tangible example for many of the fears and conspiracies associated with "Cultural Marxism," a belief that leftists are secretly attempting to erode traditional society by introducing "decadent" and "perverted" sexual norms to children.

Kinderläden were attempts to implement reflexive liberation and ideologies of cultural change as a bulwark against fascist and authoritarian movements. As such, they have profound relevance to the situation now in America, since many radicals in America either support — or are accused of supporting — changes in early education to help liberate children from oppressive ideas and to shape their worldviews so that larger cultural shifts can occur.

Debates erupt and accusations fly over the idea of introducing declarative gender and critical race theory into early education in the United States. Local populist reactions to changes in school curricula have occurred in many places, and they appear to be stoked by right-wing media figures and programs. However, some of the policies they're reacting against indeed exist, including policies regarding education about non-binary and transgender identity and pronouns in kindergarten. Also, despite the often very overblown and extremist rhetoric about critical race theory in schools coming from the media, educators have indeed introduced the ideas of white privilege and anti-racist discrimination to children in lower grades.

Radicals and leftists often publicly deny such things even occur, and ascribe the anger to manufactured controversy. On the other hand, however, many also then express support for actually existing instances of such things.

Something similar occurred with the *Kinderläden*. Official narratives often downplayed or even denied the existence of the radical core of the projects to the outside world, but as can be seen in written records from the educational movement itself, people were quite frank in their goals and explicitly supportive of the principles behind them.

The theories behind the *Kinderläden* would likely sound very familiar and even self-evident to many American anarchists and others steeped in radical politics now. Put plainly, the founders of the day cares believed that the nuclear family and traditional moral stances on sexuality were negative forces in society. Those forces reproduced authoritarian behavior by repressing sexual desire and expression, limiting the development of liberated personalities and inculcating psychological problems in children which later manifested in oppressive and aggressive enforcement of hierarchies (the patriarchy, for example).[120]

Kinderläden were designed as a way to break these cycles. Within the day cares, children were encouraged to explore their bodies and the bodies of others in an environment absent of shame, judgment, and "authoritarian" sexual limits. To ensure the children in the *Kinderläden* were protected and liberated from these negative influences, the adult teachers and the parents of the children were also encouraged to examine how authoritarianism and sexual repression existed in their own lives, and to do everything possible to counteract them.

---

120 John Money — who we met earlier (he invented the idea of gender expression and performed forced sex changes on children) — was also a proponent of these ideas about child sexual repression leading to authoritarianism.

This included avoiding at all costs any interventions into disputes between the children, and actively avoiding setting any rules or limits, as German historian Dagmar Herzog explains:

> *Kinderladen* activists' celebrations of child sexuality and lamentations about adult dysfunctionality were inextricably linked to a more broadly held New Left conviction that the nuclear family was a diseased and pernicious institution for which collective arrangements were the sole possible remedy. Declaring the nuclear family to be "rotten to the core," many Kinderladen activists not only rotated caregiving at the preschools, but actually worked to rupture what they called parent-child "fixations." The deliberate rotation of caregivers within the Kinderladen was not just designed to reduce burdens on the grown-ups; the main aim was to give children many adult reference points rather than just one or two. And the insistence that children manage their own conflicts and that the adult caregivers avoid intervening if at all possible was yet another aspect of the Kinderladen's efforts to destabilize children's dependence on parents, for even beneficent authority was still authority. Only in collective experiences, activists believed, could people develop attitudes of solidarity, overcome their fear of authorities, and develop shared strategies for resisting oppression.[121]

The larger framework for these ideas derived from a general belief on the part of radicals regarding the origins of fascism. Within this framework, the mass convulsions of fascist political expression which had overtaken Germany during the Nazi regime were thought to be manifestations of sublimated and repressed sexuality, as well as of

---

121 See Herzog, 2007, pp 170–171.

psychological and cultural indoctrination of authoritarian personality traits. To prevent fascism from ever happening again, an anti-authoritarian culture needed to emerge and take hold of the masses, and the only true way to create that culture was to start with children.

Why with children? Theorists believed that the sexual inhibitions which led to authoritarian and fascist personalities began in childhood. As the German journal *Spiegel* describes the logic:

> To them, it seemed obvious that liberation should begin at an early age. Once sexual inhibitions had taken root, they reasoned, everything that followed was merely the treatment of symptoms. They were convinced that it was much better to prevent those inhibitions from developing in the first place. Hardly any leftist texts of the day did not address the subject of sexuality.
>
> For instance, "Revolution der Erziehung" ("The Revolution in Education"), a work published by Rowohlt in 1971, which quickly became a bestseller, addresses sexuality as follows: "The de-eroticization of family life, from the prohibition of sexual activity among children to the taboo of incest, serves as preparation for total assimilation — as preparation for the hostile treatment of sexual pleasure in school and voluntary subjugation to a dehumanizing labor system."
>
> Issue 17 of the cultural magazine *Kursbuch*, published in June 1969, described the revolutionaries' position in practical terms.... In the summer of 1967, three women and four men moved into an apartment in an old building on Giesebrechtstrasse, together with two small children, a three-year-old girl, Grischa, and a four-year-old boy, Nessim...
>
> ...On April 4, 1968, Eberhard Schultz describes how he is lying in bed with little Grischa, and how she begins

to stroke him, first in the face, then on the stomach and buttocks, and finally on his penis, until he becomes "very excited" and his "cock gets hard." The little girl pulls down her tights and asks Schultz to "stick it in," to which he responds that his penis is "probably too big." Then he strokes the girl's vagina.

Kursbuch 17 contained a series of poster-sized photos. Under the headline "Love Play in the Children's Room," it depicted Nessim and Grischa, both naked. The oversized images are of the sort that one would expect to see in a magazine for pedophiles today — certainly not in an influential publication of the leftist intelligentsia. The caption reads: "Grischa walks over to the mirror, looks at her body, bends forward several times, encircling her buttocks with her hands, and says: 'Look, my vagina.'"[122]

A peculiar aspect of the *Kinderläden* has particular parallels with the problem of cancellations in radical culture now. Because the *Kinderläden* were seen as anti-authoritarian, revolutionary, and antifascist projects, those who criticized them were therefore seen as likely harboring internalized authoritarian, fascist and counter-revolutionary psychoses. Parents and teachers involved in the *Kinderläden* who expressed reluctance, doubt, or moral hesitation about the sexual liberation of these children later reported having censored these misgivings so as to not be accused themselves.

As explained by the *Spiegel* article:

The records of a Stuttgart *Kinderladen* from December 1969 include an account by a mother who suddenly found several children reaching under her skirt. When one of the boys began pulling her pubic hair, the woman wasn't sure how to

---

122 See Hollersen and Fleichhauer, 2010.

react. On the one hand, she didn't want to seem inhibited, but on the other hand, the situation was unpleasant for her. "That hurts," she finally said, "I don't like that."

An account by the sociologist Monika Seifert, who described her experiences in the "Parents' Collective of the Frankfurt Children's School" in the magazine *Vorgänge* (excerpts of which later appeared in SPIEGEL in the fall of 1970), reveals how difficult it was for the *Kinderladen* parents to eventually decide between their own ideological expectations and their sense of right and wrong.

In the account, Seifert critically asks herself why, in her project, "no cases of attempted, direct, purposeful sexual activity between a child and an adult were observed." It should be noted that she sees this as a shortcoming, not a success. As a mother, Seifert concludes that the "inhibitions and insecurities of the adults" were probably to blame for their passivity, and that the children were likely "suppressing their sexual curiosity in this regard because of the subconscious reactions of the adults."[123]

Again, parents and teachers were encouraged to let their children sexually explore their bodies — their own and *also* the bodies of their parents. The logic here was that sexual repression was an authoritarian tool and ultimately led to fascism. Thus, if a child wanted to play with his father's penis or mother's vagina, to tell him no would be to do the work of the authoritarian state. Further, any parent who admitted to feeling uncomfortable with all this was thought to be actually admitting their own authoritarian tendencies and sexual repression.

To be clear, the current moves towards educating young public school children about declarative gender and anti-racist theory are not the same as the sexual liberation theory

---

123 Ibid.

of the *Kinderläden*. However, both the older experiment and these newer ones share the same larger political and psychological framework. That framework asserts that societal and cultural problems are rooted in the inner life, thought patterns, and worldviews of people. Thus, social and cultural change can and must begin with children: changing the course of their development early on changes larger society. In other words, to create a better and more equal society, people — and especially children — need to be trained to see the world differently.

Along with this comes the idea that those who might stand in the way of this training — or even express doubts and misgivings — are not just resisting these cultural changes but are actually enemies of those changes. Parents who expressed doubt or confusion about the pedagogical policies in the *Kinderläden* were often smeared as reactionaries or even fascists, just as parents of children in America who express misgivings or criticisms about educational changes are likewise smeared. Here the situation is a little different, because for the *Kinderläden*, the parents at least had a choice as to whether or not their children would become part of them. In American public education, usually only very wealthy parents can choose to move their children to other schools.

To understand how the *Kinderläden* came about and how they went wrong, and to understand the larger framework they share with current movements to implement cultural change, we need to look to these radical critiques of fascism. We also need to delve into a very old tension between two opposing views regarding the potential of revolutionary actions against capitalism.

Enlightening the Masses

As we saw with the problem of anti-rural sentiment, the urban or bourgeois roots of anarchism and socialism influenced their development. Because of their urban context, they inherited many aspects of the bourgeois (urban) moral constellations, particularly Protestant morality. This included a belief that rural people who were more likely to be Catholic and thus superstitious, ignorant, and backwards, represented a kind of reactionary force against enlightenment and progress.

This meant that anarchists and socialists — especially utopian socialists — believed that rural people could only be liberated after they gave up their religious beliefs and customs. Since this was such an overwhelming task, revolution would first need to occur in the cities, and be enacted by the already enlightened urban radicals. Those urban radicals could then spread liberation to the unwashed masses in the countryside.

These ideas absolutely still persist in leftism, despite the obvious problem this framing ignores: there has always been — until very recently — a much, much greater population of rural people than urban dwellers. Therefore, as far as sheer numbers go, any revolution which started in the cities would find itself surrounded by an overwhelmingly reactionary population of "ignorant" rural people who would thus be the enemies of the revolution.

We find very little acknowledgement of this problem in early anarchist and utopian socialist theories, though Marxism (which arose after these other tendencies), despite Marx's very negative descriptions of the reactionary rural dweller, was much more optimistic about the potential for rural liberation. Because of the Marxist focus on material conditions, organized labor became a significant force in Europe, the United Kingdom, and the United States, while anarchism has always remained a small movement. The one exception to this was the International Workers of the World (IWW, or Wobblies) movement in the early twentieth century. Their success was only possible because they, like Marxist unions, focused on the material conditions of urban and rural workers rather than first attempting to convert those workers to bourgeois moral values.

Organizing around material conditions was so successful because workers weren't expected to renounce their religious beliefs or cultural framework in order to get higher wages or an eight-hour work day. A worker did not need to subscribe to an entire leftist program or set of doctrines to be seen as a participant in collective anti-capitalist action. While this organizing framework was often atheistic, or at least materialist, workers did not need to be atheists. Even more importantly, they did not need to accept more esoteric corollary ideas about family relations, the history of primitive accumulation, "permanent revolution," or the need for a "vanguard" party in order to be part of a union.

The very simplicity of that older form of leftist organizing is what led to its many successes early on. It's much easier to explain to a person that their boss is paying them less than they deserve than it is to convince them there is no god. Explaining to someone that other people are in the very same position they are, and that if they all work together they can force the bosses to listen to them, is a concrete argument that has direct relevance to their daily lives.

That is, such organizing doesn't require that a person accept an entire cultural framework in which the organizational ideas make sense. You can believe Jesus was born of a virgin and also believe that your boss should pay you more — without any contradiction at all. In fact, in many ways the already existing cultural framework of Christianity, at least in its more populist manifestations, often provided the very metaphors and slogans many of the poor used to express their revolutionary desires both before and after the birth of leftism. One of the oldest manifestations of this was the phrase, originating with John Bell in the fourteenth century and later repeated throughout the following centuries: "When Adam delved and Eve span / Who then was the gentleman?"

Later, the Levellers and then the Chartists relied heavily on Christian language to express their political beliefs, but not out of a cynical ploy to convince the masses of the rightness of their cause. Instead, many within these movements were themselves what can be described as "Christian radicals," forming a movement that manifested again in Catholic radicalism, such as the Irish Catholic socialism of James Connolly, Dorothy Day's Catholic Worker's Movement, and the overtly communist framework of Catholic liberation theology. Of particular note, as well, is that the League of the Just, a Catholic communist society, merged with the Communist Correspondence Society to form the Communist League. It was this group that then asked Marx and Engels to write *The Communist Manifesto* for them.

The Vanguard

Despite this legacy, later socialist, communist, and anarchist doctrines argued for the end of religion and an embrace of atheism as a prerequisite for revolution. Lenin, Trotsky, and Stalin all expressed deeply anti-religious sentiment, but the greatest hatred towards religion came from early anarchists. The phrase "No Gods, No Masters" ("*Ni Dieu Ni Maitre*," more correctly translated as "Neither God nor Master") originated in the late 1800s in the beliefs and newspaper of French anarchist Auguste Blanqui. The slogan was then popularized internationally by Alexander Kropotkin.

Auguste Blanqui was not only a fierce atheist, he also believed that convincing the ignorant masses to revolt was a lost cause. Instead, he argued that revolution should be carried out by a small group of conspirators who would force a revolutionary moment upon society. That group would then institute a temporary dictatorship to implement a revolutionary program. Then, at some later and undefined point, they would hand control back to the people. Blanqui's strain of radicalism was heavily criticized by other socialists, including Marx and Engels, because at its core was a belief that the working class was too ignorant to be able to act as informed political agents.

Unfortunately, despite opposition to this framework by the actual founders of Marxism, it appeared again in Lenin's iteration of vanguardism. Vanguardism asserts that revolutionary movements must be led by a small enlightened sector of the working class who lead organizations and build revolutionary institutions. Those institutions would then draw in other parts of the working classes. The purpose of such an arrangement was specifically to gatekeep revolutionary doctrine while educating away the "false consciousness" of the working classes preventing them from understanding their revolutionary potential.

Both Blanquism and Leninist vanguardism are founded upon the idea that the masses are too brainwashed or uneducated to see their true material conditions. They need leaders to guide them to seek what is best for them, and it falls upon those leaders to educate away the ignorance, superstition, and false consciousness of the masses. This framework was fleshed out further by Antonio Gramsci, who can probably be named as the true father of Cultural Marxism.

Gramsci asserted that there were two types of revolutionary strategy required to liberate the masses from the capitalists: the War of Position and the War of Maneuver. The latter strategy, the War of Maneuver, is what we generally think of as revolution — the physical acts, strikes, and seizure of institutional power which compose the actual transition from an old order into a new one. However, Gramsci believed that these maneuvers cannot be accomplished without first instilling in the masses a revolutionary consciousness through a War of Position.

Gramsci argued that the War of Position requires changing the cultural forms and beliefs of the working classes to be in opposition to the cultural hegemony of the capitalists. In order to desire revolution, the masses must first understand how they are being exploited and how the cultural institutions they accept as natural or good are actually created to harm them. This means changing the beliefs of the masses, including by teaching them to stop relying on their common-sense observations of the world, with which they can only perceive the situation within the capitalist social order itself.

For Gramsci, this shift is only possible if the working classes develop, support, and listen to their own intellectuals, those who work in opposition to the intellectuals of the bourgeoisie. In his conception, the dominant order produces its own intellectuals — artists, writers, journalists, scientists, and so forth. Those people, because of their privileged position within the capitalist order, will inevitably only ever argue for its continuation.

So, Gramsci asserted that the capitalists can only be overthrown if a new kind of working-class intellectual arises, one who is part of the working class yet who has simultaneously risen above the limiting common sense of the masses. These intellectuals must fully give themselves over to the task, becoming "permanent persuaders," in Gramsci's words, and must ultimately provide a popular cultural framework which can compete with the cultural hegemony of the capitalist order.

To put this all more simply, Gramsci extended Auguste Blanqui's idea of the vanguard into culture, and presented this cultural vanguard as a necessity for any successful revolution. Artists, journalists, scientists, and others were needed to create cultural forms that could compete with the capitalist forms, and once they succeeded in their War of Position, the War of Maneuver (the actual physical revolution) could proceed.

Here it's worth returning again to John and Barbara Ehrenreich's critique of the PMC and its similarities to Gramsci's understanding. It would seem that Gramsci accurately predicted the birth of the PMC, and they seem to fulfill the precise role which Gramsci predicted: creating and sustaining the hegemonic cultural and societal forms of capitalism so that the masses do not attempt to change capitalist social relations.[124]

Cultural Marxism and the "Breast Action"

I mentioned that Antonio Gramsci could be named the father of Cultural Marxism; however, that term is more likely to be heard from the mouth of a right-wing conspiracist than from a leftist. Beginning in the early 1990s, "Cultural Marxism" was the label applied to the beliefs and theories of the critical theorists of the Frankfurt School, especially Adorno, Habermas, and Horkheimer. Conspiracies about Cultural Marxism assert that the Frankfurt School's ultimate goal was the destruction of Western civilization, and that they sought to infiltrate education and the media

---

124 We'll return to this point in the final chapter.

to undermine cultural institutions and forms such as marriage, the church, sexual difference, heterosexuality, and the nuclear family.

"Cultural Marxism" is sometimes the label applied to social justice identity politics, and it isn't difficult to see why. In fact, many radical activists and theorists argue specifically for the end of those cultural institutions and forms, conceiving of them as key parts in the larger apparatus of oppression. Also, it's common to hear criticisms of radical ideas dismissed as mere reiterations of right-wing (often antisemitic) conspiracies about Cultural Marxism.

Often in conspiracy theories, the sense that something has happened or is happening is correct, but the causation or agency is wrong.[125] The conspiracies about Cultural Marxism are no different in this regard, because the ideas of the Frankfurt School did indeed lay down the intellectual foundation for the core ideological framework of social justice identity politics. However, we need only point to the complete absence of (and animosity towards) class analysis in this newer form of politics to notice there's nothing Marxist about it.

The matter of the Frankfurt School is complicated, as many of its theorists identified as Marxist or used Marx's analyses of the relationship between social and material conditions in their own theories. Additionally, though their ideas were not monolithic, a general point of agreement was the Gramscian idea of cultural hegemony, and that social and cultural change were prerequisites for a change in the material conditions of humans.

Theodor Adorno, in particular, is often cited as the primary architect of the conspiracy of Cultural Marxism. However, one of the most common criticisms levied against

---

125 See Lagalisse, 2018, for an excellent explanation of this point.

him by Marxists (his contemporaries and those living now) is that his work relied both on a misinterpretation of Marx and on a complete rejection of Marx's optimism regarding the potential of the working classes. At least in this second aspect, his Marxist critics are very correct: Adorno was deeply pessimistic regarding the masses. Experiences in his own life no doubt contributed to his pessimism, including the rise of National Socialism in Germany (which caused the Frankfurt School to exile itself to the United States) and later interactions with radical students which seem shockingly to prefigure the eructations of radical activism in our current day.

After the uprisings in May 1968, and concurrent with the *Kinderläden*, the student movement in West Germany began to extend their criticism of capitalism to academics who either did not go far enough in their critiques or who, to the students, represented a reactionary traditionalism inimical to revolution. Many of their ideas were inspired by Adorno, Habermas, Marcuse, and others of the Frankfurt School, which makes what then happened to Adorno seem not only ironic but almost hilarious.

Early in 1969, a group of student protestors led by Hans-Jürgen Krahl occupied a room in the Institute for Social Research and threatened Adorno, leading him to call the police to have them removed. This came after several months of his public criticizing of what he saw as protestors' brutish and undirected tactics. Though he supported their goals, he also came to fear the rage they directed at academics and their lack of analysis regarding fascism.

A few months later, in April 1969, on the opening day of a new lecture series on "Dialectical Thinking" that Adorno offered, a student action occurred. Attendees began to shout and otherwise harass him, while another wrote on the chalkboard, "If Adorno is left in peace, capitalism will never cease." This action, called the *Busenaktion* ("breast action"), ended with three female students surrounding the old man, baring their breasts at him, and covering him with flower petals.

Adorno would later write to his colleague, friend, and the former director of the Institute for Social Research that the student movement he and Marcuse had helped inspire was in danger of converting to a kind of "left fascism":

I would have to deny everything that I think and know about the objective tendency if I wanted to believe that the student protest movement in Germany had even the tiniest prospect of effecting a social intervention. Because, however, it cannot do that its effect is questionable in two respects. Firstly, inasmuch as it inflames an undiminished fascist potential in Germany, without even caring about it. Secondly, insofar as it breeds in itself tendencies which — and here too we must differ — directly converge with fascism. I name as symptomatic of this the technique of calling for a discussion, only to then make one impossible; the barbaric inhumanity of a mode of behaviour that is regressive and even confuses regression with revolution; the blind primacy of action; the formalism which is indifferent to the content and shape of that against which one revolts, namely our theory. Here in Frankfurt, and certainly in Berlin as well, the word "professor" is used condescendingly to dismiss people, or as they so nicely put it "to put them down," just as the Nazis used the word Jew in their day. I no longer regard the total complex of what has confronted me permanently over the past two months as an agglomeration of a few incidents. To re-use a word that made us both smile in days gone by, the whole forms a syndrome. Dialectics means, amongst other things, that ends are not indifferent to means; what is going on here drastically demonstrates, right down to the smallest details, such as the bureaucratic clinging to agendas, "binding decisions," countless committees and suchlike, the features of just such a technocratization that they claim they want to oppose, and which we actually oppose. I take much more seriously than you the danger of the student movement flipping over into fascism.[126]

The term "left fascism," sometimes now used by both right and left critics to describe social justice identity politics, actually originates with another of the core ideologues of the Frankfurt School, Jürgen Habermas. The phrase first appeared in a lecture he gave regarding the student revolts in Germany, entitled "The Phantom Revolution and Its Children." For both Habermas and Adorno (but less so for Marcuse), student radicals had given themselves over to "voluntarism," a belief that the conditions of revolution were already at hand, no more theory was needed, and all that remained was the need for action.

Both Habermas and Adorno had lived in Germany during the rise of German fascism; Habermas himself had been a member of the Hitler Youth (he was nine years old when Hitler was named chancellor), while Adorno — who was Jewish — left Germany in 1934 after his right to teach was revoked due to his being non-Aryan. Thus, both had direct experience of really existing fascism, which none of the students who harassed and threatened them in the late Sixties could have claimed. More so, Adorno was the primary author of a book which, in the first decade after its

---

126 See Adorno and Marcuse.

1950 publication, became seen as the authoritative work on fascism: *The Authoritarian Personality*.[127]

Through no insignificant irony, both men — as well as the entire Frankfurt School — had laid the foundations for the radicalism that swept through students in West Germany, in France, and in the United States during the 1960s. Particularly influential were their rejections of positivism as relevant to sociology, meaning that the ways of finding knowledge and testing theories in the natural sciences (biology, physics, and so on) were useless for social sciences. This led to an elevation of personal experience and psychological "structures" over observable material conditions and theories regarding historical forces.

Along with this belief came an interrogation of how the "authoritarian personality" developed within people. Mixing both Freudian and structural analysis, many in the Frankfurt School believed that fascist movements tapped into or exacerbated psychological phenomena that occurred in early child development, especially in families with severe discipline. A child raised in a deeply authoritarian family structure — with a strong and severe father and an obedient and subservient mother — would learn to see the world as a matter of hierarchy and obedience. This would then result in adults who fell in line under strong leaders and who unquestioningly followed their commands.

It's particularly in this analysis that the conspiracy theories about Cultural Marxism begin to correctly identify a social change, though they inaccurately describe its causes and intentions. According to the conspiracy, the Frankfurt School sought to undermine the traditional family in order to bring about a revolution through feminism, the propagation

---

127 This is the same book which significantly influenced the anti-authoritarian framework of the *Kinderläden* movement and John Money's later work on "psychohormonal" studies.

of homosexuality, and a culture of disobedience, sexual deviance, and rebellion, all of which were evident in the youth protests of the late Sixties. Here the kernel of truth is obvious: the Frankfurt School's ideas indeed contributed to the theoretical analysis which informed much of the "sexual revolution" and student protests of the Sixties. On the other hand, as evident in Adorno's correspondence with Marcuse and Habermas's public criticisms of the "children" of this phantom revolution, it's clear that what was occurring was not something the "Cultural Marxists" of the Frankfurt School predicted or supported.

In the Shadow of Fascism

To understand what happened then — and to understand what is happening now — we need to remember what the theorists of the Frankfurt School were responding to. Like many other radicals — whether theorists or otherwise — they had seen the great failure of the November Revolution in Germany at the end of World War I transform over the next decade and a half into the rise of National Socialism and the ascendency of Adolf Hitler. While Marx's ideas had taken hold of the Russian proletariat and resulted in the Union of Soviet Socialist Republics, the Germans ultimately rejected these ideas in favor of Nazism.

The ideological, psychological, and mythic power of the Nazi order became a matter of both terror and intellectual fascination for the Frankfurt School. How had so many ordinary Germans become so swept up into an authoritarian machine, eagerly obeying violent orders and supporting the purge of Jews and others from Europe? Gramsci, who was not part of the Frankfurt School, and who had only seen the failure of the German revolution and the beginning of fascism in both Italy and Germany (but not their full terror), answered this question by asserting that it was the cultural forms of the Germans that led them to become fascist rather than communist.

Walter Benjamin, another Marxist theorist associated with the Frankfurt School, and also a friend of Adorno, likewise attributed the failure of communism and the success of fascism to the question of culture. However, Benjamin insisted it was not a buried psychological or inherent cultural trait within the German people or anyone else that leads to fascism, but rather the very nature of capitalist cultural production itself. In *The Work of Art in the Age of Mechanical Reproduction*, which highly influenced the work of French theorist Jean Baudrillard, Benjamin asserted that fascism succeeded because it re-channeled the revolutionary desire of the lower classes into mass cultural expression along the lines of industrial production:

> The increasing proletarianization of modern man and the increasing formation of masses are two sides of the same process. Fascism attempts to organize the newly proletarianized masses while leaving intact the property relations which they strive to abolish. It sees its salvation in granting expression to the masses — but on no account granting them rights. The masses have a right to changed property relations, fascism seeks to give them expression in keeping these relations unchanged. The logical outcome of fascism is an aesthetizing of political life.[128]

For Walter Benjamin, fascism succeeded because it was better able to manipulate cultural forms produced by the capitalist cultural hegemony. Communism, on the other hand, required people to think differently about their position in society and their relationships to each other. Especially in Germany, fascism had managed to channel the

---

128 See Benjamin, 2008, p.41.

revolutionary anger of the lower classes into a nationalist and authoritarian project, which only further alienated the working classes from themselves and their labor.

Fighting the Fascists Within

Adorno, Habermas, Marcuse, and many others associated with the Frankfurt School generally agreed with this understanding, but instead looked for the psychological roots of the shift towards fascism. It's particularly in their subsequent theories that we see the early framework for social justice identity politics now.

Especially influential was their development of critical theory as a complication of the concurrent movement of structuralism. Structuralism posits that individual and group beliefs and cultural forms can only be understood in relation to larger "structures" or "systems," often originating on a linguistic or mental level. Critical theory generally accepts this premise, but focuses on understanding these structures or systems towards the aim of changing them or creating different systems which lead towards revolutionary — or at least more egalitarian — ends.

We hear earlier echoes of the Frankfurt School now when radicals speak of "systems of oppression" or "systemic racism," as well as structural inequality and cis-heteronormativity. However, none of these ideas actually originated with the thinkers of the Frankfurt School. What did originate with them is this way of thinking about political and social inequality.

Consider the concept of cis-heteronormativity. What it basically states is that straight, non-trans people (the vast majority of the world) are considered the normal or default state of humans. The sense that they are normal then shapes the social, cultural, and political world. In other words, they exert hegemonic control over culture, and the very small minority of people who are not cis or heterosexual have their lives dominated by this cultural norm. This is the Gramscian idea of cultural hegemony, but stripped of its Marxist content and filtered through the Frankfurt School's work on sociological and psychological structures.

The same can be shown of many other radical concepts, particularly regarding gender. Butler's theory of performative gender relies on the structuralist idea that gender operates on a symbolic or linguistic level in the mind. We believe gender exists as it does only because there is a hegemonic idea of what it means to be a man or a woman, and this idea is not actually connected to physical sexual differences. Being a man, therefore, is an idea or role we perform according to the symbolic (structural) cultural codes and cues created and dictated by the larger hegemonic system of gender difference.

Again, this is not a conclusion reached by the thinkers of the Frankfurt School but rather the result of others using their framework. The problem in these subsequent uses is that they no longer retain the original Marxist context of the Frankfurt School's theories. The Frankfurt School theorists, like Gramsci, were attempting to answer a specific and very urgent question posed by the failure of the German revolution and the subsequent rise of Hitler and Mussolini: Why had the lower classes rejected communism and instead embraced fascism?

However, we do see the shadow of fascism continue to persist within the social justice framework. Consider again the role of fascism in Judith Butler's recent editorials and interviews where she asserts that rejection of the new formulations of gender is fascist. That is, according to her view, what people are opposing in their critiques of declarative gender theory is an antifascist political formation, one that seeks to liberate people from authoritarian cultural norms such as the gender binary and sexual dimorphism. Populist — and especially working-class — resistance to these newer gender formulations and ever-expanding lists of new sexual orientations is thus seen as a symptom of a new fascist surge in Europe and the rest of the world.[129]

Other theorists and activists in these newer ideological formations share this analysis, though the specific things against which the lower classes are reacting are identified in other ways. For instance, the backlash against the teaching or implementation of critical race theory in schools is also seen as a fascist reaction, a reactionary move away from a revolution in thinking about race relations. Thus, to oppose critical race theory or Kendian-style anti-racism is to embrace white supremacy instead, which is itself an authoritarian and fascist political and cultural framework.

What is particularly absent in these framings of the problem is the reflexive criticism characteristic of the Frankfurt School. Adorno's correspondence with Marcuse and Habermas's speech about the excesses of the student protests both display this self-criticism, an acknowledgment that their theories have influenced the praxis of the protesters and that something has gone very wrong. On the matter of their influence, Marcuse wrote to Adorno:

We cannot abolish from the world the fact that these students are influenced by us (and certainly not least by you) — I am proud of that and am willing to come to terms with patricide, even though it hurts sometimes.[130]

---

129 This is also the position of some feminist theorists in Europe. See Graff, A. and Korolczuk, 2022; Case, 2019; Kováts Eszter, Poim, M. and Pető Andrea, 2015.

130 See Adorno and Marcuse, 1969.

RHYD WILDERMUTH

Adorno acknowledged this in his reply, but insisted that something else was at work, that something else was happening that went further than theory:

> I know that we are quite close on the question of the relation between theory and practice, although we really do need to discuss this relationship thoroughly some time (I am just working on theses that deal with this matter). I would also concede to you that there are moments in which theory is pushed on further by practice. But such a situation neither exists objectively today, nor does the barren and brutal practicism that confronts us here have the slightest thing to do with theory anyhow.[131]

It's unfortunately difficult to imagine such an exchange occurring now regarding, for instance, the student protests, harassments, and threats that occurred against professor Kathleen Stock at the University of Sussex in October 2021. Stock, a lesbian who had repeatedly expressed support for social protections of trans-identified people yet who remains critical of declarative gender, was the subject of an anonymous student campaign to get her fired. Soon after, an open letter from other professors was circulated in support of the protest against her, and police advised her that they could not adequately protect her. Despite official support from the university, Stock chose to resign in the face of the pressure from students.[132]

Stock's situation looks much like what occurred to Bret Weinstein at the Evergreen State College in 2017 (including the police advisement that they could not adequately protect the professor from the students), as well as like the very frequent "de-platforming" of other academics

---

131 Ibid.
132 See Kelly, 2021.

(including Adolph Reed in 2019). Beyond the remarkably similar scenarios in each case, what all these incidents have in common — with each other and with the student protests against Adorno — is that they redefine what is acceptable critique from within radical movements. They also further divorce social justice identity politics from traditional Marxist analysis.

Consider how the attacks on Adolph Reed were directed at his insistence that the replacement of class analysis by race analysis was harming the left and ensuring the perpetuation of race-thinking (in other words, reifying race). His ideas were smeared as "reactionary" and "class-reductionist," and Reed was accused of contributing to racism. Another way of framing these conflicts, and one that seems to more accurately describe the fundamental weakness of current radical political projects, is that the ideological conflict is over the question of material reality.

Marxists in particular insist that, though there may be ideological forms and structural systems which shape the way humans understand themselves, there is nevertheless a material, physical reality against which those structures and forms must be judged. Therefore, any revolutionary cultural shift must account for this material reality. In this way, Marxists are more in line with Pierre Bourdieu's analysis of social constructions as ways of instituting and maintaining divisions. For Bourdieu, such divisions can only be effective if they appear to accurately describe material conditions. The idea of gender as an instituted division functions because it *initially* appears to accurately describe sexual difference, just as race appears *initially* to accurately describe cultural and economic differences.

The theorists of anti-racism and intersectional feminism often accept that these categories of divisions are constructions, but they avoid analyzing the underlying material reality of the people for whom those categories of division are instituted. Categorizing people according to their race initially appears to give accurate explanations for why people labeled as black tend to be poorer than people labeled as white. However, they can only be accurate if they exclude the existence of rich black people and of poor white people. Put another way, social justice identity politics concludes that black people are poor because of systemic or structural racism. A class analysis, on the other hand, concludes that poor black people are poor for the same reason white poor people are poor: capitalism.

This tension between the material causes of oppression and the cultural or social causes is the true point of separation between social justice identity politics and Marxism. For social justice identity politics, the reasons for injustice are "structural" and "systematic," which means they are social, cultural, and most of all psychological. Internalized homophobia and racism, as well as patriarchal ideas regarding the gender binary and sexual difference, are the primary causes of oppression against black, queer, transgender, and non-binary people. Once these beliefs have been fully educated and disciplined out of the masses, true liberation can finally occur.

Again, in the social justice framework, authoritarianism and oppressive behavior — just like the "felt sense" of gender and the intergenerational trauma of blackness — exist outside the material realm in a secondary realm, both internal and external to the physical body. They are problems of psychological development, learned behaviors, and internal beliefs that cannot be explained by material conditions or class analysis. And here, yet again, we should keep in mind that the meaning of one of the Greek roots which form the word "psychological" is *psyche*, or soul.

CHAPTER NINE: ANARCHISTS AND ANTIFA

Just as the specter of fascism loomed heavily over the theorists of the Frankfurt School and radical experiments such as the *Kinderläden*, we've seen that it also figures in the political analysis of many radical theorists. Fascism persists as a threat to the messianic promise of democratic societies finally free of racism, the gender binary, and unequal social relations across identities.

Judith Butler's framing of the conflict regarding gender as a struggle between an ever-increasing diversity of expressions and fascism is hardly the only example of this.[133] Other theorists have consistently asserted connections between resistance to newer conceptions of gender and backlashes against anti-racism discrimination policies and the emergence of white supremacist or fascist movements.

This narrative has only remained cohesive due to recent political events in the United States, the influential rise of the movement known as Antifa, and the dominance of American anarchist political thought over Marxist class analysis. There is a story here, and it is a personal one.

For many years, I identified as an anarchist and also as part of Antifa. Years of writing on both these subjects has been compiled on multiple anarchist internet archives and sold on the shelves of anarchist bookstores and infoshops. In 2015, I co-founded a print publishing house and online journal initially focused on anarchist and antifascist politics

---

133 Butler, J., 2021.

as well as neopagan belief; some of my own articles and those I've published have been viewed over one hundred thousand times.

Some of those essays I wish I could rewrite, especially those in which I employed the framework of social justice identity politics to explain the political situation of the United States. Others, I'd happily stand by and defend. What I cannot and will not defend, however, is Antifa itself.

An Unfortunate Coincidence

A few years ago, I received a terrifying email from a journalist inquiring about a murder:

> I'm reaching out to you because Mr. Michael Reinoehl, who is a person of interest in the shooting Saturday night, is registered to vote at *[address redacted]*, and nonprofit records show that address was, at least at one point, associated with Gods&Radicals.[134]

Gods&Radicals Press is the name of the non-profit publishing house I co-founded. Michael Reinoehl was an anarchist and Antifa activist who, on 29 August 2020, gunned down a man associated with the right-wing group Patriot Prayer, Aaron Danielson, in Portland, Oregon. According to Reinoehl's statements, he killed Danielson in "self-defense," though Reinoelhl's social media posts had proclaimed an intention to use violence:

> We truly have an opportunity right now to fix everything. But it will be a fight like no other! It will be a war and like all wars there will be casualties."[135]

---

134 From a personal email.
135 See Specia, 2020.

Reinoehl was the first anarchist in the United States involved in Antifa to kill a political opponent during the Trump years, and his subsequent death at the hands of police further increased the attention given to the matter. Reinoehl had fled from the scene of the shooting, becoming a fugitive while giving several interviews to journalists (but not, apparently, to the journalist who had contacted me). On 3 September 2020, he was shot and killed by US Marshals outside of Lacey, Washington, a suburb of Olympia, Washington.[136] His fugitive status and subsequent killing were unsurprising to many of us, as were the outpourings of support for him from anarchists and from Antifa-branded media accounts, with almost no public statements suggesting his murder of Aaron Danielson had gone too far.

What was surprising to me was the email. I did not personally know the man, though we did run in similar political crowds, and I later learned several anarchist friends had known him. The reason the journalist had contacted me, however, turned out to be only an unfortunate coincidence. Reinoehl previously lived at the same address as someone I knew, a person who had been involved in setting up the non-profit board for the publishing house I directed. They never knew each other, either. There was no connection between them, nor was there any connection between Reinoehl and Gods&Radicals. It was just a dumb stroke of coincidence.

I was terrified regardless, and also angry. That anger came slower, however, and lasted much longer than the

---

136 This is about ten miles or sixteen kilometres from the
  Evergreen State College. While there was no connection
  between Reinoehl and Evergreen, Olympia and Lacey are both
  known to have very large and politically active anarchist and
  Antifa populations, and many anarchists from those towns
  joined in the protests against Bret Weinstein in 2017.

fear. I had quickly contacted quite a few of my anarchist friends — including a prominent Antifa activist and journalist — to find out what was up, how I should respond, and how worried I should be. In all cases they told me I was not only over-reacting but that I should also be completely proud to be associated with such a "hero."

Another World Is... Nevermind

I've been politically active now for more than twenty years. The World Trade Organization (WTO) meetings and protests in Seattle radicalized me, as I think they did many others my age. I was twenty-two, just turning twenty-three. Before then, though I'd had some exposure to leftist political thinking and a vague understanding of capitalism — by which I mean I didn't like it because I was poor — I hadn't yet connected anything I had thought to anything actually happening in the world.

At the end of 1999, the WTO held a meeting in Seattle which was met with massive protests. The protestors who showed up were generally what we would call "leftist," but not all of them. Many were just union members, out because their leadership had called them to be there. Some were diehard anarchists (the famed "Eugene Anarchists" blamed by the mayor of Seattle, Paul Schell, for the majority of the violence), others were part of more organized socialist groups like the now defunct International Socialist Organization (ISO)[137] and smaller groups like the Freedom Socialist Party and Socialist Alternative. Some were there

---

137 The ISO, which was one of the largest socialist organizations in the United States and existed for over forty years, was disbanded in 2019. Though the official reason for its dissolution was controversy over the mishandling of a sexual misconduct case from 2013, the ISO had also already begun

because they were environmentalists, drawn there by non-governmental organizations. Others came out because they believed there was a conspiracy by the UN and other international groups to take away individual rights and local sovereignty. And some just came out of curiosity, as forty thousand people shutting down the center of an otherwise sleepy city was something to see.

While there had been earlier and much smaller protests, the event in Seattle marked the full beginning of the anti-globalization movement, a mass politics in response to a larger political and economic shift which eventually succeeded in reshaping our world. It also meant a kind of renaissance for anarchist thought, a sudden relevance for a sub-cultural political movement few had taken seriously in the United States since the beginning of World War II.

To understand what we were all on about during that time, you need to consider what the world looked like at the end of the 1990s. Francis Fukuyama had declared "the end of history," a moment of triumph for liberal democracy and capitalism over communism and national isolationism. Before the end of the second millennium, the Berlin Wall had fallen, the Soviet Union and allied client states (like Yugoslavia) had collapsed, and the Third World was now open for pillaging.

The term "Third World" is now considered quite pejorative, but only because no one seems to remember what it actually meant. Most probably don't even know there was also a "Second World" in the equation. In that particular geo-political framing, the world was seen as being divided into three parts: the First World (Western capitalist democracies), the Second World (the Soviet bloc and

---

to disintegrate due to a push to implement intersectional feminist critique as a replacement for class analysis.

allied communist states), and the Third World (unaligned nations, primarily in what we now call the Global South), over which the First and Second worlds fought. By the end of the 1990s, the Second World collapsed. This meant there was no longer any competition for the capitalists in the First World for the resources of the Third World. Before this collapse, international investment and military policy had been crafted with a constant eye towards competing with and limiting the influence of the USSR, and now all those policies were ready to be re-written.

It's hard to imagine this, maybe, but for decades the competitive pressure from the Second (state communist) World had managed to keep First World capitalists from becoming too extreme in their exploitation of their own laborers and the resources of other nations. As long as the USSR existed and was offering an alternative model for organizing society, Western capitalists had to at least maintain the pretense of giving their own people, and the people in the Third World, a good deal. With the Communists out of power, there was no longer such a need, because there was no longer any alternative. Thus, in the late 1990s, governments, capitalists, and a new breed of technocrat theorist scrambled to create new policies and frameworks that would allow them to take as much advantage as possible of this political void. Importantly, they also needed a new moral framework to justify these policies, because "fighting communism" was no longer a believable excuse. There were no more communists to fight.

That's how globalization was born. Globalization meant many things, depending on who you asked, but ultimately it meant the worldwide spread of Western capitalist modes of production, financing, development, and the Western capitalist worldview itself. Now that there was no alternative, the missionaries of the enlightened capitalist order could spread across the globe, teaching the previously "primitive" and "backwards" peoples how to live in the brave new present. We were all connected in a universal fellowship of consumers and producers: all over the world we could have strawberries in wintertime, a Starbucks in every town center, a representative democracy, and access to a global network of information called the internet, which would bring us all closer together.

In those early days, the propaganda was intoxicating. Even for those of us who opposed this new global ordering of the world based on Anglo-American capitalist values, we still had the sense that some new world was being born. That's why, while in English the opposition to this new political formation was called anti-globalization, in Europe and the Global South the movement was called *altermondialism*: "other-world-ism." Derived from the popular rallying cry "Another World Is Possible," the idea of altermondialism was that all these new technologies and the cessation of geo-political strife after the death of state communism could usher in a more democratic and less capitalist world.

The WTO protests, for instance, had seen the birth of several new decentralized and non-hierarchical communications technologies and organizing structures (for example, the IndyMedia collectives and infoshops, and the Direct Action Network). Also, the astounding diversity of political interests and ethnic concerns that had come together for the protest (and many subsequent ones) was seen as a model of what a new resistance movement could look like. First Nations tribal leaders marching alongside union leaders and migrant farm workers, listening to speakers from India and Brazil, reading texts from African activists and Italian anarchists: this looked to many like a true other world being born.

Of course it didn't happen that way. What we got instead was the globalization of capital. We also got a new form of state and corporate repression, one that that has proven itself far more efficient than the political repression in the failed communist states. We also got an acceleration of capitalist destruction in the Global South, and of human-caused climate change.

Black Bloc and True Believers

The anti-globalization movement saw the rebirth of anarchism as a serious political ideology. Before then, though there were always small groups and various individuals who described themselves as anarchists, anarchism as a political force had largely disappeared in the previous decades, except in a few European countries, especially Italy, Greece, and Germany.

In the lead up to the WTO protests, anarchist political tactics and beliefs found a new popularity. Especially because of the Direct Action Network, which played a significant part in causing the disruption in Seattle that shifted the event from a protest march into a city siege, anarchist ideas such as non-hierarchical organization and masked action suddenly were taken seriously again. In particular, politicians and the media focused heavily on the black bloc anarchists, those who were responsible for the vast majority of property damage in Seattle during the WTO.

"Black bloc" isn't the name of an ideological tendency or even of a group — there is technically no such thing as a "black bloc Anarchist" — but rather of a tactic. In a black bloc, people don masks and wear black in order to disguise their identities and make themselves indistinguishable from others in a group. The point of doing so is to make it difficult for police or others to identify individuals, while also emboldening those individuals to take more aggressive actions. Basically you become — at least during the action — anonymous and practically invisible. This means you can get away with a lot more. You can break windows and smash cars and steal whatever you like even in plain sight, because all anyone can actually report is that they saw someone wearing all black doing those things. Thus, anything you do gets attributed instead to a group identity, rather than to an individual identity. As long as you were disguised, you can leave the action at the end of the day with no repercussions.

Not only is this tactic not new, it's also politically neutral. Disguising yourself for political actions is what the Boston Tea Party was all about. The white robes and hoods of the Ku Klux Klan are also an example of the same tactic, as was the cross-dressing of the anti-enclosure actions in England, Wales, and Ireland. In all cases, the goal of the disguise is to allow you to act with impunity, which also emboldens you to take actions you might not otherwise take because of the fear of getting caught.[138]

I was part of several black bloc actions in the first few years of the 2000s, and witnessed many more of them. I can attest that it's all quite a rush: you feel invulnerable in a way you never get to feel in your everyday life. Also, there is a profoundly spiritual dimension to all of this. Masking and disguising has always been part of indigenous and pagan rituals: changing the way you look for a ritual allows you to

---

138 This is also the tactic behind the frequent "smash-and-grab" looting events in the United States. A mob of people all wearing similar clothing swarm a store, mall, or even individuals at the same time and take what they can. Then the mob flees in different directions, leaving police and the individuals affected powerless to identify the culprits.

"channel" something other than what you are.[139] In a black bloc, then, your own identity isn't just disguised: you take on a new one.

The other anarchists I knew were an interesting lot. Many of them fit the mainstream stereotype of what an anarchist is: young, angry, straight men, not always but very often from financially well-off families. Several of those I knew turned out to be extremely abusive to their partners, women who also participated in the actions with them but then later left because the violence didn't just stop with shop windows. Others were more like me, though. They were people who had become newly radicalized and really wanted to change things, and who had just been given a copy of Ward Churchhill's *Pacifism as Pathology*,[140] or who had picked up a copy of *Adbusters*. However, people like me were often suspect. Because we were new to all this, we hadn't yet adopted the cultural signifiers of anarchism (being vegan, for instance, or loudly bemoaning Kronstadt), and so we were often seen as potential infiltrators.

There were three signs we were taught to look for, clear giveaways that someone might actually be a cop rather than a true believer. The first was the age of their black Carhartt jeans,[141] because it takes a long time for them to look worn. New ones meant they were "new" anarchists

---

139 Whether that is just a sublimated aspect of your own personality, a ritualized identity, or something else entirely depends on what framework you use to try to understand this. Regardless, the feeling of "channeling" another self is profound when engaging in this practice.

140 That book was literally everywhere in Seattle. You could find stacks of it left in coffee shops and distributed at parties and protests. It was a kind of anarchist bible for a while.

141 Carhartt jeans were the official uniform of American anarchy for many years, never mind their price.

and quite possibly infiltrators or cops. Secondly, their body weight was super important. If a man looked well fed, he was obviously a "pig": anarchy meant looking hungry. The third telltale sign is the most interesting though, as it has a lot of bearing on how Antifa later developed. That sign? Being critical of any action, expressing doubt in its efficacy, or suggesting other actions instead. That is, if at any point you wondered aloud if breaking shop windows might not be as effective as the less glamorous work of organizing the workers against those shop owners, you were at best a hopeless liberal or a communist, but more likely you were a police saboteur.

I don't know how to make clear how thoroughly paranoid I and my anarchist friends were in the early part of the 2000s, even before the organized police infiltration of our groups. Everyone was certain there were saboteurs, though at that time there probably were not. They did soon arrive, of course, *en force*, and they came in a way that anarchists had made themselves too blind to counter. While everyone was on guard against doubters, omnivores, and people with healthy body weights, the government infiltrated with people whose apparent belief in the cause of anarchy was even stronger than ours. Suddenly, there was a new breed of anarchist who was urging even more spectacular actions, questioning the real commitment of the previous "non-leader" leaders.[142]

This all led to several high-profile entrapment schemes that destroyed what remained of any real organized political movement.[143] In these schemes, FBI and police actors would

---

142 Anarchists have leaders no matter how much they believe they don't. It's this denialism that allows them to be so easily manipulated by infiltrators and charismatic narcissists.

143 One such event that particularly hit many prominent anarchist leaders in Seattle involved a long police setup in

join groups and urge them towards more extreme actions, very similar to the way many "Islamic terrorist" stings have occurred. This tactic works incredibly well, because it exploits the core weakness of any true believer: their self-doubt. For a person who believes fully in any political or religious dogma, the one thing they cannot countenance is their own misgivings. Are they being faithful enough? Are they doing all they can to serve their cause? And are there cracks appearing in the foundation of their belief?

An infiltrator only needs to act more faithful and more devoted than all the others, and those others will soon fall in line. Why? Because it is ultimately only faith and commitment to the cause which provides cohesion for the group. Even in the absence of infiltrators, members of the group are constantly challenging each other and themselves over any signs of doubt or apostasy. Add in a saboteur who understands this dynamic, and this faith mechanism becomes the group's downfall.

During the middle and later part of the 2000s, I had multiple people I considered friends just disappear out of my life. Some of them were likely to have been saboteurs. Others fled to Canada during grand jury hearings regarding environmental terrorism.[144] Some of them just left all

---

which an agent actually funded cocaine deals and paid the rent for anarchist organizing spaces. See Kiley, 2011, for this story, which involved some of my friends. Also relevant are the entrapment schemes targeting many eco-anarchists, including the use of romantic attachment by saboteurs, as in the case of of Eric McDavid. See Pilkington, 2015.

144 This occurred during a period in the United States now called the Green Scare. During the Green Scare, the federal government infiltrated many environmental organizations and set up grand juries to investigate individuals with suspected ties to eco-sabotage. Refusing to testify during

political action altogether out of disgust and fear over what they had seen, both from fellow activists and from government repression.

From Anti-Capitalism to Anti-Oppression

A deep depression came over me and many of my friends during that time. We had gone from feeling like we were on the front lines of an international movement against global capitalism to feeling that we were being hunted. Worse, the fascination with and acceptance of anarchist ideas in the wider public domain had suddenly disappeared. To be an anarchist now meant just to be violent, and this wasn't only the perception of the everyday person but also of others on the left.

Two events stand out in my memory that pointed to this shift, both protest marches. One was an event against police brutality organized by several black community groups and churches. At the beginning, the organizers had made several impassioned pleas to the crowd to stay non-violent, and had specifically singled out black bloc protestors as an unwanted presence. By this point, I no longer engaged in black bloc tactics, but I was standing near friends I knew intended to mask up once the police arrived. "Fuck that," I heard one of them say, and the others with her agreed. Then, about fifteen minutes into the march, they indeed put on their masks and pelted the police with stones, leading the cops to use pepper spray on the unwitting crowd.

Another event, a year or two later, started with even more stern words directed towards any anarchists in the crowd who intended to be violent. That event was a vigil for

a grand jury can lead to prolonged imprisonment without charges, which persists until the grand jury process is completed. There are very few legal options for such individuals, as they exist in a state of legal limbo.

a homeless First Nations man killed by a police officer. The tribal elders who led it made clear that black bloc protestors were not only not welcome but would be considered no better than the police who shot their tribesman. The anarchists I talked to about this responded similarly to how I would have responded years before. "Non-violence is a tool of the state" was usually how we said it, but I wasn't really sure I believed that anymore. Violence had become the proverbial hammer before which everything was a nail, and especially for those two events it seemed more and more obvious that the anarchists in the crowd desperately just wanted to be hammers.

Around this same time, starting around the time of the election of Barack Obama in 2008 and coming into full force after the failure of the Occupy Movement during the winter of 2011–2012, a new idea had started to circulate among the anarchist groups and individuals I knew: "anti-oppression." This was the new "work," fighting oppression on personal levels rather than in large-scale protests and actions. This often meant anti-racism, but also anti-sexism and anti-speciesism,[145] all ideas which had become increasingly popular on college campuses. Also, all of a sudden people were talking about gender in new ways, citing Judith Butler and others whose writings were much more esoteric and obfuscating than the political texts that previously circulated through anarchist spaces.

Anti-oppression soon came to replace direct action as the core anarchist work, and this initially made a lot of sense. After all, direct action tactics were not only becoming less effective, they were expressly no longer tolerated by liberals. Also, this new work provided a kind of moral framework that anarchism severely lacked, and it

---

145 Generally, opposition to the privileging of human needs over those of animals and plants.

gave anarchists something to say again to others after years of being written off as angry kids.

There was some pushback to this change, mostly from older anarchist theorists and writers. They saw the shift from physical action to moral questioning as a defanging of anarchist ideals. Some saw in the anti-oppression framework a reproduction of Christian morality and an abandonment of individual liberty for a false notion of group identity. Also, some noted correctly that much of the anti-oppression framework was a continuation of some of the ideas leftists had critically discarded from the Frankfurt School, especially the belief that hierarchy and authority are psychological features that can be disciplined or trained out of children.

Unfortunately, very few of these critiques were taken seriously, and this shift from direct action to internal reflection cannot be seen any other way except as a search for relevance after anarchism's last gasp, Occupy, failed so spectacularly. Both the government repression of anarchists and community groups' justifiable frustration with anarchist tactics — especially minority groups — caused a massive identity crisis for many anarchists, paralleling what feminists had experienced in the late Seventies and early Eighties.

This all came at a time when socialist organizations were seeing increasing support, especially because of their focus on teaching and community support and their skills in organizing over longer time periods. Anarchism tends to preclude such longer-term organizing because of its anti-institutionalism and anti-hierarchical arrangements. Marxism, on the other hand, lends itself very well to organizing.

So, starting around 2009 and increasing after Occupy, anarchists shifted to moral soul-searching regarding their own oppressive behaviors in everyday personal interactions. This gave anarchists new access to the wider liberal discussion, but it also paralyzed them in a state of constant inaction. How can you act when every action might be problematic or oppressive to someone?

The larger political situation of the United States at that time — and especially the election of Barack Obama — is crucial for understanding how this happened. Anarchism in America experienced its rise to fame and relevancy during the early years of George W. Bush. A right-wing, rich white man as president is an easier target to oppose than a rich, black, liberal president. Especially when so many people saw Obama's election as a sign that liberal democracy was finally fulfilling its false promises to eventually deliver equality, criticism of the state often fell on deaf ears.

From 2009 to 2015, anarchists became largely irrelevant in the United States. That isn't to say there were no anarchist actions; in fact, mutual-aid organizing, based loosely on anarchist principles, occurred multiple times, including in the aftermath of Hurricane Sandy in 2012 (though it was nowhere near as significant as the mutual-aid response to Hurricane Katrina in 2005). And of course, anarchists were present later in the early Black Lives Matter protests, but the many stories of anarchists causing escalations of violence at those events did little for their reputation.

How Trump Made Anarchists Great Again

What changed in 2015 was the beginning of Donald Trump's presidential candidacy and the rise of the alt-right. Suddenly, anarchism was back in vogue, but it had a new name: Antifa.

Antifa has quite a lot of similarities to black bloc. Antifa doesn't really exist anymore than you can say that black bloc anarchists really exist, yet neither of these statements are fully true. Anyone can be black bloc, just as anyone can be Antifa, but the anarchists who formed black blocs at the protests I participated in were very often the same ones each time. We had no "leaders," yet we knew who the "leaders" of those groups were regardless. They were the ones who were always directing the general movements of the bloc. It was they who made the tactical decisions: when to mask up, when to unmask, when to smash things, and when to blend back into the crowd.

Antifa is the same way. Antifa has leaders who will disavow that they are leaders. Regardless, it is very often the same groups and the same individuals making the same calls to action. Most Antifa Twitter accounts or websites that call themselves "collectives," for example, are just two or three people — and often just one person. Here, it's also worth noting there's a bit of truth to a persistent right-wing accusation[146] that some of the journalists reporting on Antifa and Antifa-aligned events are also Antifa themselves. Antifa operates through series of personal relationships and via associations between "nodes." Those nodes — or really just people — are often working as journalists and self-avowed researchers while also working closely with Antifa organizers and sometimes as organizers themselves (for instance, by running Antifa social media accounts or websites).[147]

It's also worth noting that Antifa is hardly the first or only kind of antifascist organization in the United States. On the contrary, it is a rebranding and co-option of earlier modes of organization. Every Marxist group in the United

---

146 For instance, Eoin Lenihan's article in *Quillette* (see Lenihan), or right-wing muckraking journalist Andy Ngo's various reporting on Antifa in print and internet media.

147 See Burley and Ross, 2019, for a response by two exposed journalists who are also well-known organizers and leaders of Antifa organizations.

States (including the Revolutionary Communist Party, the International Socialist Organization, the Socialist Alternative, and the Freedom Socialist Party) organized actions against self-avowed Nazis and white supremacist groups well before Antifa arose. At many of these events, their community calls brought in anarchists such as myself. Antifa, on the other hand, initially organized less against specific political formations and more against bands like Death In June. Antifa actions favor threats, physical attacks, and property damage to scare business owners and promoters over drawing on organizational strength — because they have none.

Antifa is a specifically anarchist organizing tactic, rather than a general leftist one. While other leftist groups saw opposition to fascism as a natural outgrowth of their opposition to capitalism, Antifa's only purpose is in its name: antifascism. This, of course, leads to all kinds of ideological problems. Socialist groups often identify fascism as an immune response of the capitalist order, and they have concrete ways of determining whether a movement is fascist or merely just reactionary. Antifa, lacking a larger political framework, can draw only from its core anarchist ideology for such identification. Significantly, by the time Antifa fully arose in the middle of the last decade, anarchism had become so intertwined with "anti-oppression" ideology that fascism and oppression became synonymous.

The rise of Trump and the alt-right tied this ideological knot for them, while simultaneously giving anarchists something to make them relevant again. The sudden popularity of alt-right thinkers such as Richard Spencer and Milo Yiannopoulos — themselves riding the coattails of Trump's nationalist rhetoric — provided exactly the kind of heroic crisis anarchists desperately wanted. Suddenly, there were "fascists" to fight, just like in Catalonia. Except, of course, Trump was never a fascist, and neither really were any but a very small handful of the alt-right luminaries. What they were was something else entirely, an illiberal force which rejected the anti-oppression framework anarchists had for years internalized. That same anti-oppression framework now had a new name: intersectionality, or social justice identity politics.

Trump and the alt-right both rode upon a wave of populist opposition to the cultural and social effects of anti-oppression moralization. This cannot be understated: despite how much we might generally agree with the goals of social justice and anti-oppression work, the larger public tends to finds much of it ridiculous. The extreme and unhinged nature of anti-oppression work provided exactly what both Trump and the alt-right needed for their popularity as well, and they became a kind of shadow twin of the social justice absurdities for which Antifa became the ultimate champion.

The first significant show of force Antifa affected was the deplatforming of Milo Yiannopoulos at the University of California, Berkeley, in 2017. Fifteen hundred people showed up, and anarchists using black bloc tactics managed to cause $100,000 worth of damage and convinced the university to cancel his appearance. Other events soon occurred, culminating in the mass mobilization of counter-protesters in Charlottesville, Virginia, for the Unite the Right rally in 2017, an event which resulted in the death of a counter-protester, Heather Heyer.

The Fascists That Weren't

After that event, Antifa suddenly became a media darling. Anarchists had managed to re-brand themselves as the vanguard of opposition both to Trump and to the "deplorables" Hillary Clinton had urged mainstream liberals to fear. Antifa actions became increasingly bolder and more violent, especially in the Pacific Northwest, where Antifa officially started and where several primary organizers live.

This also led to the accumulation of significant influence and power by a handful of mostly anonymous Antifa organizers and related organizations. Several books were published during this period which led to increased fame (and profit) for Antifa-aligned writers, while others found themselves highly sought-after as experts for mainstream news articles and even columnist positions in foreign newspapers. Anarchists were suddenly being quoted in the *New York Times* as if they were respectable political actors rather than violent thugs who just wanted to burn down the world.

Power has its own logic and its own demands, and one of these is ensuring you get to hold on to it no matter what. That's why, at the same time that many Antifa organizers were accumulating influence and social capital, they often turned it against rival anarchists. Such a campaign to smear and deplatform a longtime anarchist publisher and organizer — one who had been critical of this new moral turn and noted the increasing social capital of Antifa organizers — first made me aware of what was happening. Aragorn!,[148] founder of the anarchist publisher and distribution service Little Black Cart, the news site *Anarchist News*, and the massive internet archive of anarchist writing called the Anarchist Library, as well as being the internet administrator for many local anarchist websites, was a figure who had been a mainstay of anarchist thought for decades. Then, suddenly, he was labeled a "fascist" by multiple Antifa organizers.

This increasingly happened to many lesser-known anarchists in the final years of the Trump presidency. Here I'll mention myself briefly, an anarchist for two decades,

---

148 This is his name, including the exclamation point.

suddenly smeared as a crypto-fascist by anonymous Antifa social media accounts. My crime was the same unpardonable sin I learned in my early days as an anarchist to avoid at all costs: *questioning tactics*. Of particular note were reactions to my assertion that trying to get right-leaning people fired from their jobs and publishing the home addresses of alleged fascists — including fellow anarchists who were being mislabeled as fascist — was a really bad idea. Also, I had become increasingly worried about the tendency to use deplatforming as a weapon against groups on social media platforms, accurately predicting that empowering corporations to police speech would backfire on anarchists as well.[149]

Most of all, I had become critical of the way identity politics — what we earlier called anti-oppression work — seemed to align the left more and more with the capitalist order and the Democratic Party's platforms. These criticisms resulted in my ejection from anarchist organizing groups, my banning from private networks, and many, many social media crusades against me.[150]

While what I experienced was bad, what others experienced was far worse. Aragorn!, the aforementioned anarchist publisher, had his tires slashed in front of his home and the books he distributed destroyed by other anarchists at bookfairs. Other anarchist writers had their home addresses and children's names published on internet sites and received repeated death threats on untraceable

---

149 Both Patreon and Facebook banned *It's Going Down* and other anarchist websites at the same time that they banned far right groups, just as I had predicted would happen. The irony here is that many of those Antifa-identified groups had led the call for public pressure to get far-right groups banned on those platforms.

150 These still occur.

blogs. This led some of them to completely stop writing and delete all social media presence.

I survived all this mostly because I no longer live in the United States. I left in 2017 and haven't been back since: in order to slash my bicycle tires, they'd have to travel quite a long way. Of course, this says nothing about the fear their actions engendered, which led me to hide any photos of my family on social media profiles while they were still in the United States (my sister lives in Europe now as well). For a while, I lived in France on an expired visa, a "cool anarchist" thing to have done and which I disclosed to no Antifa-aligned people lest they attempted to report me to the French government.

It took me quite some time to fully comprehend how I'd become as afraid of Antifa-aligned anarchists as I had been of the far-right. This was a perverse reality that only truly dawned on me when I received the email from the journalist asking about Michael Reinoehl. What had once seemed to me a beautiful kind of resistance to capitalism and the state now seemed a reckless, violent movement eager to fight an enemy that never really existed.

Yes, of course, there are actual fascists in the world. But what arose in the United States wasn't fascism but rather populist nationalism, a different kind of reaction to the same globalization of capital that anarchists fought in 1999. The mostly white working class in the United States has seen the largest changes in their standard of living on account of neoliberal policies first put into place by Bill Clinton and increasingly implemented by Bush and Obama after him. As the PMC increasingly adopted social justice identity politics and preached that white, cis, heterosexual men were the true evil in the world, Donald Trump and the alt-right appeared to many to be the only ones speaking to their material conditions.

The False Dichotomy of "Fascist" and "Antifa"

The greatest influence that Antifa has had upon the current state of radical politics is the dualistic or binary framing of all political and cultural positions, especially regarding newer conceptions of identity. Ibram X. Kendi's formulation that there is only racism and anti-racism, for instance, can only be sustained within a larger framework in which such binary framing is seen as defensible. This is also the Antifa framing of such questions: there is no other option between being fascist or antifascist.

This dichotomy seems self-evident and difficult to argue against, but only if we accept the definitions proposed by those who impose it. To see the path beyond these false choices, consider George W. Bush's famous assertion to nations reluctant to support US military actions in Afghanistan and then Iraq: "You are either with us, or with the terrorists." In other words, there are only two possibilities: pro-terrorism or anti-terrorism. This is the same formula proposed by many radicals now: fascist or antifascist, pro-trans or anti-trans, racist or anti-racist.

Recalling Pierre Bourdieu again, we must remember that these dichotomies are also acts of institution and categorization. Bush's statement did not merely present a choice, it defined the categories which composed that choice, a point we can see more clearly if we add the words "as I define them": "You are either with us, or with the terrorists as I define them." Applying this same framework, we can then see the false choice between fascism and antifascism, racism and anti-racism, and between being pro-trans and anti-trans. The question is never whether one is objectively for a thing or against a thing, but whether one agrees with the proposed category of division.

Who defines what is fascism? Is it Antifa, or are there more objective and historical measures we might use instead? Who defines what it means to be anti-trans? Is it activists who believe that hormone replacement therapy and puberty blockers should be available without parental consent to very young children, or is it the dissenting trans and other activists who propose a broader and more holistic way of looking at the questions of childhood gender dysphoria?[151] Who defines what racism is? Is it those who make statements such as "White people should never be allowed to adopt black orphans," or are there larger frameworks we might apply to determine whether a policy or position actually betters the lives of black people or merely replicates race-thinking?

Bourdieu reminds us that categorization derives from the Greek work for insult, and we should keep in mind that an insult — especially a smear — is often an act of power and abuse. An abusive person who insults his or her partner does so to weaken them, to belittle them into a state of victimhood and passivity. As many who have experienced domestic abuse can attest, these insults can reach a degree at which the sense of self, the ability to define what is right or wrong, and especially the sense of agency and will of the victim are constantly eroded. The false dichotomies — these attempts to define and institute the categories of fascist/antifascist, racist/anti-racist, pro-trans/transphobe, and against terrorism/for terrorism — often function the same way.

This, more than any other reason, is why I publicly disassociated myself from Antifa and anarchism in the United States. It felt as if we were becoming what we were

---

151 For instance, Erica Anderson and Marci Bowers, both
    trans people renowned for their work with trans patients.
    Both have become highly critical of current trans activism
    regarding young children. See Shrier, 2021.

trying to fight, acting as authoritarian, as thuggish, and as brutal as the enemies we named. As Nietzsche warned:

> Beware that, when fighting monsters, you yourself do not become a monster... for when you gaze long into the abyss. The abyss gazes also into you.[152]

---

152 See Nietzsche, 1966.

CHAPTER TEN: THE WEREWOLF

In the previous two chapters, we've seen how the threat of fascism influenced a lot of radical leftist thought. Much of the work of the Frankfurt School theorists, such as Theodor Adorno, Herbert Marcuse, and Jürgen Habermas, as well as others aligned with their ideas (Walter Benjamin, for example, and Wilhelm Reich), was aimed at understanding why fascism had taken such a hold over the lower classes in Europe in order to prevent it ever happening again. More recently, especially in the United States, many anarchists and social justice activists retooled many of their political theories and organizing tactics to deplatform and otherwise "resist" what appeared to be a rising fascist threat in the form of the alt-right and President Donald Trump.

We've also seen that many PMC theorists of gender and race have depicted those critical of the newer frameworks they articulate and defend as part of a growing fascist menace. Those opposed to "gender ideology" or critical race theory are therefore (in their view) a growing reactionary threat to vulnerable, oppressed, and marginalized people.

In the United States, Canada, and the United Kingdom, right-aligned media figures and politicians warn of "the woke," a catch-all phrase which in their usage can mean everyone from traditional Marxists to social justice and Antifa activists, Black Lives Matter protesters, and even just everyday people with generally progressive tendencies. Groups that often have little in common — and are often deeply at odds with each other over the ultimate goals of political change — are presented as one faceless hoard threatening the stability of society. In France, *"le wokisme"* has become a similar *bête noir* for extreme nationalist politicians and even centrist liberal ones alike. Though neither group can quite agree on what it precisely entails, they regardless agree it is a threat to French society and also an imperialist threat from Anglo-American political culture.

"Woke" has a slippery, unclear, and constantly relative meaning. What is woke to one person is just normal tolerance to another; however, ask a third person and those two other people now become "the woke." Not only does one's relational position determine what is woke and what is not, those whom the word "woke" is meant to describe rarely ever use the label for themselves.

Woke has a shadow term, "fascist," and this is a crucial point. What or who is fascist has no clear definition in public discourse. Though originally describing a specific political ideology articulated first by Benito Mussolini,[153] then later applied to Hitler's National Socialism and to Francisco Franco's nationalist dictatorship in Spain, "fascism" has now taken on so many other meanings that it resembles almost nothing of those actually existing political forms.

Various attempts to define what fascism really is have been made, however. One common academic definition calls it "a genus of political ideology whose mythic core in its various permutations is a palingenetic form of populist ultranationalism."[154] A more recently popular definition calls fascism "a cult of the leader who promises national restoration in the face of humiliation brought on by supposed communists, Marxists and minorities and

---

153 Incidentally, he was previously an anarcho-syndicalist.
154 See Griffin, 2003.

immigrants who are supposedly posing a threat to the character and the history of a nation."[155] Neither of these definitions get us very far in understanding what fascism actually is or who or what specifically can be accurately called fascist.

This is not a new problem, however. George Orwell noted in a 1944 essay that fascism had already come to mean something quite slippery:

> It will be seen that, as used, the word "Fascism" is almost entirely meaningless. In conversation, of course, it is used even more wildly than in print. I have heard it applied to farmers, shopkeepers, Social Credit, corporal punishment, fox-hunting, bull-fighting, the 1922 Committee, the 1941 Committee, Kipling, Gandhi, Chiang Kai-Shek, homosexuality, Priestley's broadcasts, Youth Hostels, astrology, women, dogs and I do not know what else.
>
> Yet underneath all this mess there does lie a kind of buried meaning. To begin with, it is clear that there are very great differences, some of them easy to point out and not easy to explain away, between the régimes called Fascist and those called democratic. Secondly, if "Fascist" means "in sympathy with Hitler," some of the accusations I have listed above are obviously very much more justified than others. Thirdly, even the people who recklessly fling the word "Fascist" in every direction attach at any rate an emotional significance to it. By "Fascism" they mean, roughly speaking, something cruel, unscrupulous, arrogant, obscurantist, anti-liberal and anti-working-class. Except for the relatively small number of Fascist sympathizers, almost any English person would accept "bully" as a synonym for

---

155 Liberal professor Jason Stanley's definition. See Silva and Doubek, 2020.

"Fascist." That is about as near to a definition as this much-abused word has come.[156]

In some political theories, the word "populism" has come to replace fascism as the desired term. Populism, however, also has a slippery, unclear, and relative definition. Movements generally seen as left-aligned (Black Lives Matter, Occupy, anti-globalization protests, rural resistance to development, large-scale anti-war mobilizations, and so on) are all populist movements. On the other hand, so, also, are reactionary or nationalist movements, such as anti-immigrant protests, local oppositions to the teaching of critical race theory in primary schools, "Trumpism," and European and Anglo-American opposition to gender theory. They are all populist movements, which again gets us nowhere close to clarity.

Fascism, populism, and wokeism are not the only political terms that have slipped from their original meaning and become mere insults. Even "right" and "left" rarely have agreed-upon definitions anymore. I consider myself a leftist, yet some whom I consider non-leftist have labeled my political ideas "right-wing" and even "fascist."[157] Others have described my politics as "extreme left-wing" and even "Cultural Marxist," both terms being meant as an insult.

Some of the problems of definition are certainly cultural. We often cannot see how our own context is much smaller than we imagine. What is considered left in the United States maps more closely onto center-right political views in Europe, and what is far left would be center-left in France and Germany. On the other hand, some right-wing ideas in

---

156 See Orwell, 1944.

157 A brief social media search would suffice to show you what
I mean. And no, I'm not a Satanist, either.

the United States are actually more commonly held by "far-left" anarchists and others in Europe.

Our idea of left and right is anyway derived from a unique historical moment in Europe, the seating chart of the National Assembly during the French Revolution. Those who sat on the right side were for keeping around the *ancien régime*, those on the left were for abolishing it. Yet as even Karl Marx pointed out, those defined as the left during the French Revolution were primarily the bourgeoisie: that is, the capitalist class.

I can understand if all these unclear meanings and labels lead you to despair. They did so for me, at least for a little while. It can seem as if it is quite impossible to talk about anything without being misunderstood, that all the words, as T.S. Eliot once complained, "slip, slide, perish / Decay with imprecision, will not stay in place / Will not stay still."

If we cannot talk about political movements clearly, if we cannot define what is fascist, populist, woke, left, or right without finding all the co-ordinates and goalposts have moved the next day, why even try at all? If what promises to be liberating turns into something terrifying, why fight for a better world, for economic or social justice, or even try to imagine something better?

The Werewolf

A few years ago, I found myself flipping through the pages of a very surprising book. It was a grimoire, a collection of spells and incantations, entitled *The Magic Secrets of Guidon*. Published in 1670 as an appendix to *The Grimoire of Pope Honorius*, the short text recounts various folk magic practices of Norman shepherds against all manners of ills and evils.

It's a rarely cited fact that, while the vast majority of those accused of witchcraft in Europe and Britain were women, the opposite was the case in Normandy.[158] Shepherds were often suspect, especially because their work meant they were often in the wilderness (and thus less civilized). They also had created a parallel male society with other shepherds in the same way that bandits, rogues, pirates, and other outsider groups developed.[159]

Somewhat rare for grimoires of the time, the spells in *The Magic Secrets of Guidon* are for practical matters rather than for binding demons for power and wealth. Quite a few spells are for protecting sheep and horses, or for healing ones that are sick; another protects small garden plots from rabbits. A few are directed at other people, mostly to turn away bandits and thieves or to counteract the spells of rivals. In addition, several spells are to deal with personal health problems, including bleeding, hemorrhoids, and other illnesses.

A particular health problem merits two spells: that of "mange," or scabies, a contagious affliction transmitted by touch. In the second of these two spells, we find the following peculiar curse aimed at the cause of the skin condition:

May the werewolf farrier's dick rot, because he fucked me.[160]

---

158 See Monter, 1997.

159 Such male-only societies were often accurately accused of being full of homosexuals. See Turley, 1999. Also, for background on the anarchic tendencies of such men, see Hobsbawm, 1969.

160 The original Norman French is "*Lupin ferrant à filli le grand, car il m'a fait cha*," which one translator notes means literally, "The werewolf farrier will fail to get big, because he made me a cunt."

A farrier is a blacksmith who focuses on shoeing horses, and the implication of the curse is that the farrier passed scabies along to the shepherd and to his animals after sexual relations. While this alone could merit an entire discussion of late-medieval sodomy and folk magic beliefs, most relevant here is the accusation that the farrier is also a werewolf. While less common than those regarding witchcraft, accusations that a person was a werewolf often resulted in public trials. The most prominent of these occurred in Switzerland in the early fifteenth century, alongside a significant wave of witch trials which soon spread throughout Europe. Famous accusations (such as that made against Peter Stumpp) were printed as pamphlets and distributed widely throughout Europe.

The Werewolf is much, much older than these trials. Like the Vampire, the Werewolf is also a widely known monster. The ability to change from human into an animal (or the other way around) is a core feature of many shamanic and animist traditions, and stories of humans turned into animals by the gods as punishment for some offense — or even as divine favor against an attacker — abound in animist and pagan lore throughout the world, especially in European beliefs.

The ability to shapeshift into animals was a common accusation against witches in the medieval and pre-capitalist period of Europe: indictments against people accused of being werewolves often occurred alongside the witch hunts, though — as with Norman shepherds — suspected werewolves were rarely women and most often men. Unlike the Vampire or the Zombie, though, the Werewolf is a living human. It is neither a ghost nor a revenant, nor does the Werewolf lack a wandering soul or animating spirit. Instead, like the Cyborg, the Werewolf is fully human, fully alive, but also a hybrid being as well.

Accusations of werewolfery often followed a similar pattern to those of witchcraft, except for one significant difference. Witches supposedly knew they were witches, were accused of actively seeking relations with the Devil or demons and of actively performing *malefica* (curses), and were otherwise accused of choosing to be witches. Those who accused others of being werewolves, on the other hand, assumed their target didn't even realize what they were.

The Threat of the Wolf

The vast majority of recorded accounts we have about the Werewolf are from France, but the word we use for it in English is specifically Germanic. In fact, the French word for them, *loup-garou*, is derivative of the word the Germanic Frankish peoples used for it, "*werawulf*", which means "man wolf."[161] For ancient Germanic peoples, the Werewolf was both a mythic creature and also an exile or outcast marked for death and reliant only upon the gods for protection.

To understand how these two ideas were related, we need first to contemplate actual wolves and their relationship to settled society, or "civilization." In Europe particularly, wolves were the primary threat to the keeping of cattle, sheep, and other animals for meat, milk, and wool. A wolf could quickly destroy a family's personal herd (usually just a handful of animals) before the humans could even intervene. Such a loss meant not just the loss of a few animals but also loss of wealth and even life due to starvation.

---

161 Werawulf became *garulphus* in Latin and then *garou* in French. Thus, the French term for the Werewolf, *loup-garou*, actually means "wolf-manwolf."

Without attacking a single person, a small group of wolves could cause the death of an entire village by killing off their livestock. As such, in many places wolves took on a symbolic sense of destruction, famine, and also of an unstoppable natural or external threat to society. They also were sometimes seen as a form of punishment sent by displeased gods or ancestors, or as a herald of a change in rulership, since leaders and kings who couldn't protect their people from such threats were soon replaced.

Wolves themselves became part of the rituals of punishment within society, including in one of the oldest recorded prescriptions for ritual capital punishment, the "*poena cullei*." In that ritual, the condemned first had his head covered with a wolf skin before he was put into a sack with other animals and thrown from a cliff or drowned in a river. In his excellent book *Homo Sacer: Sovereign Power and Bare Life*, Giorgio Agamben details how the connection between punishment for severe, unpardonable crimes and wolf-men extended from both ancient German and Roman law into the medieval period of Europe. Men who were exiled as murderers or bandits were defined as werewolves or "wolf heads" even in English law:

The laws of Edward the Confessor (1030–35) define the bandit as a *wulfesheud* (a wolf's head) and assimilate him to the werewolf (*lupinum enim gerit caput a die utlagationis suae, quod ab anglis wulfesheud vacatur*, "He bears a wolf's head from the day of his expulsion, and the English call this *wulfesheud*"). What had to remain in the collective unconscious as a monstrous hybrid of human and animal, divided between the forest and the city — the werewolf — is, therefore, in its origin the figure of the man who has been banned from the city. That such a man is defined as a wolf-man and not simply as a wolf (the expression *caput lupinum* has the form of a juridical statute) is decisive here.

The life of the bandit, like that of the sacred man, is not a piece of animal nature without any relation to law and the city. It is, rather, a threshold of indistinction and of passage between animal and man, *physis* and *nomos*, exclusion and inclusion: the life of the bandit is the life of the *loup garou*, the werewolf, who is precisely neither man nor beast, and who dwells paradoxically within both while belonging to neither. [162]

Perhaps you noticed something in Agamben's final sentence. He calls the Werewolf "a threshold of indistinction and of passage between animal and man," adding that it is "precisely neither man nor beast" and "dwells paradoxically within both while belonging to neither." That is, the Werewolf is the shadow of the Cyborg, or rather they are inverse twins of each other. The Cyborg is part human, part machine, a hybrid being with one foot in the human world and one foot in our technological dreaming. The Werewolf, on the other hand, is part animal, part human. Each are both and neither, both part human but not fully human, part animal or machine but not fully those things, either.

This leads to several immediate conclusions. First of all, the Cyborg is not the first monster to have arisen into our consciousness when our definitions of what it means to be human have become unclear. The Werewolf is a much older monster who arose from the very same sort of problem concerning the complications of understanding how we are different from the rest of the world and from what we create.

Secondly, both the Cyborg and the Werewolf relate to political questions. The Cyborg appeared just at the point when capitalist societies began trying to overcome naturalistic ideas of what life is and what humans are

---

162 See Agamben.

capable of doing. Technologies that allowed for the extending of life, the replacing of human organs and functions with machines, and even the surgical changing of genitals to switch people's gender and sex created not only theological and philosophical questions but political ones also. If "natural" laws or limits could be transcended and even shown not to exist at all, then the very basis of "natural" rights and protections, as well as of questions of race and identity, seemed to fall away underneath us.

What's Beyond the Pale?

The Werewolf appeared in similar times to that of the Cyborg, and because of similar questions, but rather than technology being the trigger for these crises, it was civilization itself. "Civilization" and "politics" are both words that derive from ancient words for city: "*civitas*" (Roman) and "*polis*" (Greek). "*Civitas*" forms the root of the words "civil" and "civilian," while the words "polite" and "police" both come from "*polis*."

To be "civil" and "polite" both originally implied acting correctly according to urban or societal norms. Those who were neither civil nor polite, who failed to act civilized or according to the political norms of society, were often thought of as being too natural, too rural, and too much like animals. They were in essence barbarians or outlaws, people outside the reach of urban law and power. Such people inspired the word "pagan," originally a Roman slur for uncivilized people who lived past certain boundary markers ("*pagus*") between the city and rural land. They were also the "heathens," the Germanic word for those who lived on the rural heaths and which was later used by Christians to denote non-Christians. The English phrase "beyond the pale" was also likely derived from a similar idea: those in Ireland who lived past certain border poles ("pales"), outside the reach of English law, were considered savages, primitives, and dangerous people.

It's hard not to notice that the very same places which inspired the words "pagan" and "heathen" and the phrase "beyond the pale" were also places where wolves would have been common. Wolves tend to avoid extensively settled areas, hunting instead in wilder, more sparsely populated areas. Such places were also where political exiles, bandits, and other societal outcasts lived, since it was only in places far from settlements that they were not in danger of execution by civil authorities.

So, while the Cyborg is the monster of hybridity between human and technology, the Werewolf was the hybrid of human society and the wild. Instead of presenting a technological challenge to human society, the Werewolf was nature's challenge to it, a threat to the stability and order of settled, political life. Exiled from society yet still human, it lived just outside the reach and grasp of social understanding and governmental power. Equally human and animal but not fully either, it showed that all our political understanding, our civilizational reach, and our urban politeness and civility could not overcome some ineffable part of us that makes us wild, savage, animalistic, and ultimately ungovernable.

It's no wonder, then, that the Werewolf has stood also as a symbol for outlaws and rural resistance to political power many times throughout recent history. Here, the shadow of fascism looms particularly heavy, especially that of the Nazis. Reintroduced to German consciousness by a 1910 novel about a peasant revolt against imperial armies called *Der Wehrwolf*, the Nazis adopted an icon that had been a popular symbol of resistance during German peasant revolts in the sixteenth century. That symbol, the *wolfsangel*, was based off a barbed hook (called by the same name) that was used to trap wolves.

Inspired by the fictional account of those actually occurring revolts in *Der Wehrwolf*, the Nazis adopted the symbol as part of their regalia and even named one of their military operations Wehrwolf, after the book. Both the Werewolf and the *wolfsangel* appeared again quite recently, this time in far-right movements in the United States (Operation Werewolf and the Wolves of Vinland). The fascist-aligned Azov battalion in Ukraine also uses the *wolfsangel* on their uniforms and official military logo.

So, the *wolfsangel* has appeared both as part of lower-class resistance to empire and also as associated with anti-liberal war machines and fascist paramilitary groups. So, too, has the Werewolf, being both a symbol and an actual name for those who resist political control and choose to operate outside the law, as well as for those who wish to enforce their own power over others.

What should we make of this? What is the Werewolf trying to tell us?

One crucial reality is that resistance to totalizing political control can appear in multiple forms outside our "civilized" understanding of "left" and "right" co-ordinates. This resistance is then often subsumed into larger political formations, which use it for their own ends and then later reject it. In particular, we can see this in the way resistance to globalized capitalism was taken up early by the established left and then later completely abandoned by them. This is how "anti-globalization" became "anti-globalism": because the left abandoned opposition to neoliberal capitalism in favor of anti-oppression and social justice identity politics, the right took up the banner the left dropped.

As the Cyborg warns us of the problem of integrating technology into human existence without also losing our humanity, the Werewolf warns us that the animal, untamed, wild parts of humanity cannot ever fully be integrated into civilization or political regimes. In other words, no universal social norms or cultural revolution can ever accommodate — let alone conquer — every mode of being.

Considering the Werewolf's appearance both in peasant resistance to authoritarian rule in Europe as well as in authoritarian rule itself, it seems to have arrived at moments when some great political, social, and economic transformation was attempting to fully capture what Giorgio Agamben referred to as "bare life." Bare life is also natural or animal life, comprising our everyday existence as humans outside of political orders and abstracted from civilizational concerns. It's the "reality" of being human rather than the "reality" of being a political or economic subject; the human part of the Cyborg, or the animal part of the Werewolf.

Bare life cannot be fully integrated into political life, into law, or into societal norms. It's the private part of the individual, as opposed to the public existence determined by political categories. Bare life is who we are outside of identities, categories, and other social fictions. Put another way, it's the body-soul, rather than the wandering soul, the part that becomes a Zombie when its other soul is trapped by sorcery or trauma. As Agamben concludes:

> Today a law that seeks to transform itself wholly into life is more and more confronted with a life that has been deadened and mortified into juridical rule. Every attempt to rethink the political space of the West must begin with the clear awareness that we no longer know anything of the classical distinction between *zoē* and *bios*, between private life and political existence, between man as a simple living being at home in the house and man's political existence in the city.[163]

---

163 Ibid.

Must Everything Be Political?

Agamben's observations about the political having captured all of life seem to give a shadow meaning to the feminist slogan "The personal is political," pointing to a general tendency we see in radical thought (particularly online) to define every identity as a matter of politics.

One incident from a few years ago in the United States will illustrate what I mean. For a little while, the very expensive grocery store Whole Foods sold pre-peeled oranges in plastic containers. When news of this product became widespread, there was a maddening debate about it: on one side were those who saw it as ridiculous and hyper-capitalist; on the other side were those who insisted that critics of the pre-peeled oranges were ableist. The latter group asserted that since a disabled person who might not be able to peel an orange on their own would benefit from the product Whole Foods was selling, those who thought it was wasteful were against disabled people.

The curious fact that an orange could become a terrain of political struggle and conflict demonstrates what Agamben meant. In a way, we might say that the political has colonized every part of our life: our thoughts, our belief systems, our perceptions, and even what we eat. It is as if there is no "outside" any longer, no realm beyond the reach of the *polis* where wolves roam and political ideas have no power.

Regardless, there is still the Werewolf, with a foot outside the political realm and in the realm of nature. Of course, those who stand in both realms seem to us as monstrous, terrifying horrors that threaten the stability of everyday life, which is why we exile them and their ideas from our consciousness.

Actually existing fascists aren't werewolves, regardless of how much they might like to style themselves as such. On the contrary, they are just as civilized and part of the *polis* as the rest of us. The core aspect of historical fascism — which we forget at our peril — was that it was a political machine, a product of mass production and the production of masses. Its aim was to seize and transform society in order to "save" it from foreign and domestic threats. If anything, the fascist has much more in common with the hunters of the Werewolf and the judges presiding over those trials than with those living outside civilization's grasp.

They also have much more in common with the bourgeoisie as Marx and Engels described them. The bourgeoisie act as a transformative force in society, shaping morality, values, and our relationship to ourselves and each other according to their values. The fascist projects did the same thing, with terrifying results.

Such a fact should give us deep pause when we consider radical projects of cultural and societal transformation as well. Of course, "we" are not the same as those "others," yet it's quite easy to understand that those who stand outside our often very small radical groups and spaces might not feel the same way we do. Attempts to transform an entire society are totalizing political projects. While they may not start out as totalitarian, eventually those they exile and banish will become werewolves, threats that "must be dealt with" to maintain the political order.

Carl Jung proposed that what we exclude or fail to integrate comes back to haunt us as our shadow. No political order can ever be truly total or universal, and will always banish or exile certain humans and their ways of being and thinking in order to maintain its sense of totality. What is excluded, like the exiled men who became bandits or those with "wolf heads," then returns like the shadow to threaten the social order.

When we label those who do not fully accept, agree with, or even see the point in our radical ideas as "fascist," we hang a wolf's head upon them. Thus, we should not be surprised that we see threats everywhere, "fascists" lurking just past the boundary markers of "us" and "them." We may even sometimes be creating the monsters we claim to fight.

Werewolves themselves were not always seen as aberrant threats or secret murderers: for some peoples, the Werewolf was a divine protector of other animals and even of humans. In 1692 in what is now Estonia, for example, a man named Thiess of Kaltenbrun confessed to being a Werewolf. He explained that he and others fought demons on behalf of humans. Rather than being executed, he was instead merely flogged and then banished for admitting also to performing magic spells without calling on the Christian God for their power.

Further back, and even up to the present elsewhere, these hybrids have been revered as shamans and mystics and occupied other roles as sacred leaders. The wolf itself, we must remember, is one of many animals which shamans might entreat, learn from, and even become. How better to learn about our own wild nature than from beings which represent to us — accurately or not — the potential collapse of all our human efforts to tame and wall out nature?

Put another way, the Werewolf is a kind of antidote to the hubris we humans so relentlessly exhibit, to all the beliefs that we can conquer the rest of the natural world, and also the nature that composes us. All the grand utopian dreams of remaking human society into something that stands outside the larger reality — that we are also animal and nature — fall apart under the Werewolf's feral gaze. No matter how hard we might try to render extinct the wolf, and in many places we've almost succeeded, we cannot banish from ourselves the material reality of what we are. We can only accommodate it, make space for it, plan around it, and include it our reckonings.

The "Real State of Emergency"

What this means practically for the question of fascism is made clear by one of Giorgio Agamben's strongest influences, Walter Benjamin. In Benjamin's eighth thesis in his *On the Concept of History*, he suggests that our delusional beliefs about "progress" are what prevent us from understanding why such movements happen at all:

> The tradition of the oppressed teaches us that the "emergency situation" in which we live is the rule. We must arrive at a concept of history which corresponds to this. Then it will become clear that the task before us is the introduction of a real state of emergency; and our position in the struggle against Fascism will thereby improve. Not the least reason that the latter has a chance is that its opponents, in the name of progress, greet it as a historical norm. The astonishment that the things we are experiencing in the 20th century are "still" possible is by no means philosophical. It is not the beginning of knowledge, unless it would be the knowledge that the conception of history on which it rests is untenable.[164]

We see this same problem now in the panicked denunciations of populist movements by theorists and politicians. The condescending blindness of Hillary Clinton and the Democratic National Convention regarding the really existing concerns fueling Donald Trump's ascendency are

---

164 See Benjamin, 1940.

one such example. By dismissing everyone who didn't fully buy into her political program (more globalized capitalism in exchange for identity recognition) as "deplorable," she all but ensured their disparate concerns would coalesce into a singular movement to defeat her. Judith Butler's assertion that there is a global fascist movement against gender is yet another example, as are the re-narrations of any criticism of racialized politics as "class reductionism" at best, and more often as "white supremacy."

States of emergency — or states of exception — are a core tool of capitalist governments anytime they are under threat or when they seek to accumulate more political power over the people. In such moments, a crisis is named which then serves as justification for the suspension of specific explicit or implicit rights. In the United States, the attacks on the World Trade Center towers in New York City in 2001, for example, resulted in one such moment. The quick rush to implement a new regime of surveillance, the founding of new policing agencies with previously unheard-of authority (the Department of Homeland Security, Immigrations and Customs Enforcement, for example), the introduction of new restrictions on the freedom of movement ("no-fly" lists, intrusive security checks in airports), and the imposition of extrajudicial punishment and imprisonment (CIA black sites, coercive torture methods such as waterboarding, the suspension of *habeus corpus* for those identified as "terrorists," and so forth) all happened quite suddenly. Two decades later, few of these "emergency" measures have been relinquished by the government, and many of them have been expanded.

The same expansion of the political reach of governments has occurred throughout the United Kingdom, Europe, Canada, Australia, and to some extent the rest of the world as well. Power accumulated over the bare life of the people becomes normalized. Even those who noticed these changes come to accept them, or they forget there was ever a time we experienced less political control over our daily lives.

Initial resistance to these emergencies is often quite broad, and frequently what we might call "populist" or pre-political, but is later captured by political formations. One place we can see this quite clearly is in the recent accumulation of state power in response to the emergency of COVID-19. Early on, protests against government restrictions on movement, curfews, lockdowns, and vaccine mandates were quite widespread, and they were not immediately aligned with "left" or "right" political ideologies. However, quite soon this populist resistance was re-narrated as a right or extreme-right reactionary movement.

Without getting too deep into the controversy, we should examine at least a few of the larger principles at play in opposition to these government policies and how leftists ceded these struggles to rightist formations. Firstly, as Silvia Federici noted in her essay "In Praise of the Dancing Body," the state has always tried to accumulate power over human bodies through restrictions on movement:

> Fixation in space and time has been one of the most elementary and persistent techniques capitalism has used to take hold of the body. See the attacks throughout history on vagabonds, migrants, hobo-men. Mobility is a threat when not pursued for work-sake as it circulates knowledges, experiences, struggles. In the past the instruments of restraint were whips, chains, the stocks, mutilation, enslavement. Today, in addition to the whip and the detention centers, we have computer surveillance

and the periodic threat of epidemics as a means to control nomadism.[165]

Thus, we might have expected that the curfews and lockdowns would have been a target for leftist mobilization against the state. Instead, in the United States especially, but also in the United Kingdom and Europe, leftist journals and Antifa websites described those who opposed the lockdowns and mandatory vaccinations as reactionary, murderous, and most of all "fascist." In places where large manifestations of resistance did occur, as in Germany, the political alignments of the participants were in reality quite mixed. Both far-right and far-left activists and political figures supported them and were present. This then led to panicked news articles and analyses suggesting they were signs of a "red-brown" insurgency.

There's another way to see these moments, however. The resistance to these new state powers was based in a pre-political or anti-political desire to maintain the borders between bare life and the power of the state and capital over the lives of people. The *gilets jaunes* movement in France was another such moment, bringing people from otherwise conflicting political alignments together in resistance to increased government control over human mobility and labor. The quintessential example of this kind of resistance, however, was the anti-globalization or altermondialist manifestations, events which brought out the most dazzling array of different and otherwise opposing interests.

Unfortunately, leftists later came to divorce themselves from — and even actively denounce — these mass mobilizations. The desires that fueled those movements didn't disappear just because leftists decided they no

---

165 See Federici, 2016.

longer mattered: instead, that populist anger was captured by far-right and right tendencies. In other words, leftists ceded the desire for freedom against — and resistance to — government control over bare life to the right.

I must be direct here. We often create the very conditions of the fascism we seek to stop by "hanging a wolf's head" on anything that doesn't fit into our narrow political visions. We exile and banish everything difficult to integrate or fight for, labeling struggles that do not look like our own as those of an enemy. Resistance to neoliberalism, for example, becomes immediately suspect; the understandable concerns of precarious workers or communities disrupted by policies like NAFTA get smeared as "reactionary" and "fascist" despite having at their core the very same anti-capitalist desire the left once held.

Benjamin's solution is that, instead of believing that society is one long death march of progress interrupted by "emergencies" which sidetrack us, we must understand that these moments are inevitable products of capitalist mass society itself. When people become part of a mass — meaning they becoming alienated individuals who lose their sense of attachment to place, to culture, to familial ties, and to everything except mass identity — they become easy political tools.

We have seen this problem in earlier periods, especially in the beginnings of the capitalist period. Those displaced by the Enclosures in England lost their attachments to their older identifications (land, place, family) and later became the "whites" of British colonies. Slaves ripped from their villages in Africa had their attachments cruelly severed, and they became the "blacks" of those same colonies. These historical forces didn't end: capitalism continues to accelerate societal, technological, and cultural disruptions.

Walter Benjamin asserts that capitalism continuously produces alienated masses, and then fascism organizes those masses, redirecting their desire for a change in property relations into a desire for "expression." Populist resistance to the state and the capitalists then becomes channeled instead into the service of mass identities.

This redirection is made much easier when the left cedes anti-capitalist, populist movements to others. By dismissing or even vilifying those who desire more bare life, we practically hand them over to totalitarian ideologies. Others — including fascists — can then redirect their desire for material change back into the capitalist state's emergency situation.

Against these emergency situations, Benjamin insists we must introduce a "real state of emergency." What does such a real state of emergency look like? To the dismay of capitalists, liberals, and conservatives alike, it looks like the people refusing to acknowledge the hegemonic control of the *polis* and of capitalist property relations over their private lives. It looks like people returning to the wild, to bare life, forging their own ways of relating to each other and themselves outside the political realm. It looks like economic exchange, social forms, cultural expression, and land relations that cannot be shaped, governed, captured, commodified, directed, or regulated by the political regime and the capitalist class.

Rather than being exiled or exiling others, a real state of emergency would involve us all exiling ourselves from the reach of the *polis*. In other words, it would mean our becoming the Werewolf rather than the obedient citizen-consumer-producers that we are. To introduce such a real state of emergency, to become faithful realists to the larger reality of the world outside capital, would require a collective, organized exit. Such a moment would require us to drop the mass-identities that turn us against each other, those that make us easy tools in the hands of the capitalist. This is why no one seems more eager than the capitalists to make sure we never do so.

CHAPTER ELEVEN: BECOMING REALISTS OF A LARGER REALITY

For years, even as I watched what I considered the left transform into something that made less and less sense, I was fully on the side of these cultural changes and shifts. I initially supported them, wrote quite a few essays advocating for many of these ideas, and engaged in many social media crusades to cancel and punish people who questioned the rightness of these moral precepts.

Over more recent years, I began to notice certain contradictions and unacknowledged ideological knots in what we were arguing for. We were on the side of "justice" and "liberation," yet it seemed our side had an awful habit of acting just as oppressive as those we claimed to be fighting. Increasingly, it became harder and harder for me to ignore what we were doing. I couldn't ignore the extremely abusive behavior of many Antifa activists towards anyone who questioned the clarity and righteousness of their judgments, or the online and in-person harassment by activists of anyone not fully convinced of the declarative gender framework. I stopped being able to justify the fact that the fight against racism increasingly relied on race-thinking and the reification of race, or the way many people employed identity politics and zombified concepts such as reparations and mutual aid just to extort money from people.

The left I knew had become something else entirely. It seemed almost as if we'd given up trying to build anything that could change material circumstances for people and instead had settled for symbolic struggles with no clear end goal. Rather than fighting against exploitation, we contented ourselves with warring against the "problematic" and "systems of oppression."

What was hardest to countenance for me was the way that I and others had fallen into a pattern of denialism. We had seen and engaged in the kinds of behaviors that I now critique. We had acted like bullies to others and to each other, constantly "cancelling" and "calling out" each other for the slightest misstep or supposedly oppressive or reactionary belief.

I and others had fallen into a kind of collective denial, almost a mass psychosis. We thought we were fighting for a better world, but we were only ever fighting each other. And most of all, it felt like we were engaging in hypocrisy, claiming to be one thing yet acting in ways that showed our reality to be something else entirely.

"Hypocrisy" is a useful word for what was happening. In modern English, it usually just means claiming to be something you are not or demanding people act one way despite personally acting another way. Its older meanings, derived from Greek, referred specifically to theatrics, to playing a role or acting a part in order to convince an audience.

Hypocrisy once specifically meant "to answer." In the context of Greek theater, the word was used to describe the act of answering another actor on stage. To understand how we got from this original meaning to the present one, imagine a stage play. Everyone is dressed up and ready to act out their roles, while an audience waits patiently for the drama to begin. Then, the first actor says something, calling out to another character with accusations or a question. Imagine, then, that none of the actors answer. The words of the first actor are left hanging in the air, suspended in a place in which the collective ritual of drama remains stillborn because there is no one to carry along the fiction.

The act of answering that first actor is what actually creates the play. The moment another actor responds, even if not directly to the first person, is the moment the drama is born, the words of one carried by another, and then another, becoming a conversation that the audience witnesses as a wholly other world.

This was the original meaning of "hypocrisy": the answering of an actor by another actor. It later came to mean pretense, pretending something was the case. The connotation of "make believe" that now defines the word "pretend" is a very new sense, one that didn't arise until the late 1800s. Before then, "to pretend" meant "to lay claim to" or "to make an argument for," as in "a pretender to the throne." That's where the idea of pretense as a falsehood comes from: a pretender (someone who made claims to a throne, for example) who did not succeed was then seen as a false pretender, and those two senses later collapsed into one.

It's worth looking also at a related word (and a direct synonym of the older meaning of "hypocrisy" in English): "answer." "Answer's" original meaning is similar to what "pretend" once meant, and comes from the older Germanic word "*swerian*", meaning to speak an oath (it's the root of the word "swear").

"Answer" originally had a sacred sense to it, and was what we might call a sacred kind of speech, having more weight than normal words. Ancient peoples saw certain kinds of speech as sacred, just as they saw certain types of acts as sacred. Greek drama wasn't just for amusement, it was a kind of religious ritual. The *hypocrisy* of one actor to another was crucial to the ritual itself: it was a sacred or magical act which created the drama. "Answer," to Germanic peoples, had the same religious dimension. It was a swearing, an oath, and thus needed to be true. Giving a false answer — a false oath — was a crime not just against people but against the entire (sacred) order of meaning itself.

All this has supposedly fallen away in our modern world, but it actually hasn't. Consider the way a child reacts the first time their mother or father says something and yet does the opposite, or how we as adults feel when a leader, a lover, or someone else we have come to trust acts in a way completely contrary to their statements. That moment is always jarring to us, because it represents a sudden disconnect between the world we thought we were in and the actual material reality of that world. Loss of trust in others, that sense of betrayal and of being lied to, will always feel, at best, disorienting. In more significant moments, it can lead us to question everything we thought we knew about a person or about ourselves, creating a "crisis of faith" or a complete shattering of our ideology or worldview.

The Other Emperor's New Clothes

We all probably know the folk story written by Hans Christian Andersen "The Emperor's New Clothes." In that tale, an emperor is convinced by swindlers to wear invisible clothing which they promise is magically stunning. The emperor thus parades around completely naked. All those who see the emperor play a part in the swindle, since, when he asks them what they think of his new clothing, they answer that they find he is wearing the finest clothing they have ever seen.

The tale has been used countless times to illustrate an enlightened stance against a collective delusion. Each of the people who pretends to see the invisible clothing is a hypocrite in the original Greek sense. The emperor is an actor calling out, and they answer him: without those answers, without their sacred participation in the drama, the swindlers would never have succeeded. They collectively pretend — lay claim — to a reality that is, of course, not real, yet it nevertheless has all the weight and power of truth as long as they all keep up the hypocrisy. But then, as the story goes, a child brings the whole order of meaning crashing down on itself by blurting out that the emperor is actually naked.

Hans Christen Andersen is thought to have based his version of the story on an older Spanish tale, which itself likely had older origins. That tale was found in a book called *Libro de los enxiemplos del Conde Lucanor et de Patronio*, a collection of moral stories first published in 1355. Many of these stories were retellings of the fables of Aesop, as well as of Arabic tales, and some are thought to have come from India.

In the Spanish telling of the story, the grift is quite similar except for one brilliant detail. The monarch is given "clothing" of incomparable beauty, but is warned that it will be invisible to anyone who is not actually the child of the man he believes is his father. So, while in Andersen's version of the story it is the emperor's own vanity and his subjects' sycophantic desire to please him that prevents everyone from admitting the truth, in the Spanish tale it is something much more powerful.

Even the monarch himself has doubts about the clothing, but he cannot admit this — to say the clothing was invisible to him would be to declare he is illegitimate. So, too, for all those around him, who of course notice immediately that the man is naked. To declare the truth would be to become a target of moral outrage and face exile from the social order. Saying you didn't see the clothing was "admitting" something deeply embarrassing and destructive about yourself.

This older version is deeply relevant to our situation now. In Andersen's retelling, everyone keeps up the hypocrisy out of fear of offending the vanity of a powerful figure; in the Spanish version, anyone who violates the newly created truth risks becoming illegitimate, rootless, and ultimately nameless. To not pretend would make them a false pretender to their father's name and thus a nobody, invisible just like the clothing they claim not to see.

I can think of no better metaphor for the hypocrisy I once participated in. Admitting there was a problem with our ideas about liberation, that many of the things we thought would make the world better were actually causing more problems, would lead me to lose credibility and position in radical groups, and would even open me up to accusations of being oppressive, racist, transphobic, misogynist, or the worst thing of all, fascist.

In the Spanish account of the tale of magical clothing, what traps each person in the hypocrisy is fear about their own truth and their own place in the world. To say, "Hey, this isn't true" is to step out of a collective order of meaning which previously affirmed your own truth as well. It would be to exile yourself, to declare yourself a heretic or an apostate. This is because what is really playing out is a struggle between your own will and the sustaining hypocrisies of others, who themselves fear the repercussions of giving up the act.

Against False Choices

That's how I finally escaped all this. There finally came a moment when I realized I was playing a part I didn't want to play, answering to and for an ideology that cultivated not personal and collective power but narcissism and *ressentiment*. I had been afraid of admitting there was nothing actually there, that we were all just role-playing revolution rather than ever confronting the real of the world beyond our make-believe.

Eventually, I'd had enough. I stopped being a hypocrite, stopped re-affirming the fantasies others demanded I help them sustain. In the end it took only an act of will, a refusal to play along. "This isn't true" was one of the hardest things I ever had to say, and yet it made living an authentic and fulfilling life — and no longer needing others for legitimacy — a much easier path. It also made being a leftist a tenable position for me again, saving me from having to reject leftism wholesale because of its current conflation with social justice identity politics.

In our current situation, it's very difficult to critique any of the problems with identity politics without immediately being smeared as a racist or worse. That's not just because radical movements lack the self-reflective habits we saw in Adorno's letters to Marcuse, but also because criticizing the "woke" has become an easy way for right-aligned politicians, activists, and media figures to gain attention and to stoke outrage.

This is happening not just within the United States but increasingly elsewhere as well. For instance, in the 2022 presidential elections in France, the self-described reactionary politician Éric Zemmour made his opposition to "le wokisme" a core issue of his campaign. According to Zemmour, "woke culture" has become a successor ideology to Marxism and before that socialism, both of which were themselves successor ideologies to the true core of French democracy:

> During Balzac's time, one was liberal, patriotic, and socialist. Now one is anti-racist, feminist, ecological. Woke culture has taken the place of Marxism, which succeeded socialism, which succeeded liberalism.[166]

---

166 Translation mine: "Au temps de Balzac, on était libéral, patriote, socialiste. Aujourd'hui on est antiraciste, féministe,

Zemmour managed to win only 7 percent in the initial round, and was greatly overshadowed by the showing of the other nationalist candidate, Marine Le Pen, with 23 percent. Though both presidential candidates criticized similar issues, Zemmour's focus on "*le wokisme*" was particularly obsessive and formed a significant part of his overall vision of a return to a Gaullist version of France.

Zemmour has not been the only European politician to position himself this way. In the United Kingdom, both primary contenders for the Conservative Party leadership in 2022, Rishi Sunak and Liz Truss, vowed to fight "woke nonsense" and "woke culture." Giorgia Meloni, the far-right politician and now Italian prime minister, made many speeches vowing to protect Italian families from that same threat. Right-wing politicians in Hungary, the Czech Republic, Poland, and Germany have all cited variations of a "woke virus" and even a "woke European Union" as the primary threats to the stability of their nations.

It's worth noting that beyond the rhetoric, right-wing politicians who criticize "woke" identity politics are often themselves just as guilty of employing identity towards political ends. They are just as identitarian as those they promise to stop, meaning that the choice for voters in many places comes down only to two forms of identitarianism, with no real alternative.

With so much right-aligned criticism of social justice identity politics, it was inevitable that criticism coming from other places would be conflated with the right. However, even though the right has gained control of the narrative, we shouldn't cede that territory to them. Rather than blaming leftists who point to these problems for

écologiste, la culture "woke" a pris la place du marxisme qui avait pris la place du socialiste qui avait pris la place du libéralisme." See Agence France-Presse, 2022.

"aiding the enemy" or accusing them of being the enemy themselves, we should understand that the silencing of leftist critiques and leftists' subsequent self-censoring is precisely why far-right political formations now dominate these discussions.

In a way, it's our fault. Because we stopped offering another analysis of these problems, the only option presented as an alternative to social justice identity politics has become nationalist identity politics. Just as a false framing is inherent to the dichotomy of racism/anti-racism or fascism/antifascism, we are stuck with a false choice between two forms of identitarianism.

The crucial work here is to reject the false choice entirely. In US elections, the two-party system is often described by its critics as offering only a choice between Coca-Cola and Pepsi, with no option available for those who'd prefer something besides carbonated sugar water. Similarly, the choice between social justice and nationalist ideologies is just between two brands of the same dead-end logic.

Identity Is How Capitalism Intends to Perpetuate Itself

A few have suggested we've reached some sort of pinnacle or "peak" of "woke" politics. Before even talking about this, we need to clear up what's even meant by "woke" and "wokeness." It's a slippery term, so slippery that I've become convinced it's no longer useful for describing anything.

Words lose their original contexts as part of a natural process of meaning-drift. Before the internet, it usually took decades for this to happen. Now, however, a word can take on completely different meanings in the space of only a few years. A very recent example of this is the verb "cringe," which is now more popularly used as an adjective ("That's so cringe").

"Woke" means everything and nothing at all, depending on who you speak to. Since the people "woke" refers to no longer use it to describe themselves (they once did, for a short period before Trump), there's a good argument to be made that it's a useless term. On the other hand, just as the word "queer" was once a slur (and for older gay and lesbians it still is) and then later became an ideological principle (and a verb, to whit: "We need to queer mathematics," a phrase I still don't understand), it's quite possible we'll see "woke" become the preferred label.

"Social justice identitarianism" and "social justice identity politics" are much more accurate labels. Plenty might argue with these terms too, especially the "identitarian" part because of its association with right-wing movements. But what else do you call a politics that attempts to organize groups around their racial, sexual, and other identities against groups with different identities except "identitarian?"

In any case, the more important part of these terms is the first part, "social justice." The various movements called "woke" differ from traditional leftist movements in their focus on the social rather than the economic: they call for us to change the way humans relate to each other to affect justice, rather than to change underlying material conditions and class relations. That is, they seek to fight racism, sexism, transphobia, able-ism, and all the other "systems of oppression" as a means of making capitalism a little nicer.

So, back to the question. Have we reached "peak woke"? That is, are we at a point when the apparent expansion of these ideologies will start to decline and then even reverse? I don't think so. I tend to agree more with the conservative writer John Gray that social justice identity politics is functioning as a "successor" ideology to neoconservativism, and with black Marxist Adolph Reed that it's the core moral constellation of neoliberalism. Though coming from apparently different political traditions, they — and quite a few others — are essentially arguing the same thing: identity is how capitalism intends to perpetuate itself.

This is really a change in cosmology. Identity relations are replacing class relations as the dominant field of political struggle, which means we're replacing functional and material relations with social characteristics. Formerly, it was the capitalists against the working class, and everyone knew that these were functional positions (one owned, the other labored) rather than eternal or inherent characteristics. There was nothing inherent or intrinsic about the capitalist herself which made her the enemy, it was what she did and how she colluded with others to make sure she could keep doing it. There was nothing inherent or intrinsic to the working class that made them good or evil, but rather only the functional relationship of being exploited for their labor and the material state of having no access to land or the means of production.

Within this newer cosmology, it's a person's being cis-, or heterosexual, or able-bodied, or male, or white that makes them oppressive. None of these are functional relationships; rather, they are identity markers that point to something "inherent" about the oppressor. The same is true for being black, or female, or trans, or disabled: they, too, are all identity markers pointing to an inherent trait rather than a functional relationship.

In other words, in the older cosmology a worker is *exploited* by a capitalist. In this successor cosmology, the black disabled trans woman is *oppressed* by the white, cis, heterosexual, able-bodied man. Before, it was because of *what a person did* that injustice arose. Now, it is because of *who a person is*.

This cosmology suits capitalism quite well, because it does not challenge the exploitation of workers by the owning class. In fact, a capitalist can even claim to be oppressed and victimized by the people she exploits if she has more oppressed identity markers (by virtue of being black, trans, disabled, and so forth) than the people whose labor increases her wealth.

It's really an ideal situation for the capitalists. That's why so many corporations, banks, and neoliberal politicians have readily adopted the language of identity, as well as the aesthetic of diversity and equity in their hiring practices, management styles, and political platforms. They have every reason to be happy with this cosmological shift, since they still get to keep property relations intact as long as they offer more expression to identity concerns.

There seems to be a sudden awareness of this trajectory among many on the left. Especially as the US government and corporations have started to adopt identity discourse more openly, identity politics seems increasingly stripped of any anti-state and anti-capitalist pretensions.

Recognition that something is shifting has led to attempts to reinforce the focus on identity and to present government and capitalist adoption of identity discourse as "recuperation" or "elite capture." The theory here is that the capitalist class is adopting social justice identitarianism as a way to make its ideas impotent, to neuter its revolutionary core. We've already looked at one such attempt to salvage social justice identitarianism, Olúfẹ́mi O. Táíwò's argument in the aforementioned *Elite Capture: How the Powerful Took Over Identity Politics (and Everything Else)*. While the "real" problem for Táíwò is white "racial capitalism," elites within the oppressed groups tend to stifle actual resistance to it because they fail to include less-elite people in the conversation (or "room," as he repeatedly calls it). Black, trans, and other oppressed groups could have not only social but also economic justice if only the elites let some of the poorer members of those groups speak. In the end, Táíwò insists identity politics can eventually end capitalism, provided the elites (including, he admits, himself) start acting like a more inclusive vanguard rather than just soaking up all the attention for themselves.

There have been other attempts to argue more intensely that identity politics is the only way forward, such as in another title from the same publisher: *Fractured: Race, Class, Gender and the Hatred of Identity Politics* by Michael Richmond and Alex Charnley. Their argument is really an expansion of Táíwò's, with the added feature that they define all leftist critiques of identity as a "conservative pivot." In particular, the authors are obsessively critical of Adolph Reed and the editorial direction of the leftist journal *Jacobin* for their acceptance that there might be such a thing as neoliberalism. For them, any leftist who even accents the "wrong" syllable of Antifa (pronouncing it "Anteefa") has been manipulated by white supremacists.

The core of their political program sounds as un-actionable as Táíwò's conclusion, except with some extra family abolition and misunderstood Walter Benjamin added for flavor:

> The measure of a new society will depend on challenging racial and gendered divisions of labour, but also a working-class "community" model that does not depend on the family for social reproduction, and state policing to secure it. These are key sites of struggle, for communities of care and for the means of reproduction in a social context of widespread and differentiated crises of precarity and social isolation punctuated by bursts of "Revolutionary Time."[167]

---

167 See Richmond, M., & Charnley, A., 2022

Both books betray some degree of recognition that identity politics is becoming less and less tenable because of its adoption by the state and capitalists. While *Fractured* makes scant mention of this, the authors' focus on earlier race-based struggles reveals an attempt to wrest identity politics back from the neoliberals they claim do not actually exist. *Elite Capture*, on the other hand, more honestly admits the current state (and statist uses) of identity politics, while still insisting the problem isn't capitalism, it's "racial capitalism."

There are worried defenses of identity appearing elsewhere, of course. The intense and panicked attempts to narrate all criticism of gender as fascist (as Judith Butler did in the *Guardian*) points to a growing recognition of a natural limit to its ideological spread. The unacknowledged problem there, however, is that without state power and mass re-education (through media propaganda and schooling), it would be impossible to convince the entire world that there is no material aspect to sexual difference. This is how fears of Cultural Marxism and opposition to neoliberal policies have increasingly merged: state power is increasingly invoked as a tool with which to increase acceptance of new gender and racial frameworks.

This is a crucial problem that the left ignores at its peril. Consider the situation I cited in the discussion about race: that of the guaranteed basic income program for BIPOC families in Oakland. Such state programs, meant to rectify racial inequality, certainly seem beneficial on paper, but they also have the effect of increasing racial and other identity-based resentment. Explaining to poor white people that they cannot qualify for such assistance because of systematic racism isn't an easy sell. It should surprise none of us that right-wing identitarians might then be able to manipulate such situations to increase racial animosity.

The problem continues, however. Consider what happens when there is popular outrage against state programs such as this. Politicians and theorists can then cite this outrage as proof there is a rising tide of reactionary populism against anti-racist policies. Through such narrations, the conflict is presented as being only about race, rather than as a complex reaction to an economic program favoring one group or another. When social justice activists and others then come to the defense of the state, they appear unsympathetic to the plight of those barred from such programs and also lend more legitimacy to the state itself.

This mechanism has been repeating itself relentlessly over the last two decades. In Europe, the mass anger over austerity measures and carbon reductions which target certain workers but not others (like the one which sparked the *gilets jaunes* movement) has been re-narrated as reactionary or racist anger. Brexit (the exit of the United Kingdom from the European Union) is yet another example: the anger over European Union policies which favored certain groups over others was re-narrated as reactionary racism and xenophobia (despite there also being leftist support for Brexit). In this case, the neoliberal European Union came to be seen as the defender of social justice, and all those who thought otherwise were therefore enemies of oppressed minorities.

This mechanism is how identity politics and neoliberalism have now fully fused in the minds of many, if they were ever truly separate. The problem everywhere becomes racism and anti-genderism, not capitalism, meaning that the solution everywhere becomes identity politics, not anti-capitalist revolt. In this new cosmology, the core theorists of identity politics have become like the early church fathers or the Reformation figures, providing the sacred cosmology for capitalism's continuation.

Expression? Or Revolution?

Identity has become the primary framework both for neoliberalism and also for right-wing opposition to neoliberalism. Walter Benjamin's critique of fascism as aestheticization is especially helpful for understanding how this has happened. Recall again his observation in *The Work of Art in the Age of Mechanical Reproduction*:

> The increasing proletarianization of modern man and the increasing formation of masses are two sides of the same process. Fascism attempts to organize the newly proletarianized masses while leaving intact the property relations which they strive to abolish. It sees its salvation in granting expression to the masses — but on no account granting them rights. The masses have a right to changed property relations, fascism seeks to give them expression in keeping these relations unchanged. The logical outcome of fascism is an aesthetizing of political life.

Taking Benjamin's point seriously, we can begin to suspect that identitarianism itself is a mass politics of expression. We see this quite easily in nationalist, fundamentalist, and fascist identitarianisms, each of which predicates their political program upon identity. Islamic extremism as manifested in the last few decades, for example, frames political struggle along the lines of Islamic identity against all those who would seek to annihilate its beliefs and religious expressions (US imperialists, Israel, European secularism, and so on). European identitarian and nationalist movements use the same mechanism, framing Europeans (or the French, or the English) as the oppressed identity group being invaded, colonized, or made extinct by foreign peoples and their religious and cultural forms.

Regardless of its different goals, however, social justice identity politics uses the very same mechanism and framing: all the various marginalized people, with their countless and ever-expanding intersecting identities, struggling against a hegemonic and existential threat. Micro- and macro-aggressions are everywhere, oppression constantly enacted, and privilege relentlessly manifested by a dominant majority.

Of course, the apparent goals of social justice and nationalist identitarianisms are different, and if we were forced to choose between societies dominated by one or the other, the choice would be a very simple one. However, it's a false choice, since neither of them offers the masses what Benjamin called "a right to changed property relations." Instead, they only offer expression of that desire, and channel the desire itself back into sustaining the capitalist system.

The role of state power and the capture of institutions are inherent features of identitarian movements of all types. European identity movements ultimately strive to control the state, since this is the only way their visions can be achieved. The ultimate goal of Islamic extremists is the transformation of existing states or their full replacement with an Islamic state or caliphate. As their name suggests, white nationalists in the United States, Canada, and Australia all argue for the creation of a "white nation" in which only white people can wield political power. Social justice identity politics is predicated upon the same seizure of power, wresting control of the government, the courts, the presidency, and all other political institutions from the white cis-heteropatriarchy and placing them all firmly in the hands of the marginalized and oppressed.

Benjamin's point — that the expression offered to the masses by fascism is a way of keeping property relations unchanged — is part of a larger analysis of fascism as an emergency switch for the capitalist class in the face of mass revolt. That is, rather than being a third option between capitalism and communism, fascism is a last-ditch effort by the capitalists to hold on to power.

The actually existing fascist regimes in Germany, Italy, and Spain during the last century offer evidence that Benjamin's analysis is correct. Consider Benjamin's own experience with the situation in Germany during the Weimar Republic, and especially with runaway inflation and economic turmoil leading to mass social unrest. Communism during that time presented a very significant threat to the ruling capitalist class because of its potential to channel and organize the anger and disaffection of the working classes towards revolution.

The Nazi Party, however, offered something completely different. Capitalist social relations would stay intact, but identity would determine who was allowed to accumulate capital and who could engage in capitalist and labor exchanges. One very small part of the capitalist class (the small number of Jewish capitalists) would have their capital seized, and one small part of the working class (Jewish workers) would be prevented from selling their labor to the capitalists. The remainder, the "true" Aryan race of Germans, would then get to fully express themselves and their racial potential.

For the German capitalists, fascist identitarianism offered a way of maintaining property relations unchanged, albeit with a different aesthetic (one which resulted in the horrors of the concentration camps and the Holocaust). Offering expression by changing the identity composition of the capitalist and the working class succeeded in staving off anti-capitalist revolution and keeping capitalism intact.

Social justice identity politics isn't fascism, but it offers a similar bargain to the capitalists. At the expense of changing the composition of the capitalist class (fewer white and male capitalists, more black trans women and disabled, non-binary capitalists of color), capitalism can remain intact and unchallenged. It's the proposition that Benjamin noted fascism offers the masses: expression rather than any meaningful change in property relations. Greater representation of identity concerns in government and more individuals from oppressed identity groups being represented in the capitalist class may look like change, but it will have no real effect on property relations within capitalism.

Consider again the legacy of Barack Obama, the first black (or mixed-race) president of the United States. Obama's presidency offered a symbolic win for racial justice without ever resulting in significant changes affecting the lives of black people. In other words, Obama was "mere expression," rather than representing any change in property, class, or racial relations. In fact, the mass expressions of anger regarding police killings of black individuals, the Black Lives Matter protests, first began during the final years of his presidency. During his eight years as president, no significant change occurred in the rate of killings of black people by police, and that same rate continued throughout Donald Trump's presidency as well. All that was offered to the black masses in the form of a black president was a sense of representation, the feeling of having someone with the same skin color in power.

In order to affect significant political change, identitarianism — in whatever its form — requires that identity category be the primary ground of identification. A black president would need to identify more with being black than with all his other concerns (including material concerns) and see black people or blackness as the sole ground of political struggle. The same is true for a Muslim, Catholic, trans, or disabled political figure: they must care more for their identity and those who share it than for all other concerns.

Likewise, the masses themselves would need to jettison all other concerns and all other identities except those which give them an esoteric sense of community with an identity group. Black people would need to see "black" as a coherent political category and care more about blackness — just as trans people would need to identify more with their transness — than about anything else they are. A black factory worker would therefore need to identify more with a black boss than a white worker at the same factory; a trans customer at a cafe would need to identify more with the trans owner of that cafe than with the non-trans workers actually making their coffee.

Intersectionality is proposed as the work-around for this inherent problem. Rather than identifying only with a specific oppression identity, the oppressed must identify with all oppression identities themselves. As we've already seen, however, once oppression identities are proposed as the grounds of political solidarity, a hierarchy of oppression (with black, trans, disabled people being the most oppressed) necessarily arises, and the ultimate enemy becomes not oppression or capitalism but the apex-oppressor himself, the white, cis, heterosexual, able-bodied male.

The Larger Reality of Capitalist Exploitation

Despite my earlier criticisms of the work, Donna Haraway's observations about economic and technological disruption in "A Cyborg Manifesto" offer a guide out of this problem. Though it's often forgotten or even willfully obscured by those who cite her, she presents the Cyborg as an alternative to the politics of identity which the Combahee River Collective had proposed.

Haraway's analysis was that "woman" had been shown to be an inadequate and impossible category for natural solidarity, since there was nothing which naturally connected middle-class (or PMC) white women to non-white and working-class women. Decades later, we can see this problem even more clearly, especially in the failed presidential candidacy of Hillary Clinton and the many online eruptions against "white feminism" or "white women's tears."

Though Haraway didn't address them directly, we can see the exact same problem existing within all other identity categories. Also, we must remember that the crisis to which Haraway was reacting in "A Cyborg Manifesto" was not just one of identity (what makes us human, what makes us women or men, and so forth), but also one of capitalist economic disruption. The Sixties, Seventies, and early Eighties saw a massive shift in industrial production and distribution, which greatly changed the relationship between capitalists and the working class. In the United States, two technologies forever altered the composition of the working classes and the previously stable relationship organized labor had maintained with the owners of capitalist manufacturing.

One of the most radical changes during that period had become almost completely invisible to the modern world until March of 2021, when a large freighter happened to get stuck in the Suez Canal. Current international shipping relies fully upon the standardized use of shipping containers. Those containers were developed in the late 1950s, but it was not until the 1970s that the US government deregulated US shipping and allowed their use.

Previous to this, the cost of outsourcing parts of the manufacturing chain (for instance, materials for automobiles) was prohibitively expensive for capitalists. This meant that along almost every part of the manufacturing chain, the labor employed was primarily all located within the same country. The workers mining the raw materials, the workers transforming them into other materials in foundries, the workers finishing those materials into parts, and the workers assembling those parts into finished products — as well as the workers transporting those materials from one part of the manufacturing chain to another — all usually shared a national or geographic identity.

Just as importantly, so too did their bosses and the primary consumers of the products of their labor. This fact is what enabled organized labor in many nations — especially the United States, France, Germany, and the United Kingdom — to become such a powerful force. Unions not only could organize the specific workers they represented, they could also co-ordinate with unions of other workers to force capitalist concessions on wages and working conditions.

The de-regulation and standardization of international shipping radically altered these relations. Because shipping materials in from overseas was suddenly an affordable option for the capitalists, if the national labor organizations demanded too much, the capitalist could now just go elsewhere. The power of unions was eroded, which meant the power of laborers to make demands for better wages became eroded, too. The end result is the root of the constant modern lament heard from younger people regarding generational inequality. They accurately and justifiably complain that their parents and grandparents were able to afford a home, college, and a generally good life on the income of only one wage earner, while now no such possibility is on offer even for two wage earners pooling their resources.

The second industrial shift which began at this time was the birth and increasing adoption of computerized automation, a transformation which Haraway devotes quite a bit of ink to in "A Cyborg Manifesto." While international shipping had deeply eroded the power of organized labor, computers were eroding the idea of labor itself. If a machine could perform complex labor tasks that only human laborers could previously perform, then what did it mean to be a human laborer at all?

The root of this existential crisis is found in Marxism itself, since Marx presents labor as an intimate relationship between a human and the world around him or her. When we labor, we transform the things around us into things of value. That value is the basis of human economic relationships: I use my labor to transform wood into a chair, that chair has value because it is something I or others use and would like to use, and because of the value of the chair, others will exchange the products of their own labor (including money) for it. For Marx, the alienation of humans from their labor is what capitalist exploitation is founded upon. A capitalist pays others to make chairs for him, he then sells those chairs to customers and pays the workers who made the chairs much less than the amount he received for them.

Fighting Capital or Fighting Each Other

We should look once again at the matter of social and economic disruption, particularly the point Marx and Engels made about it being the core consequence of capitalist class relations in *The Communist Manifesto*:

> The bourgeoisie cannot exist without constantly revolutionising the instruments of production, and thereby the relations of production, and with them the

whole relations of society. Conservation of the old modes of production in unaltered form, was, on the contrary, the first condition of existence for all earlier industrial classes. Constant revolutionising of production, uninterrupted disturbance of all social conditions, everlasting uncertainty and agitation distinguish the bourgeois epoch from all earlier ones. All fixed, fast-frozen relations, with their train of ancient and venerable prejudices and opinions, are swept away, all new-formed ones become antiquated before they can ossify. All that is solid melts into air, all that is holy is profaned, and man is at last compelled to face with sober senses his real conditions of life, and his relations with his kind.[168]

Capital constantly disrupts social relations in order to create new markets and new forms of accumulation. Capital constantly affects the way we think about ourselves and each other, what and who we think of as valuable or worthless, and even what we need and do not need.

It has especially changed how we think of time, our bodies, and the land around us. This is Silvia Federici's point in her previously cited essay, "In Praise of the Dancing Body":

One of capitalism's main social tasks from its beginning to the present has been the transformation of our energies and corporeal powers into labor-powers.

...Capitalism was born from the separation of people from the land and its first task was to make work independent of the seasons and to lengthen the workday beyond the limits of our endurance. Generally, we stress the economic aspect of this process, the economic dependence capitalism has created on monetary relations, and its role

---

168 See Marx et al, 2022.

in the formation of a wage proletariat. What we have not always seen is what the separation from the land and nature has meant for our body, which has been pauperized and stripped of the powers that pre-capitalist populations attributed to it.

In order to convert humans into the proletariat — in other words, to create the labor force it needed to accumulate more wealth — capitalists needed us to think of ourselves in new and ahistorical ways. This is also how race became a "real" thing for us, a way of thinking about ourselves and each other. As capitalism began to require a more versatile and mobile workforce, we began to change the way we saw sexual difference as well as our attachment to local communities and older cultural forms.

These shifts in how we see ourselves were what Marx and Engels identified in their manifesto. The same process of social disruption was what Walter Benjamin observed in his opus on art, industrial production, and fascism. It was also the same mechanism Donna Haraway noticed when she wrote "A Cyborg Manifesto," and it is still the mechanism of capitalism which we see today.

For Marx and Engels, the attempt to revive moribund forms of social relations (for instance, feudal relations) as an act of resistance to capital was reactionary, because doing so would not actually change the exploitative property relations that capitalism had introduced, it would merely replace them with other forms. The embrace of identity as a political category now should be seen as representing the same reactionary trap. Giving expression to the masses — whether that is in the form of reified racial, religious, or nationalist identities — can never change the function of the capitalist machine itself, only the identities of its pilots and operators.

Though some might object that the working class and previous understandings of labor relations are likewise no longer relevant, they're actually even more relevant now. Just because there is less and less manufacturing and far fewer factories in the "Western world" doesn't mean there's any less of this type of labor being done. In fact, there's much more of it, but because it is dispersed and displaced into poorer nations, especially in the Global South, it's easy to forget it's there. The Mexican immigrants picking tomatoes and strawberries, the Chinese and other Asian women working in textile and technology factories, the African children mining rare Earth minerals for computer and mobile phone manufacturing, the South American laborers picking and cleaning coffee beans for world markets, and yes — even all the lighter-skinned workers in Europe and the United States — share a material *reality* that social justice identity politics does not and cannot address.

Worse than merely not addressing this reality, identity politics pits each of those groups against each other, making it harder for them to develop any kind of practical, reality-based solidarity. We must insist on being realists of that larger reality, the reality of capitalist exploitation. To get to this point, we'll need to re-orient radical politics away from identity and instead back towards material concerns.

Being Faithful Realists

What that might look like isn't very hard to imagine, as it's what the left has already been in many places and at many times throughout history. While easy to imagine, however, it may at first be a bit difficult to implement, because it will require significant changes in the way we talk about what is possible through political action, and especially a harsh realism about our previous mistakes.

The example I cited of the *Kinderläden* in Germany is a good place to begin examining how we might reclaim our connection with a larger reality. Few, if any, would suggest that the radical experiments in child sexuality which informed the *Kinderladen* philosophy were successful. More so, the fact that they even occurred might seem hard to believe, a denialism which I myself committed when I first learned of them.

Instead of denying that they happened, the best and most honest path is to admit they did and then figure out if the theories behind them should be discarded as well. Perhaps this should lead us also to decide that it's best to leave children out of radical politics, or that any political program that attempts to change society by re-educating children is maybe just as coercive as any other kind of indoctrination.

Even if we do not collectively reach this conclusion, it's at least helpful to consider how it explains why there is so much anger against the teaching of critical race theory or alternative gender expression in early education. Regardless of whether what parents are specifically complaining about is really happening, we can at least understand how and why the current trend towards identity-based education might feel like coercive indoctrination. Especially as many of these ideas are very new and hardly even a majority opinion in adult society, it's perhaps better to just focus instead on changing the minds of people *who can actually consent to having their minds changed.*

Becoming faithful realists requires us also to look soberly at the way radical political discourse occurs now. Social media is a cesspool of toxic political discussions, and we must admit that, yes, radicals say and do some very awful things online. Being honest about such behavior, rather than denying it, would also serve to take away a powerful weapon we have given right-aligned critics through our silence and denial.

Currently, they are able to position themselves as telling the truth that leftists deny, and as revealing excesses and absurdities which we refuse to address. What if, instead of denying such things, we nodded in agreement? "Yes, you're right: this happens," we might say. "And it's awful, but those people don't speak for me. Now, let's talk about getting you access to healthcare."

Such a focus on reality and material conditions won't be initially easy, and the issue of *ressentiment* is a problem that leftists will need to address; that vampiric gaze which levels and cripples both the person experiencing resentment and those who love them. As I noted in the chapter on the Vampire, the opposite of *ressentiment* is agency, the sense that each of us can be and are active participants in our own lives and own circumstances. Unresolved trauma can take away that sense of agency, but so too can our own patterns of looking for others to blame for our own unhappiness.

To overcome *ressentiment* and its influence on radical politics, we must help restore to people their own sense of agency and power. This, anyway, was the point of Marxism and some anarchist thought at the very beginning: to help the lower classes see that they are the ones who create wealth and value for the capitalists, not the other way around. Empowering workers — just as for anyone else — really only requires helping them understand they've been powerful all along. They can affect the world around them, rather than having to wait for some politician or boss to do it for them.

There's another way to help with *ressentiment* that is much more practical. It's something I learned from older friends in my life, a tactic they used whenever they noticed I was upset or angry about things I couldn't control. After a few patient moments of listening to me rage about all the injustices in the world, they'd ask calmly, "Are you hungry? Are you getting enough to eat?" Besides expressing the obvious observation that much of our anxiety often begins in the body — and that what feels like a mental crisis can sometimes just be the result of our being hungry, tired, thirsty, or stressed — their questions also helped me learn to return my attention towards material conditions and circumstances.

We can do the same, not just by asking individuals if they need anything tangible, but also by applying the logic of that question to political ideas as well. Would this theory or idea result in people being fed, in their being materially better off than they were before? Or does it instead focus on something that cannot be easily changed or truly fought? Does this argument seek tangible changes in the physical existence of the people it discusses, or does it rely on a utopian ideal that may never manifest or an esoteric struggle that has no end?

What the Past Can Teach Us

Becoming realists of a larger reality doesn't require dreaming new realities out of whole cloth. This is particularly an important point with regard to gender identity conflicts in modern society, struggles made much more contentious because we pretend we are the first people to ever deal with gender variation. Countless pre-capitalist and non-capitalist societies have recognized variant gender expressions and often treated these variations as sacred. Within cosmological views where a person has multiple souls (a body-soul and a wandering soul), the idea that a person could be one sex while some other part of them was something else isn't a problem.

The term "two spirit," which is a modern term adapted by First Nations peoples in North America, reflects this idea.

Serving as a catch-all phrase for the many different ways of recognizing these variations in individual tribal cultures, two-spirit people are recognized as being physically sexed one way while also having aspects of the other sex. In many tribes, such people are seen as having essential spiritual roles in the community precisely because they have feet in both worlds.

Perhaps the most intriguing of these non-capitalist forms is that of the Bugis people in Indonesia, who have five genders. While attempts have been made to map modern formulations of gender onto their society, no easy correspondences can be truly made. The two primary groupings are analogous to (cis) men and women, but the second set of groupings, the *calalai* and the *calabai*, are biological men or women who take on specific artisan roles that Westerners might associate with the other sex. For instance, the *calalai* are women who dress and act in masculine ways, while the *calabai* are men who dress and act in feminine ways. Their roles in society are a bit akin to many of the Western stereotypes of gay men and lesbian women: *calabai* are the hairdressers and wedding planners, while the *calalai* craft tools and do other "masculine" work. A fifth group, the *bissu*, are seen as equally embodying the roles of the four other groups while also standing outside them all. As with many two-spirit figures among First Nations peoples, the bissu's specific place within society leads them to be seen as spiritual leaders of the people.

Attempts to make the Bugis gender system fit current Western ideas (transgender, non-binary, and so on) are of course fraught with problems because they lead to the assumption that cultural forms can be separated from the cosmologies that create them. The same problem occurs when attempting to translate same-sex relationships from Ancient Rome and Greece into modern ideas of homosexuality or to relabel historic figures such as Joan of Arc as non-binary. Rather than attempting to make the past fit the present or to categorize non-capitalist cultural forms as capitalist ones, a more honest framework would involve letting those other forms inform and instruct our understanding. This shows that what is missing in modern capitalist frameworks of gender and sexuality is the recognition that a person can be multiple things at once, and that no part of the multitude negates any other part. Just as the Zombie shows us that a body-soul without its wandering soul is lost and without agency, a cultural framework without the idea of a second self or multiple selves cannot accommodate the full range of human existence.

The implications of such a framework are quite profound. For one, it would break us out of the problem of "being trapped in the wrong body." In the Western, Christian-informed framework, the soul inhabits the body, and therefore we can feel as if our soul (mistakenly believed to be our "true self") is in the wrong house. In animist frameworks, the body-soul and the wandering soul (and sometimes other souls) all live together in the same being as companions to each other. Thus, a person can have a male body-soul and a female wandering soul and find peace (and societal recognition) in accepting both equally rather than trying to change one to conform to the other. In other words, we need not be at war with our multiple selves.

This framework could first of all remove a lot of pressure currently upon people who identify as gender non-conforming, trans, or non-binary. If the communities around them acknowledge that feeling oneself to be one thing while physically being something different is a natural, human, and important experience, gender dysphoria might no longer be seen as an ailment to be treated but rather as just one aspect of being human.

Such a framework likely makes some atheist-inclined readers bristle, and it may not feel sufficient for some radicals who believe declarative gender to be a liberating project. Such concerns I can only answer with two observations. First of all, though in our modern capitalist societies we claim not to believe in a soul, I've already pointed out in this book many occasions in which we act as if we do regardless. Declarative gender especially depends upon the notion of a psychological container in which we place interior experiences (the "felt sense"), and Adolph Reed's observations about transracialism and neoliberal anti-racism reveal that some belief in a soul persists. If we regardless act as if there is a soul, why not bring these beliefs to the surface and wrestle with them?

Secondly, for those who believe the declarative gender framework is liberating, I'd like to ask that you consider the legacy of earlier radical projects that rushed into new understandings without accounting for potential harm, then ask if this current framework can ever truly be implemented everywhere without coercion. Projects to liberate children through education have especially led to horrid ends and very severe societal reactions. Also, accounts of people who've come to regret early gender transition, especially those of women who underwent mastectomies and genital surgery at young ages, should at least give us pause. Leftists need to take both the positive and negative experiences of people who have transitioned seriously, without dismissing either group because they don't fit into our current narratives.

Becoming Friends Again

Embracing a sense of multiple selves (or souls) would also help solve the deadlock of identity where intersectionality has failed. This is a solution which both the Cyborg and the

Werewolf point to: humans are never just one thing but rather are composed also of other existences and inhabit other realms. We are social, political, economic, and also natural beings, as well as spiritual, cultural, and many other kinds of being as well. We cannot be reduced to one identity, nor even to a discrete set of intersecting identities: there is always something of us that cannot be defined.

What we all are, past that multitude of identities, is human; bodies who labor, who desire, who need, who create, and who are in the end much more like each other than different. This is the only place leftist politics can start from: our shared needs, our common material conditions, the exploitation of our labor, and the political control over our existence as bodies.

A politics of bodies is a materialist politics, but it is also a kind of anti-politics. Agamben's lament that all our lives are now subject to the realm of the political, that there is no longer any real distinction between the public and private self, need not be a funeral dirge. Resisting the politicization of every part of life might seem like the most difficult task of all, but it's also the most important.

And it's easier than you might think, because this is what friendship is. Friendships, especially the strongest ones, are rarely ever forged upon political ideas or identitarian thinking. We befriend each other not just despite our differences but often because of them. The best friends are the ones who refuse to always say what you want to hear, and who rather say what you most need to hear. They reflect back not our idealized versions of ourselves but glimpses of the larger reality of who we really are to them and to the world.

The greatest friends I've had were the ones who never demanded I think like them, and who never demanded I hate others. It's unfortunately taken me a long time to identify and end friendships based on coercion and manipulation, all of which turned out to have been founded upon the false premises of political conformity. In other words, they were more like gangs than friendships.

I am not alone in this, I am sure. Perhaps this is one of the reasons you have been reading this book. Perhaps you, too, have seen people you thought were friends turn upon you or upon others in order to be good social justice activists. Maybe you did this to others, just as I did. Perhaps you found, like I did, that though you thought you were fighting monsters, you were becoming one yourself. Perhaps, like me, you found that when you thought we were fighting capitalism, we were only fighting each other.

Friendships that resist the politicization of everyday life are where we learn how to understand each other beyond all the political rhetoric that reduces us to identities. It's from such friendships that I finally understood how my political views were shaped more by idealism and beliefs than by physical reality or even my own material conditions and observations. Such friendships showed me how to speak as a human, rather than an identity, and how to find commonalities grounded not in political conformity but rather in shared human struggle.

If we are ever to become something more than hypocrites, actors in political dramas we have little control over, internally divided between our beliefs and our actions, we must embrace this kind of friendship again. We are many selves and many beings, and we are also human. That human part is where we start from, where friendships form and relationships are made. Past the borders of the political is the realm of monsters, monsters who look remarkably like us.

WORKS CITED

Adorno, T. and Marcuse, H. (1969). Correspondence on the German Student Movement. *FIELD*. Available at: http://field-journal.com/editorial/theodor-adorno-and-herbert-marcuse-correspondence-on-the-german-student-movement (Accessed 13 May 2022).

AFROSOCialist and Socialists of Color Caucus (no date). Reed response covid 19 - Demand to debate Reed, Google Docs. Google. Available at: https://docs.google.com/document/d/1GnMhl9Mi1UKKbBdX2ygsbAOT9IBlzfrtlPmoxDtdJ5k/edit?fbclid=IwAR1-vyxJKlxwCdmSRZC6NuCpaz32xT1XnaPTEtKmgi4ciie98IOmgnrBYiA (Accessed 14 October 2022).

Agamben, G. (2016) *Homo Sacer: Sovereign Power and Bare Life*. Translated by D. Heller-Roazen. Stanford: Stanford University Press.

Agence France-Presse (2022) Apôtres du wokisme: LE "peuple a raison d'en Vouloir " aux Journalistes, dit Eric Zemmour. *La Presse*. Available at: https://www.lapresse.ca/international/europe/2022-01-10/apotres-du-wokisme/le-peuple-a-raison-d-en-vouloir-aux-journalistes-dit-eric-zemmour.php (Accessed: 14 January 2023).

Agiesta, J. (2016) The anatomy of a white, working-class Trump voter. *CNN*. Available at: https://edition.cnn.com/2016/09/19/politics/trump-supporters-working-class-white-kaiser-family-foundation-infographic/ [(Accessed: 14 May 2022).

Akomolafe, B. (2018) When You Meet the Monster, Anoint Its Feet. *Emergence Magazine*. Available at: https://

emergencemagazine.org/essay/when-you-meet-the-monster/ (Accessed: 14 October 2022).

Archuleta, I. (2022) LGBTQIA+: Can you be transgender without transitioning? *iAmClinic*. Available at: https://www.iamclinic. org/blog/can-you-be-transgender-without-transitioning/ (Accessed: 14 October 2022).

Beckett, L. and Levin, S. (2021) Person charged with indecent exposure at LA spa after viral Instagram video. *The Guardian*. Available at: https://www.theguardian.com/us-news/2021/ sep/02/person-charged-with-indecent-exposure-at-la-spa- after-viral-instagram-video (Accessed: 13 May 2022).

Benjamin, W. (1940) On the concept of history (excerpt of *Theses on History*). Marxists.Org. Available at: https://www.marxists. org/reference/archive/benjamin/1940/history.htm (Accessed: 14 January 2023).

Benjamin, W. (2008) *The Work of Art in the Age of Its Technological Reproducibility, and Other Writings on Media*. Cambridge: Harvard University Press.

Blake Psychology (no date) Gender Identity. *Blake Psychology*. Available at: https://www.blakepsychology.com/services/ gender-identity/ (Accessed: 13 May 2022).

Bourdieu, P. (1992) *Language and Symbolic Power*. Cambridge: Polity Press.

Bray, M. (2017) *Antifa: The Antifascist Handbook*. Brooklyn: Melville House Publishing. Available at: https://theanarchistlibrary. org/library/mark-bray-antifa-the-antifascist-handbook (Accessed: 14 May 2022).

Burley, S. and Ross, A.R. (2019) Opinion: What happened when I was the target of alt-right death threats. *The Independent*. Available at: https://www.independent.co.uk/voices/alt- right-antifa-death-threats-doxxing-quillette-a8966176.html (Accessed: 22 May 2022).

Butler, J. (2021) Why is the idea of "gender" provoking backlash the world over? *The Guardian*. Available at: https://www.theguardian.com/us-news/commentisfree/2021/oct/23/judith-butler-gender-ideology-backlash (Accessed: 13 May 2022).

Canadian Observatory on Homelessness (no date) Single women. *The Homeless Hub*. Available at: https://www.homelesshub.ca/about-homelessness/population-specific/single-women (Accessed: March 13, 2023).

Capon, T. (2021) Rough sleeping in the UK: 2002 to 2021, Census 2021. *Office for National Statistics*. Available at: https://www.ons.gov.uk/peoplepopulationandcommunity/housing/articles/roughsleepingintheuk/2002to2021 (Accessed: March 13, 2023).

Capuano, G. (2018) Who are Australia's homeless?, *.id blog*. Informed Decisions. Available at: https://blog.id.com.au/2018/population/australian-census/who-are-australias-homeless/ (Accessed: March 13, 2023).

Case, M.A. (2019) Trans formations in the Vatican's war on "Gender ideology." *Signs: Journal of Women in Culture and Society*. 44(3). Available at: https://www.journals.uchicago.edu/doi/abs/10.1086/701498 (Accessed: 14 October 2022).

Central Intelligence Agency (2021) (untitled). YouTube. Available at: https://youtu.be/jpJDnyZqfLw (Accessed: 14 October 2022).

Clynes, M.E. and Kline, N.S. (1960) Cyborgs and Space, Astronautics. *The New York Times*. Available at: https://archive.nytimes.com/www.nytimes.com/library/cyber/surf/022697surf-cyborg.html (Accessed: 14 October 2022).

Coates, T. (2017) The First White President. *The Atlantic*. Available at: https://www.theatlantic.com/magazine/archive/2017/10/the-first-white-president-ta-nehisi-coates/537909/ (Accessed: 13 May 2022).

Colapinto, J. (2018) *As Nature Made Him: The Boy Who Was Raised as a Girl*. Vancouver: Langara College.

Coontz, S. (2016) Why the white working class ditched Clinton. CNN. Available at: https://edition.cnn.com/2016/11/10/opinions/how-clinton-lost-the-working-class-coontz/index.html (Accessed: 14 May 2022).

Crenshaw, K.W. (1989) Demarginalizing the intersection of race and sex: A black feminist critique of antidiscrimination doctrine, feminist theory and antiracist politics. Scholarship Archive. Available at: https://scholarship.law.columbia.edu/faculty_scholarship/3007 (Accessed: 14 October 2022).

Deleuze, G. (1983) *Nietzsche and Philosophy*. Translated by H. Tomlinson. New York: Columbia University Press.

Deleuze, G. and Guattari, F. (2019) *Anti-Oedipus: Capitalism and Schizophrenia*. London: Bloomsbury Academic.

Dembroff, R. and Payton, D. (2020) Why We Shouldn't Compare Transracial to Transgender Identity. *Boston Review*. Available at: https://bostonreview.net/articles/robin-dembroff-dee-payton-breaking-analogy-between-race-and-gender/ (Accessed: 13 May 2022).

Ehrenreich, B. and Ehrenreich, J. (1977) The Professional-Managerial Class. *Radical America*, Volume 11, Number 2, March-April 1977, p.13.

Elm, S. (2021) A Ring Around Utopia. *RITONA // A Beautiful Resistance*. Available at: https://abeautifulresistance.org/another-world-1/2021/6/30/a-ring-around-utopia (Accessed: 14 May 2022).

Etymonline.com. (2022) Gender. Etymonline. Available at: https://www.etymonline.com/word/gender (Accessed: 13 May 2022).

Evergreen State College (2022) Academic Catalog. The Evergreen State College. Available at: https://www.evergreen.edu/catalog (Accessed: 13 May 2022).

Federici, S. (1975) *Wages against Housework*. Montpelier: Falling Wall Press.

Federici, S. (2016) In praise of the dancing body. *RITONA // A Beautiful Resistance*. Available at: https://abeautifulresistance. org/site/2016/08/22/in-praise-of-the-dancing-body (Accessed: September 14, 2022).

Federici, S. (2020) *Beyond the Periphery of the Skin: Rethinking, Remaking, and Reclaiming the Body in Contemporary Capitalism*. Toronto: Between the Lines.

Fisher, M. (2013) Exiting the Vampire Castle. *OpenDemocracy*. Available at: https://www.opendemocracy.net/en/opendemocracyuk/ exiting-vampire-castle/ (Accessed: 14 May 2022).

Garcia-Navarro, L. (2021) Understanding Multiracial Whiteness And Trump Supporters. *NPR*. Available at: https://www.npr. org/2021/01/24/960060957/understanding-multiracial-whiteness-and-trump-supporters (Accessed: 13 May 2022).

GLAAD (2022) GLAAD Media Reference Guide - LGBTQ terms, GLAAD. Available at: https://www.glaad.org/reference/terms (Accessed: March 13, 2023).

Gleeson, J.J. (2021) The deleted Judith Butler answer (guardian US). Patreon.com. Available at: https://www.patreon.com/ posts/55912898 (Accessed: 14 October 2022).

Global Industry Analysts (2021) With Global Spending Projected to Reach $15.4 Billion by 2026, Diversity, Equity & Inclusion Takes the Lead Role in the Creation of Stronger Businesses. Prnewswire.com. Available at: https://www.prnewswire.com/ news-releases/with-global-spending-projected-to-reach-15-4-billion-by-2026--diversity-equity--inclusion-takes-the-lead-role-in-the-creation-of-stronger-businesses-301413808.html (Accessed: 14 May 2022).

Goldman Sachs (no date) Diversity and Inclusion — Racial Equity. Goldman Sachs. Available at: https://www.goldmansachs.com/ our-commitments/diversity-and-inclusion/racial--equity/ index.html (Accessed: 14 May 2022).

Graff, A. and Korolczuk, E. (2022) *Anti-Gender Politics in the Populist Moment*. London: Routledge.

Gray, J. (2020) American unreality. *New Statesman*. Available at: https://www.newstatesman.com/uncategorized/2020/10/american-unreality (Accessed: 13 May 2022).

Griffin, R. (2003) The palingenetic core of fascist ideology. Library of Social Science. Available at: https://www.libraryofsocialscience.com/ideologies/resources/griffin-the-palingenetic-core/ (Accessed: 14 January 2023).

Haraway, D. (2016) *Manifestly Haraway*. Minneapolis: University of Minnesota Press.

Herzog, D. (2007) *Sex after Fascism*. Princeton: Princeton University Press.

Hobsbawm, E.J. (1969) *Bandits*. London: Weidenfeld & Nicolson.

Hollersen, W. and Fleichhauer, J. (2010) The Sexual Revolution and Children: How the Left Took Things Too Far. *Spiegel*. Available at: https://www.spiegel.de/international/zeitgeist/the-sexual-revolution-and-children-how-the-left-took-things-too-far-a-702679.html (Accessed: 13 May 2022).

Ideal (no date) What Diversity, Equity and Inclusion Really Mean. *Ideal*. Available at: https://ideal.com/diversity-equity-inclusion/ (Accessed: 14 May 2022).

Igoe, K.J. (2022) A comprehensive list of sexualities to know, from pomosexual to heteroflexible. *Cosmopolitan*. Available at: https://www.cosmopolitan.com/sex-love/a39186738/list-of-sexualities/ (Accessed: 14 January 2023).

Institut National d'Etudes Démographiques (no date) The homeless in France, *Ined*. Available at: https://www.ined.fr/en/everything_about_population/demographic-facts-sheets/focus-on/the-homeless-in-france/ (Accessed: March 13, 2023).

Jones, M. (2015) 5 Reasons We Need Black-Only Spaces (And No, Reverse Racism Isn't One of Them). *Everyday Feminism*. Available at: https://everydayfeminism.com/2015/09/why-need-black-only-spaces/ (Accessed: 14 May 2022).

Kelly, J. (2021) Kathleen Stock — free speech and fear on campus. *Financial Times*. Available at: https://www.ft.com/

content/9504baa4-5cf9-40b5-87b5-04d24f19f2b6 (Accessed: 13 May 2022).

Kendi, I. (2019) *How to Be an Antiracist*. London: Bodley Head.

Kendi, I. (2003) Living with the white race. *The Famuan*. Available at: http://www.thefamuanonline.com/2003/09/09/living-with-the-white-race (Accessed: 14 October 2022).

Kierkegaard, S. (2010) *The Present Age*. Translated by A. Dru and W. Kaufmann. New York: Harper Perennial.

Kiley, B. (2011) The Long Con. *The Stranger*. Available at: https://www.thestranger.com/seattle/the-long-con/Content?oid=7989613 (Accessed: 14 May 2022).

King, H. (2021) Juneteenth prompts Venmo, Cash App reparations. *Axios*. Available at: https://www.axios.com/2021/06/25/reparations-online-twitter-venmo-cashapp (Accessed: 14 May 2022).

Knudson, C.A. (2020) Beyond the periphery of the skin — Silvia Federici. *Full Stop*. Available at: http://www.full-stop.net/2020/05/28/reviews/cory-austin-knudson/beyond-the-periphery-of-the-skin-silvia-federici/ (Accessed: 14 October 2022).

Kováts, E., Poim, M., and Pető, A. (2015) *Gender as Symbolic Glue: The Position and Role of Conservative and Far-Right Parties in the Anti-Gender Mobilizations In Europe*. Brussels: Foundation for European Progressive Studies.

Lagalisse, E. (2018) *Occult Features of Anarchism. With Attention to the Conspiracy of Kings and the Conspiracy of the Peoples*. Oakland: PM Press.

Lansing, R. (2021) Alleged Trans incident at upscale LA Spa may have been staged. *Los Angeles Blade*. Available at: https://www.losangelesblade.com/2021/07/07/alleged-trans-incident-at-upscale-la-spa-may-have-been-staged/ (Accessed: 13 May 2022).

Le Guin, U.K. (2014) The National Book Foundation Medal for Distinguished Contribution to American Letters. Ursula K. Le

Guin. Available at: https://www.ursulakleguin.com/nbf-medal (Accessed: 14 October 2022).

Lee, F. (2017) Excommunicate Me from the Church of Social Justice. *Autostraddle*. Available at: https://www.autostraddle.com/kin-aesthetics-excommunicate-me-from-the-church-of-social-justice-386640/ (Accessed: 14 May 2022).

Lenihan, E. (2019) It's Not Your Imagination: The Journalists Writing About Antifa Are Often Their Cheerleaders. *Quillette*. Available at: https://quillette.com/2019/05/29/its-not-your-imagination-the-journalists-writing-about-antifa-are-often-their-cheerleaders/ (Accessed: 14 May 2022).

Linebaugh, P. and Rediker, M. (2012) *The Many-Headed Hydra: The Hidden History of the Revolutionary Atlantic*. London: Verso.

Lussenhop, J. (2016) Safety Pin Box aims to get white people to step out of theirs. *BBC News*. Available at: https://www.bbc.com/news/world-us-canada-38306294 (Accessed: 14 May 2022).

M4BL (no date) REPARATIONS. *M4BL*. Available at: https://m4bl.org/policy-platforms/reparations/ (Accessed: 14 May 2022).

Manchester, C. (2022) Day of Absence Changes Form. *The Cooper Point Journal*. Available at: https://www.cooperpointjournal.com/2017/04/10/day-of-absence-changes-form/ (Accessed: 13 May 2022).

Marcus, E. (2021) A Guide to Neopronouns. *The New York Times*. Available at: https://www.nytimes.com/2021/04/08/style/neopronouns-nonbinary-explainer.html (Accessed: 14 May 2022).

Marx, K. (1996). *Das Kapital*. Edited by F. Engels. Washington: Regnery Publishing.

Marx, K. et al. (2022) *Manifesto of the Communist Party: A Modern Edition*. London: Verso.

Marzorati, G. (2021) Oakland Guaranteed Income Program now says it's not exclusively for people of color. *KQED*. Available at: https://www.kqed.org/news/11867881/oakland-guaranteed-income-program-now-says-its-not-exclusively-for-people-of-color (Accessed: 14 September 2022).

Money, J., Hampson, J.G., and Hampson, J.L. (1955) An examination of some basic sexual concepts: the evidence of human hermaphroditism, *Bulletin of Johns Hopkins Hospital*, 97(4), pp. 309–319.

Monter, W. (1997) Toads and Eucharists: The male witches of Normandy, 1564–1660. *French Historical Studies*, 20(4), p. 563

National Alliance to End Homelessness (2019) *Demographic data project: Gender and individual homelessness*, *National Alliance to End Homelessness*. Available at: https://endhomelessness. org/demographic-data-project-gender-and-individual-homelessness/ (Accessed: March 13, 2023).

Newman, C. (2017) Chimamanda Ngozi Adichie on feminism. *Channel 4 News*. Available at: https://www.channel4.com/news/chimamanda-ngozi-adichie-on-feminism (Accessed: 14 October 2022).

Ngo, A. (2021) Sex offending suspect claims transgender harassment in Wi Spa case. *New York Post*. Available at: https://nypost.com/2021/09/02/charges-filed-against-sex-offender-in-wi-spa-casecharges-filed-against-sex-offender-in-notorious-wi-spa-incident/ (Accessed: 14 October 2022).

Nietzsche, F. (1923) *The Genealogy of Morals; a Polemic*. Translated by H.B. Samuel. New York: Macmillan & Co.

Nietzsche, F. (1966) *Beyond Good and Evil: Prelude to a Philosophy of the Future*. Translated by W. Kaufmann. New York: Vintage Books.

Oakland, City of (2021) Mayor Schaaf Announces Guaranteed Income Pilot, Oakland resilient..., City of Oakland. Available at: https://www.oaklandca.gov/news/2021/mayor-schaaf-announces-guaranteed-income-pilot-oakland-resilient-families (Accessed: 14 October 2022).

Oluo, I. (2017) The Heart of Whiteness: Ijeoma Oluo Interviews Rachel Dolezal, the White Woman Who Identifies as Black. *The Stranger*. Available at: https://www.thestranger.com/

features/2017/04/19/25082450/the-heart-of-whiteness-ijeoma-oluo-interviews-rachel-dolezal-the-white-woman-who-identifies-as-black (Accessed: 13 May 2022).

Orwell, G. (1944) What is Fascism? Orwell.Ru. Available at: https://www.orwell.ru/library/articles/As_I_Please/english/efasc (Accessed: 14 January 2023).

Pilkington, E. (2015) Role of FBI informant in eco-terrorism case probed after documents hint at entrapment. *The Guardian*. Available at: https://www.theguardian.com/us-news/2015/jan/13/fbi-informant-anna-eric-mcdavid-eco-terrorism (Accessed: 14 May 2022).

Press, A. (2022) On the Origins of the Professional-Managerial Class: An Interview with Barbara Ehrenreich. *Dissent Magazine*. Available at: https://www.dissentmagazine.org/online_articles/on-the-origins-of-the-professional-managerial-class-an-interview-with-barbara-ehrenreich (Accessed: 13 May 2022).

Quinn, J.L., McGahan, J., and Dolak, K.A. (2022) Exclusive: Transgender fugitive who spurred Wi Spa riots bares all. *Los Angeles Magazine*. Available at: https://www.lamag.com/citythinkblog/exclusive-transgender-fugitive-who-spurred-wi-spa-riots-bares-all/ (Accessed: 5 January 2023).

Reed, A. (2015) From Jenner to Dolezal: One Trans Good, the Other Not So Much. *Common Dreams*. Available at: https://www.commondreams.org/views/2015/06/15/jenner-dolezal-one-trans-good-other-not-so-much (Accessed: 13 May 2022).

Reed, A. (2018a) Black Politics After 2016. *Nonsite*. Available at: https://nonsite.org/black-politics-after-2016/ (Accessed: 13 May 2022).

Reed, A. (2018b) Antiracism: a neoliberal alternative to a left. *Dialectical Anthropology*, 42(2), pp.105–115.

Reed, A. (2019) What materialist black political history actually looks like. *Nonsite*. Available at: https://nonsite.org/what-materialist-black-political-history-actually-looks-like (Accessed: 14 September 2022).

Reed, A. (2020) How Racial Disparity Does Not Help Make Sense of Patterns of Police Violence. *Nonsite*. Available at: https://nonsite.org/how-racial-disparity-does-not-help-make-sense-of-patterns-of-police-violence-2 (Accessed: 13 May 2022).

Reese, H. (2021) Adolph Reed Jr.: The Perils of Race Reductionism. *JSTOR Daily*. Available at: https://daily.jstor.org/adolph-reed-jr-the-perils-of-race-reductionism/ (Accessed: 13 May 2022).

Richmond, M., & Charnley, A. (2022). *Fractured: Race, Class, Gender and the Hatred of Identity Politics*. Pluto Press.

Salihbegovic, A.S. (2020) Women watch porn, too — but why? *Deutsche Welle*. Available at: https://www.dw.com/en/women-watch-porn-too-but-why/a-55710197 (Accessed: 14 October 2022).

Shrider, E.A. (2022) Income and poverty in the United States: 2020, *Census.gov*. Available at: https://www.census.gov/library/publications/2021/demo/p60-273.html (Accessed: March 13, 2023).

Shrier, A. (2021) Top trans doctors blow the whistle on "sloppy" care. *The Free Press*. Available at: https://www.commonsense.news/p/top-trans-doctors-blow-the-whistle (Accessed: 14 October 2023).

Silva, C. and Doubek, J. (2020) Fascism scholar says U.S. is "losing its Democratic status." *NPR*. Available at: https://www.npr.org/2020/09/06/910320018/fascism-scholar-says-u-s-is-losing-its-democratic-status (Accessed: 14 May 2023).

Simeon, A. (2019) 3 black women get honest about light-skin privilege. *Refinery 29*. Available at: https://www.refinery29.com/en-us/light-skin-privilege-colorism (Accessed: 14 October 2023).

Specia, M. (2020) What we know about the death of the suspect in the Portland shooting. *New York Times*. Available at: https://www.nytimes.com/2020/09/04/us/michael-forest-reinoehl-portland.html (Accessed: 14 May 2022).

Táíwò, O. O. (2022) *Elite Capture: How the Powerful Took Over Identity Politics (And Everything Else)*. Chicago: Haymarket Books.

The Combahee River Collective (1977) A Black feminist statement. In *The Second Wave: A Reader in Feminist Theory*. Edited by L. Nicholson. New York: Routledge, pp. 63–70.

Tognotti, C. (2015) Spokane is a very white city. *Bustle*. Available at: https://www.bustle.com/articles/89959-what-percentage-of-spokane-washington-is-black-theres-a-staggering-lack-of-diversity (Accessed: 13 May 2022).

Turley, H. (1999) *Rum, Sodomy, and the Lash: Piracy, Sexuality, and Masculine Identity*. New York: New York University Press.

US Army (2021) Emma: The calling. YouTube. United States Army YouTube Channel. Available at: https://youtu.be/MIYGFSONKbk (Accessed: 14 October 2023).

Uwujaren, J. (2020) Why our feminism must be intersectional (and 3 ways to practice it). *Everyday Feminism*. Available at: https://everydayfeminism.com/2015/01/why-our-feminism-must-be-intersectional (Accessed: 14 October 2022).

Vincent, I. (2020) Protester in Seattle's CHAZ demands white people give out cash. *New York Post*. Available at: https://nypost.com/2020/06/13/protester-in-seattles-chaz-demands-white-people-give-out-cash/ (Accessed: 14 May 2022).

Volokh, E. (2022) Professor told he's not safe on campus after college protest at Evergreen State College. *Washington Post*. Available at: https://www.washingtonpost.com/news/volokh-conspiracy/wp/2017/05/26/professor-told-hes-not-safe-on-campus-after-college-protests-at-evergreen-state-university-washington/ (Accessed: 13 May 2022).

Wedia (2019) *Homelessness on the rise in Germany, IamExpat*. Iam Epat. Available at: https://www.iamexpat.de/expat-info/german-expat-news/homelessness-rise-germany (Accessed: March 13, 2023).

Weigel, D. (2016) Clinton in Nevada: "Not everything is about an economic theory." *Washington Post*. Available at: https://www.

washingtonpost.com/news/post-politics/wp/2016/02/13/
clinton-in-nevada-not-everything-is-about-an-economic-
theory/ (Accessed: 14 May 2022).

Wildermuth, R. (2020) Reclaiming the body of the Witch: A
review of *Beyond the Periphery of the Skin* from Silvia Federici.
RITONA // A Beautiful Resistance. Available at: https://
abeautifulresistance.org/site/2020/6/4/reclaiming-the-body-
of-the-witch-a-review-of-beyond-the-periphery-of-the-skin-
from-silvia-federici (Accessed: 14 October 2022).

Wildermuth, R. (2022) Why I am not a family abolitionist. *Compact
Mag*. Available at: https://compactmag.com/article/why-i-am-
not-a-family-abolitionist (Accessed: 14 November 2022).

RHYD WILDERMUTH is a writer, a theorist, a publisher, and a druid. Originally from Appalachia and now living in the Ardennes, he's the author of several books on paganism, animism, and anti-capitalism, including *Being Pagan: A Guide to Re-Enchant Your Life* and *All That Is Sacred Is Profaned: A Pagan Guide to Marxism*.

You can find more of his writing at *From The Forests of Arduinna* (rhyd.substack.com) or at RhydWildermuth.com.

REPEATER BOOKS

is dedicated to the creation of a new reality. The landscape of twenty-first-century arts and letters is faded and inert, riven by fashionable cynicism, egotistical self-reference and a nostalgia for the recent past. Repeater intends to add its voice to those movements that wish to enter history and assert control over its currents, gathering together scattered and isolated voices with those who have already called for an escape from Capitalist Realism. Our desire is to publish in every sphere and genre, combining vigorous dissent and a pragmatic willingness to succeed where messianic abstraction and quiescent co-option have stalled: abstention is not an option: we are alive and we don't agree.